The
Regional Vocabulary
of Texas

The
Regional Vocabulary
of Texas

By

E. Bagby Atwood

UNIVERSITY OF TEXAS PRESS, AUSTIN

Published with the assistance of a grant from the Ford Foundation under its program for the support of publications in the humanities and social sciences

International Standard Book Number 0–292–77008–1

Library of Congress Catalog Card Number 62–9784
Copyright © 1962 by E. Bagby Atwood
Printed in the United States of America

First Paperback Printing, 1975
Second Paperback Printing, 1980

To Tad and Laurie

who may possibly take after their Opa

FOREWORD

The present study deals with a vocabulary which, although still in use, is to a great extent obsolescent. Many regional words reflect an era of the not-too-distant past when most citizens were rural, or at least knew something of rural life, before mechanization had become commonplace. Most of these terms will, nevertheless, still be familiar to anyone who is old enough to have had such simple experiences as hitching a mule to a *singletree*, or gathering a mess of *roasting ears* or *snap beans* from the garden, or merely sitting on the *front gallery* in a *settee*.

The word usages were collected in direct interviews with men and women of the Southwest, by a method that is explained fully in Chapter II. What should be emphasized here is that such a project was, by its very nature, a work of collaboration. Those who were, in a sense, co-authors would make up a very long list.

I am indebted first of all to the "informants"—several hundred staunch and respected citizens who obligingly permitted themselves to be interviewed on their vocabulary usage. Their kindliness and long-suffering patience on many an occasion were more than exemplary.

Next, I am highly appreciative of the efforts of the fieldworkers—mostly advanced students in Southwestern colleges and universities, who went forth with questionnaires to interview acquaintances or kinsmen in many remote areas. As Sherlock Holmes said of the Baker Street Irregulars, "[they] go everywhere and hear everything. They are as sharp as needles, too; all they want is organization."

For invaluable aid in the organization of field work, I am grateful to a considerable number of colleagues in other institutions; their names and locations are listed in Chapter II.

The authors of theses and dissertations provided much material on the trends of usage in several key areas. Worthy of special mention is the late Mima Babington, whose data on southern Louisiana made possible the establishing of many contrasts with Texas usage.

To many other persons and groups my thanks are likewise due:

To the University of Texas Bureau of Business Research, particularly to Professor John R. Stockton for suggestions regarding changes in the Texas economy, and to Mrs. Roberta B. Steele for valuable counsel on the preparation of maps.

To Professor Barnes F. Lathrop, for aid in matters pertaining to the settlement of Texas.

To Professors Mody C. Boatright and J. Frank Dobie, for help in clarifying many dubious points regarding the regional culture.

To Professor Américo Paredes, for valuable information regarding usage in Texas Spanish.

To Professor Lorrin G. Kennamer, for his careful examination of the preliminary maps, and for his suggestions regarding their improvement.

To Professor Rudolph Willard, for his reading of the manuscript and for the impeccable taste of his suggested revisions.

To Mrs. Joyce E. Cope of the University of Texas Testing and Counseling Center, for her expert "programming" of the raw data for efficient handling by IBM machines.

To my wife, Mary Bell Atwood, for her typing of masses of semilegible script, as well as for her constant sympathy and encouragement.

To the University of Texas Research Institute, for funds to permit the machine handling of the data, and to the Ford Foundation for a grant in aid of publication.

All of the figures and maps were drafted in final form by Thomas R. Doebbler. Although I myself am responsible for their accuracy, I can take no credit for their appearance. To Mr. Doebbler I am also indebted for the design of the jacket.

E. B. A.

CONTENTS

ILLUSTRATIONS

TABLES

Showing the Percentages of Usage in the Age Groups

The
Regional Vocabulary
of Texas

I THE AREA

GEOGRAPHY

The present vocabulary survey is concerned primarily with Texas, which—although no longer the largest state—is of considerable geographic extent. It lies roughly between the 26th and 36th parallels and between the 94th and 107th meridians. It is bounded on the south by Mexico and the Gulf of Mexico, on the west by New Mexico, on the north by Oklahoma, and on the east by Arkansas and Louisiana. It covers an area of over 267,000 square miles and has a population of a little more than 9,500,000. This is rather sparse in comparison with that of most Eastern States; moreover, it is very unevenly distributed. While some of the counties (Dallas, Tarrant, Harris, Bexar) have a population density of over 500 per square mile, there are others, predominantly in the western portions, which average less than one person to the square mile: Hudspeth, Culberson, Jeff Davis, Loving, and Kenedy.[1] Of the nine counties that lie to the west of the Pecos River, only El Paso has a density of more than 6.6.

In spite of the impression of monotony experienced by some travelers, Texas is quite varied in its topography. In general, the altitude increases by gradual stages from the southeastern corner, which is very little above sea level, to the northwestern, parts of which have an elevation of about 3,000 feet. The Trans-Pecos region is exceptional, in that there are several mountain peaks in that area which reach a height of more than 6,000 feet. The rivers of Texas all flow in a southeasterly direction; the most important of these are, from west to east: the Rio Grande, the Pecos, the Nueces, the Guadalupe, the Colorado, the Brazos, the Trinity, the Neches, and the Sabine.

The geographical subdivisions of Texas are demarcated differently by different authorities and for different purposes; it is agreed, however, that the main Texas areas are extensions or counterparts of regions that extend far into other parts of the country: the Coastal Plain of the

[1] *Texas Almanac 1958–1959* (Dallas, A. H. Belo Corporation), pp. 104–106.

Atlantic and the Gulf of Mexico; the Great Plains; the Rocky Mountain system; and probably the Midwestern Prairies or "Corn Belt."[2]

The accompanying map (Fig. 1) represents the geographic regions according to William T. Chambers.[3] The divisions are ultimately based on rather complex geological phenomena; still, the transitions from one region to another are usually easily perceptible to an observant layman on the basis of external features alone. To mention a few examples, vegetation varies from the tall pines of East Texas to the mesquites of the southwest and the "bear grass" (yucca) of the Trans-Pecos. The soil of the Blackland belt is so different from the "caliche" (thin, gravelly limestone) of the Edwards Plateau that even a city-dweller can distinguish them at a glance. The High Plains are rimmed by the Caprock, an abrupt elevation that can be seen for a good many miles.

Annual rainfall in the state varies from more than fifty inches in the southeastern portion to less than eight inches in the El Paso area[4]. Winter temperatures usually dip well below zero in the northern High Plains,[5] whereas freezing weather is rare in the lower Rio Grande Valley. Summer weather is uniformly hot in all areas; it is not unusual for such weather stations as Presidio and Laredo to report the highest temperature in the nation.

All of these natural features have had a bearing on the peopling of the state and on its economic growth, although, as will appear later, the geographic regions have been exploited in strikingly different ways in different eras.

SETTLEMENT

The area that we now know as Texas had been, more or less continuously, a part of "New Spain" from the time of the early explorations in the sixteenth century until the gaining of independence by Mexico in 1821. During much of that period, attempts at settlement had been made, principally by means of the mission system that had

[2] Elmer H. Johnson, *The Natural Regions of Texas* (Austin, University of Texas, 1931); William T. Chambers, "Geographic Regions of Texas," *Texas Geographic Magazine*, XII, No. 1 (1948), 7–15; R. N. Richardson, *Texas the Lone Star State*, second edition (New York, Prentice-Hall, 1958), pp. 2–5; W. P. Webb and H. B. Carroll, *Handbook of Texas* (Austin, Texas State Historical Association, 1952), II, 261; *Texas Almanac 1958–1959*, pp. 135–139.

[3] By the kind permission of the Bureau of Business Research of the University of Texas.

[4] *Texas Almanac 1958–1959*, p. 157.

[5] E.g., Johnson, *Natural Regions of Texas*, pp. 39 ff.

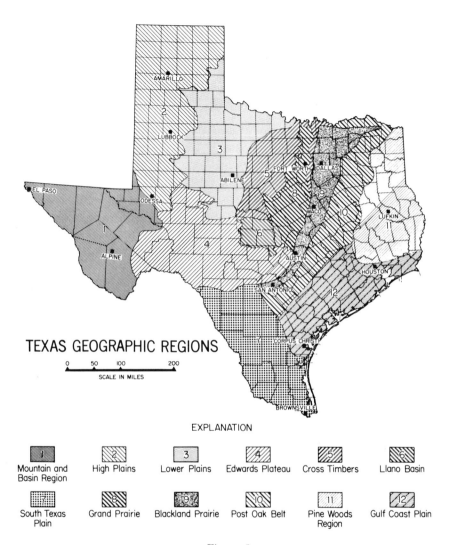

TEXAS GEOGRAPHIC REGIONS

0   50   100   200
SCALE IN MILES

EXPLANATION

1	2	3	4	5	6
Mountain and Basin Region	High Plains	Lower Plains	Edwards Plateau	Cross Timbers	Llano Basin

7	8	9	10	11	12
South Texas Plain	Grand Prairie	Blackland Prairie	Post Oak Belt	Pine Woods Region	Gulf Coast Plain

Figure 1

Adapted from William T. Chambers, "Geographic Regions of Texas," *Texas Geographic Magazine*, Spring 1948. Through the courtesy of the Bureau of Business Research, the University of Texas.

been successful in other areas of sparse European settlement. The steps in the failure of that system and of the attempts to settle the area need not be related; but the fact is that in 1821 only three missions or settlements remained: San Antonio de Bexar, La Bahía del Espíritu Santo (Goliad), and the pueblo at Nacogdoches.[6] In 1809 the non-native population of Texas was estimated at only 4,155 persons, and more than a thousand of these were soldiers.[7] Thus, when the Anglo-Americans arrived, they entered a domain that was virtually unpopulated, so far as settlers of European origin were concerned. Yet the Spanish left a full and vivid record of their former presence in the place names of the state: El Paso, Amarillo, San Antonio, Lamesa, San Angelo, Llano, San Jacinto—the list could be extended indefinitely, and would include the names of most of the Texas rivers and quite a few of the counties.

A number of "indigenous" Indian tribes inhabited the area of earliest settlement: the Tonkawa, the Karankawa, the Bidai, the Caddo, the Hasinai, and others,[8] but these offered few obstacles to settlement. The same cannot be said of the "intrusive" tribes—those forced into Texas from pressure of other tribes or from Anglo-American expansion: the Comanche, the Wichita, the Kiowa, and the Kiowa-Apache; but these in general occupied the territory farther to the north and west than that of the early Anglo-American settlements.[9]

Before the days of Texas independence, and to some extent afterwards, colonization was carried out by means of the *empresario* system. That is, an individual or a group would, under contract, assume responsibility for the settlement of a certain number of families within a given area. The first of these *empresario* contracts was negotiated by Moses Austin in 1821, but he died in that year and left the fulfillment of his plans to his son Stephen F. Austin. The latter succeeded in renewing his father's contract with the government of Mexico, and he received permission to settle three hundred families on the Gulf Coast Plain between the San Antonio and the Brazos rivers. This plan he shortly carried out; his original families were later known as the Old Three Hundred, and descent from one of these is now regarded as a distinction. Grants of land to these settlers consisted of one *labor* (177 acres) to a

[6] Webb and Carroll, *Handbook of Texas*, II, 2; Richardson, *Texas*, p. 34.

[7] Richardson, *Texas*, p. 34.

[8] One often hears of the Tejas Indians, but this is a term applied by the early explorers and settlers to a confederation of the Hasinai and their neighbors. Richardson, *Texas*, p. 9.

[9] *Handbook of Texas*, I, 883–884; H. E. Driver and others, *Indian Tribes of North America* (Baltimore, Waverly Press, 1953), insert map (back cover).

family engaged in farming, or one *sitio* (about 4428 acres) to one engaged in the raising of livestock. It is not surprising that most of the colonists put themselves in the category of cattle raisers,[10] although in actuality they probably engaged in both activities.

Austin later settled many more families, both within the original area and in lands farther to the north and west. There were a number of other *empresarios* in the colonial period, among whom were Green DeWitt, Sterling C. Robertson, David G. Burnet, Lorenzo de Zavala, and Arthur G. Wavell. Most of the successful colonies were located in the eastern one-third of Texas (by present boundaries), although John McMullen, an Irishman, succeeded in settling 84 families in an area to the northwest of Corpus Christi.[11]

It is not possible in most cases to determine where the earliest Texas colonists came from. Austin left no record of the places of emigration of the first three hundred families; but after 1825 he kept a register of those who applied for land, recording, among other facts, the place of emigration. Of 864 such applicants, 201 came from Louisiana, 111 from Alabama, 90 from Arkansas, 89 from Tennessee, 72 from Missouri, and so on in descending order through Mississippi, New York, Kentucky, Ohio, and several other states and territories.[12] This is really only an indication of the places through which the colonists passed, since, as E. C. Barker has pointed out, most of the area to the west of the Appalachians was unsettled until after 1800, so that "few adults who arrived in Texas prior to 1831 could have been born in the west."[13]

Of those who fought at the Battle of San Jacinto (21 April 1836), birthplaces have been determined for over 400.[14] Of these troops, more were born in Tennessee than in any other two states combined.[15] Reduced to percentages, the figures are: Tennessee, 23.5; Kentucky, 9; Alabama, 8.5; Georgia, 6.6; Virginia, 6.4; New York, 4.9, and so on. It is perhaps interesting that only 20 per cent were born in the states to the north of the Potomac and the Ohio rivers.

It has also been possible to trace the birthplaces of those who came

[10] Lester G. Bugbee, "The Old Three Hundred," *Quarterly of the Texas Historical Association*, I (1897–1898), 108–117.

[11] Richardson, *Texas*, pp. 55–59.

[12] E. C. Barker, "Notes on the Colonization of Texas," *Southwestern Historical Quarterly*, XXVII (1923–1924), 108–119.

[13] *Ibid.*, p. 117.

[14] S. H. Dixon and L. W. Kemp, *The Heroes of San Jacinto* (Houston, Anson Jones Press, 1932).

[15] This may be due partly to the fact that General Houston himself had been a resident of Tennessee, and had served as governor there from 1827 to 1829.

to the Peters Colony in North Texas. This colony was a rather unsuccessful venture undertaken under an *empresario* contract negotiated
after the independence of Texas. The percentages of the birthplaces
are as follows: Tennessee, 23.1; Kentucky, 17.6; Virginia, 9.9; North
Carolina, 8.9; Missouri, 8.3; Illinois, 5.5; Indiana, 4.8; South Carolina,
3.6; Georgia, 2.5; Arkansas, 1.7. Although a slight majority of colonists
came from states that were later to make up the Confederacy, it is
significant that only a small proportion were born in the Coastal Southern states; the predominant group (about 61 per cent) came from the
inland South, plus the neighboring states of Indiana, Illinois, and
Missouri.[16]

For what we know of immigration into Texas in the years following
independence, we are indebted to the research of Barnes F. Lathrop[17]
and of his pupil Homer Lee Kerr.[18] Lathrop, in his study of nineteen
East Texas counties, systematically examined the manuscript census
returns of the period, and put into application the "child-ladder"
method—that is, a study of the children's birthplaces—as a means of
determining the previous residences of each family that entered Texas.
The results show that, for the area as a whole, the preponderant proportion of immigrants came through the Gulf Coast states; the percentages
are: Alabama, 20.8; Tennessee, 16.4; Mississippi, 15.6; Arkansas,
10.1; Georgia, 9.3; Louisiana, 8.8; Missouri, 6.5; Kentucky, 3.4;
Illinois, 2.2. There are, however, clear signs of cleavage in different
parts of the area. In the four northern counties (Grayson, Hopkins,
Kaufman, Lamar), immigrants from Tennessee, Arkansas, and Missouri made up the majority (55.9 per cent). On the other hand, in the
southeastern counties (Angelina, Jasper, Liberty, Chambers, Polk, and
Sabine), the majority (68.4 per cent) came from the Gulf Coast states
of Alabama, Mississippi, and Louisiana, the last of which contributed
the larger proportion (27 per cent).[19]

In his study of the later period of immigration (Fig. 2), Kerr established the streams of migration (Coastal as against Inland Southern)
somewhat more clearly. He was also able to carry his study considerably
farther to the westward, but not into the northwestern part of the state,

[16] All of this information is from Seymour V. Connor, *The Peters Colony of
Texas* (Austin, Texas State Historical Association, 1959), p. 107.

[17] Barnes F. Lathrop, *Migration into East Texas 1835–1860* (Austin, Texas
State Historical Association, 1949).

[18] Homer Lee Kerr, "Migration into Texas, 1865–1880" (Doctoral dissertation. University of Texas, 1953—typescript).

[19] Lathrop, *Migration into East Texas*, p. 35.

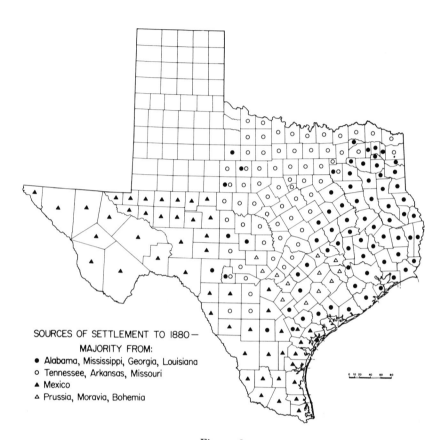

Figure 2

Data from H. L. Kerr, "Migration into Texas, 1865–1880" (doctoral dissertation, University of Texas, 1953).

where settlement was even more recent. His results, which are here presented in a very simplified form, show that, in the period concerned, the Pine Woods area, the Post Oak belt, and most of the Gulf Coast Plain were occupied by settlers the majority of whom came from the Gulf states of Alabama, Mississippi, Georgia, and Louisiana. Louisiana settlement strongly predominated in the southeastern and southern portions of this area (Figs. 2 and 3). Nearly all of the Blackland belt and the areas to the westward show a preponderance of settlers from the inland states of Tennessee, Arkansas, and Missouri. Arkansas settlement was heaviest in the northern counties, although it reached farther to the south in the Cross Timbers area (Fig. 4).

Although Richardson's statement that, in the days before the Civil War, "ninety per cent of the white immigrants to Texas had come from the Old South"[20] is probably an oversimplification, still there is no doubt that this element was very strong. If we include Tennessee among them, the plantation states certainly provided the leading group, both in numbers and in priority of arrival—the latter of which inevitably confers prestige in a newly settled area.

The earliest German immigration came in the days of the Republic, and resulted in the founding of such settlements as New Braunfels and Fredericksburg.[21] This immigration continued after the Civil War; Kerr designates no less than twelve counties in Central Texas which owe the preponderance of their population to Prussia, Moravia, and Bohemia (Fig. 2). Some of these immigrants, however, were certainly speakers of Czech rather than German.

Although there are many old, and much respected, Latin families in Texas, the great majority of Latin-Americans came in by immigration in the latter half of the nineteenth century and the early part of the twentieth. As Kerr has shown, the South Texas Plain, the Edwards Plateau, and the Trans-Pecos area derived the largest proportion of their early population from Mexican immigration (Fig. 2). It should be noted that the actual numbers of immigrants were not large; most of these areas were, and still are, very sparsely populated. Latin population is still heavily concentrated in the southern and western extremities of the state (Fig. 5).

Of course, a great many Negro slaves were brought to Texas, in spite of objections to slavery in the early days of colonization. Austin was forced to tolerate slavery, and indeed by 1825 his colony contained 443 slaves as against 1,347 whites. After the independence of Texas,

[20] Richardson, *Texas*, p. 181.
[21] *Ibid.*, p. 144.

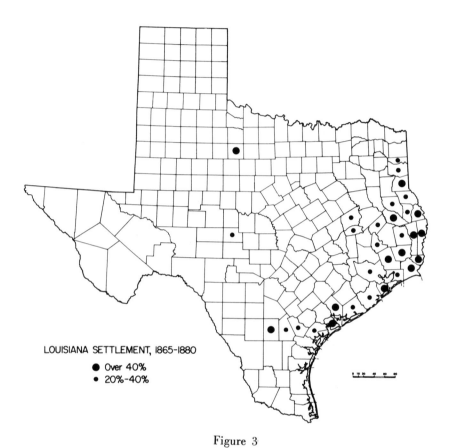

Figure 3

Data from H. L. Kerr, "Migration into Texas, 1865–1880" (doctoral dissertation, University of Texas, 1953).

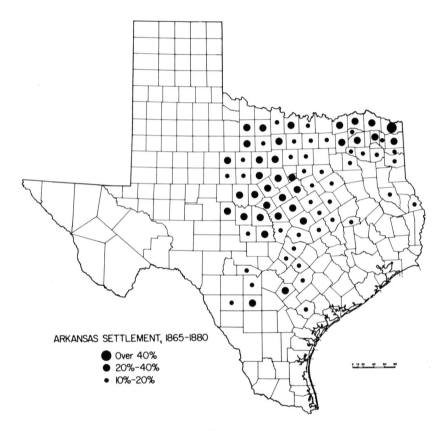

Figure 4

Data from H. L. Kerr, "Migration into Texas, 1865–1880" (doctoral dissertation, University of Texas, 1953).

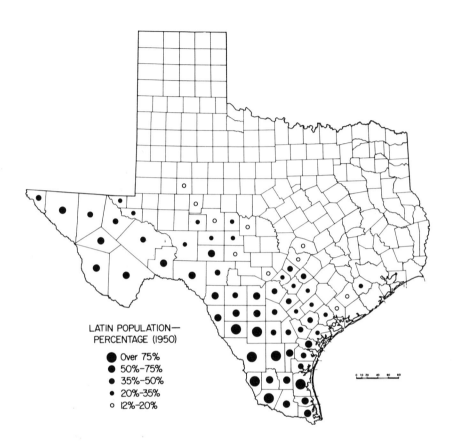

Figure 5

Data from the *Texas Almanac 1958–1959* (Dallas, A. H. Belo Corporation).

slavery continued to flourish, so that by 1860 about 30 per cent of the population were slaves. As elsewhere in the South, only a minority (less than 28 per cent) of the white families owned slaves,[22] but the influence and prestige of these families were so far out of proportion to their numbers that there was never any doubt that Texas was a slave state at the outbreak of the Civil War.[23] The heaviest concentration of Negroes, both slave and free, has always been in the eastern portion of the state,[24] where it is still to be found (Fig. 6). If the planters moved to West Texas, their former slaves did not go with them.

As has been stated, there are no reliable figures on the origin of the Anglo-American population in the western portion of Texas, since this area was mostly settled very late, and no manuscript census returns are as yet accessible for the appropriate period. Indeed, for this survey it was difficult to find older informants who were lifelong residents of the area. Of seventy-three informants[25] interviewed in the South Plains (approximately from Plainview to San Angelo),[26] only thirteen were born in the area. Of the remainder, forty (or two-thirds) were born farther to the eastward in Texas—predominantly in North or Central Texas. This situation may or may not be characteristic of the population as a whole, but at any rate it is true of the persons whose speech is actually represented in the survey.

CHANGES IN THE ECONOMY

An extended account of the economic history of Texas would be unnecessary and out of place here, yet a few essential facts must be presented. Most people outside of Texas are sure that the eastern portion of the state is a vast cotton plantation, that the western part is an even more vast cattle ranch, and that in both areas there is an oil well in every back yard. At one time there was a general sort of truth in this notion, but time has brought about some remarkable changes.

[22] *Ibid.*, especially pp. 64, 162, 163.

[23] In the crucial election of 1860, Lincoln received no votes, Douglas 410, Bell 15,463, and Breckinridge (the planters' candidate) 47,548 (*Ibid.*, p. 183).

[24] Charles O. Paullin and John K. Wright, *Atlas of the Historical Geography of the United States* (Washington and New York, Carnegie Institution, 1932), Plates 68–70.

[25] Not all of the results of these interviews were actually used, since in some communities there were more informants than were needed.

[26] Note that the plural form *plains* by accepted usage has become applicable to the level terrain in the northwestern part of the state. The singular *plain* would apply to a similar but lower area in the south and southeast. Thus, *South Plains* is a familiar and accepted term for the area dealt with here (see Fig. 1).

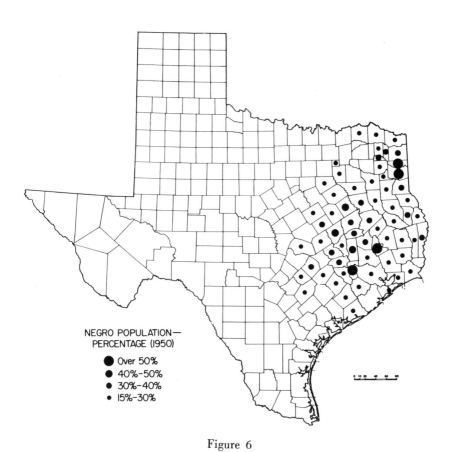

Figure 6

Data from the *Texas Almanac 1958–1959* (Dallas, A. H. Belo Corporation).

Cattle raising began in the colonial period of Texas, when far more land was offered to raisers of livestock than to farmers. However, because of the lack of markets, the industry did not flourish at that time. Herds had also been maintained previously on the missions, particularly those near Goliad. But it was not until the middle of the nineteenth century that what is known as the "cattle kingdom" had its beginning. This was in the South Texas Plain to the southward of San Antonio and to the westward of the present Corpus Christi.

For centuries, in this and other parts of the country, a type of "Spanish" cattle had run wild, and these were often hunted for food. They had remained undomesticated for so long that they are described by one observer (in Texas) as "wilder than the deer" and by another (in California) as "more dangerous to footmen than grizzly bears."[27] The Mexican vaqueros had learned the art of managing and exploiting ("domesticating" would not be the right word) herds of these cattle, by methods foreign to Anglo-Americans from the East. The details need not be given, but the essential feature, according to Webb, was the use of horsemen for herding.[28] Not only the methods, but also in many cases the cattle themselves, were taken over by the Anglo-Americans.[29] From a mixture of these cattle with various other strains, there developed the Texas longhorn, and the hardiness of this breed has made it a symbol of early Texas.[30] These animals were driven overland to the markets, along the now-famous cattle trails which led originally to Missouri, later to Dodge City and Abilene in Kansas.

By the outbreak of the Civil War ranching had spread to North Texas, and from there began to push westward.[31] After the War, and after the Plains Indians had been sufficiently subdued, the industry advanced into the western portions of the state. In an amazingly short period cattle raising had spread over the entire Great Plains and the slopes of the Rockies.[32]

To sum up briefly, the range cattle industry developed from a unique

[27] J. Frank Dobie, *The Longhorns* (Boston, Little, Brown & Company, 1941), pp. 10, 21.

[28] Walter P. Webb, *The Great Plains* (Boston, Ginn and Company, 1931), p. 207.

[29] Dobie, *The Longhorns*, pp. 26–28.

[30] The athletic teams at the University of Texas are known as the "Longhorns"; and no less than eighteen business establishments in Austin, according to the telephone directory, have the word *Longhorn* in their names.

[31] Richardson, *Texas*, p. 248.

[32] Webb, *The Great Plains*, pp. 216–227. No more than fifteen years were required for this spread (*Ibid.*, p. 225).

combination of circumstances, the most important of which were: the technique of mounted herding learned from the vaqueros; the development of a breed of cattle sufficiently hardy to withstand long drives; and the availability of almost unlimited pasturage.

In Texas the area of the large ranches extended from the southern-most tip to the northern Panhandle, including most of the Trans-Pecos area, but not, for the most part, the Edwards Plateau. The extent of this "kingdom" is indicated on Figure 7;[33] it will be referred to as the "old ranch country" in the ensuing discussion of ranching vocabulary.

In the twentieth century the cattle-raising industry in the western portions of Texas has declined, gradually but none the less strikingly. Roger B. Letz[34] has shown that the cattle population of Texas moved steadily eastward between 1900 and 1954, as the western counties for the most part decreased markedly in production (see Figs. 7–8). According to his tally, the two adjoining East Texas counties of Harris and Brazoria produced more cattle in 1954 than all of the nine large counties lying to the west of the Pecos. This change is due to a number of factors: drouth in the far western areas; the reduction of farming acreage in the east as a result of national farm policy; and probably foremost, the realization that East Texas is better suited to cattle raising than to farming, whereas parts of the west, particularly the High Plains and the lower Rio Grande Valley, are extremely well adapted to certain kinds of agriculture. Only sheep raising has remained stable; the Edwards Plateau has always been, and still is, the area where most of the Texas sheep are produced (Fig. 9).

Although largely uncelebrated in fiction and folklore, the kingdom of cotton has also had its striking migrations. In the days of the Republic, the raising of cotton was confined to the river bottoms of the Gulf Coast Plain and to the northeastern corner of the state. As late as 1860 most of the cotton was still produced in these areas.[35] Later, cotton moved into the Blackland belt and tended to be concentrated there; and this situation continued until about 1916 (Fig. 10). Within ten years, however, rather heavy cotton production had moved westward into the lower plains and even beyond the Caprock, as well as southward to the Corpus Christi and Brownsville areas (Fig. 11). This trend continued very strikingly; in 1959 by far the heaviest concentrations of Texas cotton

[33] The information is based on J. W. Williams, *The Big Ranch Country* (Wichita Falls, Texas, Terry Brothers, 1954).

[34] "Changes in Texas Cattle Population," *The Cattleman*, XLII (December, 1955), pp. 23–29.

[35] Richardson, *Texas*, p. 156.

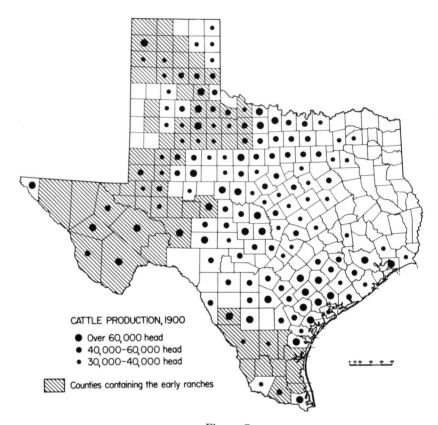

CATTLE PRODUCTION, 1900
● Over 60,000 head
● 40,000-60,000 head
• 30,000-40,000 head

▨ Counties containing the early ranches

Figure 7

Data from R. B. Letz, "Changes in Texas Cattle Population," *The Cattle-man*, December 1955, pp. 23–29; and from J. W. Williams, *The Big Ranch Country* (Wichita Falls, Texas, Terry Brothers, 1954).

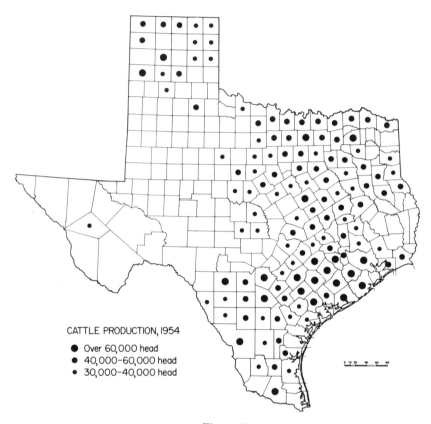

Figure 8

Data from R. B. Letz, "Changes in Texas Cattle Population," *The Cattle-man*, December 1955, pp. 23–29.

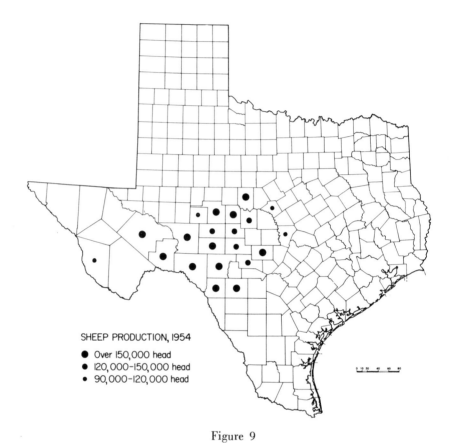

Figure 9

Data from the *Texas Almanac 1961–1962* (Dallas, A. H. Belo Corporation).

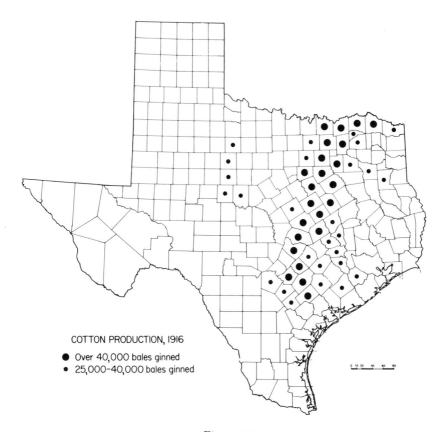

Figure 10

Data from the *Texas Almanac 1961–1962* (Dallas, A. H. Belo Corporation).

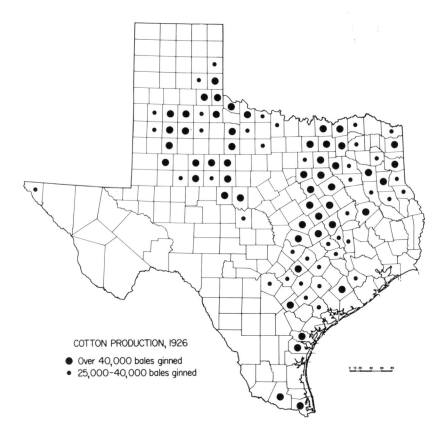

Figure 11

Data from the *Texas Almanac 1961–1962* (Dallas, A. H. Belo Corporation).

production were in the southern High Plains and in the lower Rio Grande Valley (Fig. 12). Indeed, these two areas have now become the real centers of Texas agriculture. The High Plains area has more actual acres under cultivation than any other Texas region;[36] it is a heavy producer of wheat and grain sorghums as well as cotton. Much of the High Plains acreage is under irrigation from "shallow wells," and this makes the land immensely productive. As for the Lower Valley, its production of citrus fruits and vegetables is well known; cotton is relatively new but gives great promise.

Agriculture in general—not alone cotton growing—has declined in East Texas as cattle raising has increased. In the Pine Woods belt less than 6 per cent of the land is under cultivation.[37] To be sure, the Blackland belt continues to be the leading area of corn production (Fig. 13), whereas rice is profitably raised in the eastern portion of the Gulf Coast Plain. But the major trend is clear; one can no longer speak in the old terms of the farming and the ranching portions of Texas and still make sense. The kingdoms of cattle and cotton have exchanged a major portion of their domains.

For our purposes a discussion of the oil industry will be unnecessary. We should observe, however, that heavy oil production has developed in various widely separated regions (Fig. 14).[38] The western fields undoubtedly played a major part in the rapid settlement of the area; the growth of such cities as Odessa and Borger has been phenomenal.[39] The production of oil also promoted considerable mobility of population; many a young man has spent a profitable period as a "roustabout" before settling down. As for the vocabulary of the oil industry, it is a matter for specialized study, and well deserving of attention; in the present general survey it was thought best not to attempt the task.

Certainly many other aspects of social history might have a bearing on dialect, but an enumeration of them would probably be more tedious than profitable. The land itself, the people who came to it, and their ways of exploiting it remain the leading factors that determine the distribution of the regional vocabulary.

[36] Chambers, "Geographic Regions," p. 14.

[37] *Ibid.*, p. 8.

[38] Sources of information are given below each figure. In general, particularly in the case of the *Texas Almanac*, the information was given in the form of tables rather than maps.

[39] The population of Odessa in 1930 was only 3,500; in 1960 it was a little over 80,000. Borger, founded in 1926, had a population of 45,000 within eight months *(Handbook of Texas).* Its 1960 population, however, was only 20,911.

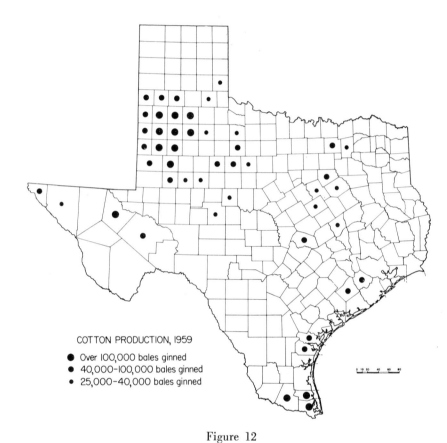

Figure 12

Data from the *Texas Almanac 1961–1962* (Dallas, A. H. Belo Corporation).

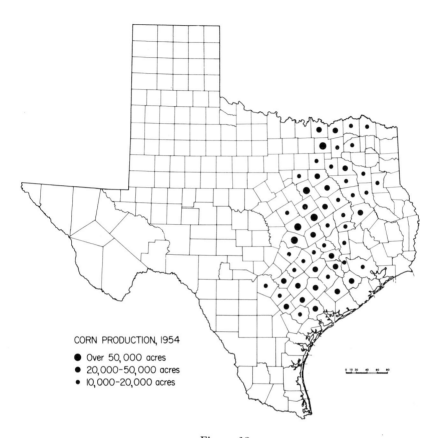

CORN PRODUCTION, 1954

● Over 50,000 acres
● 20,000-50,000 acres
• 10,000-20,000 acres

Figure 13

Data from the *Texas Almanac 1956–1957* (Dallas, A. H. Belo Corporation).

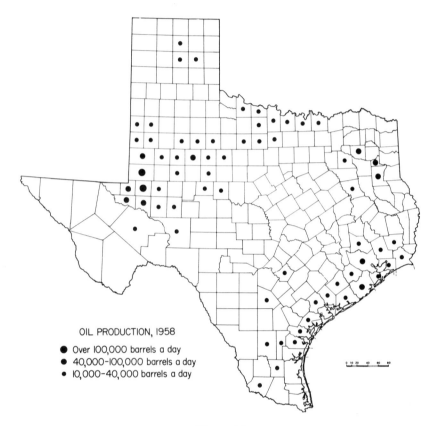

Figure 14

Data from the *Texas Almanac 1961–1962* (Dallas, A. H. Belo Corporation).

II THE METHOD

BACKGROUND AND RELATED STUDIES

The collection of "dialect" in the United States has in recent decades become far more systematic than it was in the nineteenth century and the early part of the twentieth. In those earlier days, most studies of pronunciation were confined to a single community or at any rate to a small area,[1] whereas vocabulary was, in general, collected by rather haphazard methods, such as holding conversations on someone's front porch and trying to jot down or remember his "quaint" words and sayings. A good many "word lists" were published as a result of these investigations, and they are by no means worthless;[2] but they do not contain truly comparable material, in that no uniform set of questions had been adopted, and thus there is no way of knowing whether a given usage might also have occurred a hundred miles away, or indeed throughout the country. Moreover, the lists had a strong tendency to emanate from isolated communities in the mountains or on the seashore —where academic people were likely to spend their vacations—and little attention was given to the large agricultural areas. *The American Dialect Dictionary*, compiled by Harold Wentworth,[3] reflected the imperfections in method that have been mentioned, since it drew its materials from the previously published lists.

By far the strongest influence on modern dialect studies, in the United States as well as in Europe, has been that of Jules Gilliéron, who, in collaboration with his field worker Edmond Edmont, prepared

---

[1] For example, O. F. Emerson, *The Ithaca Dialect* (Boston, J. S. Cushing, 1891). For a fuller summary of the development of dialect studies in the United States see Raven I. McDavid, Jr., "The Dialects of American English," in W. Nelson Francis, *The Structure of American English* (New York, The Ronald Press Company, 1958), pp. 480–543.

[2] For example, L. W. Payne, *A Word List from East Alabama*, Austin, University of Texas Bulletin, 1909).

[3] Harold Wentworth, *American Dialect Dictionary* (New York, Thomas Y. Crowell Company, 1944).

and published the *Atlas linguistique de la France*.[4] Gilliéron's procedure had the following requisites: (1) the use of one living speaker ("informant") for each community—secondhand reports were never accepted; (2) the use of a standardized questionnaire, so that each speaker was asked for the same items of usage; (3) the conducting of all interviews by the same fieldworker, who must be well trained and able to record responses in a phonetic alphabet; and (4) the printing of all responses on the faces of large maps, exactly as the fieldworker wrote them down.

These methods were essentially followed in the preparation of the later European linguistic atlases, for example, that of Italy by Jaberg and Jud.[5] Some of these atlases departed from Gilliéron in minor particulars, such as the use of several fieldworkers rather than one, and sometimes the inclusion of certain "ethnographic" information; that is, combining the study of language with that of various artifacts which were found to be in use in different areas.

The Linguistic Atlas of the United States and Canada was planned according to the principles that have been mentioned. This project, during its early years, was supported partially by the American Council of Learned Societies, as well as by certain colleges and universities. Preparations for it began as early as 1930, and field work was under way by 1931. For the first geographical segment that was covered—the New England States—nine fieldworkers conducted the interviews, under the supervision of Hans Kurath, the editor and director. Close phonetic transcription was used in all cases, but, as might be expected, some interviewers were much more accurate than others. The questionnaire included items to bring out variants in pronunciation (such as *Tuesday*), in morphology (*riz* as against *rose*), and in vocabulary (*tonic* as against *soda pop*). The New England materials were edited by Hans Kurath and a staff of assistants. Publication of the *Linguistic Atlas of New England* began in 1939 and ended in 1943.[6] Responses of informants were entered in phonetic symbols on the faces of the maps, after the fashion of the great European atlases, and often full commentaries were provided (beside the maps) to explain matters that could not well be entered on the maps themselves. A separate

---

[4] Jules Gilliéron and Edmond Edmont, *Atlas linguistique de la France* (Paris, H. Champion, 1902–1910).

[5] Karl Jaberg and Jakob Jud, *Sprach- und Sachatlas Italiens und der Sudschweiz*, 8 vols. (Zofingen, Ringier and Co., 1928–1940).

[6] Hans Kurath, Bernard Bloch, and others, *Linguistic Atlas of New England*, 3 vols. in 6 parts (Providence, R. I., Brown University, 1939–1943).

Handbook[7] explained the methods of the *Atlas* and provided valuable bibliographies.

For most of the Middle Atlantic and South Atlantic states, a single fieldworker, Guy S. Lowman, did most of the interviewing. After Lowman's death in 1941 Raven I. McDavid, Jr., continued work in the remaining areas, and finally brought it to an end in 1949. The materials from this portion of the East have never been published, nor even completely edited. The manuscript field records, however, are kept at the Linguistic Atlas headquarters (now at the University of Michigan), and Kurath has always made them accessible to interested scholars. It was on these records, plus those of the New England *Atlas*, that Kurath based his vocabulary survey, *A Word Geography of the Eastern United States.*[8]

In the areas to the westward, the Linguistic Atlas has taken the form of separate studies and projects carried out under the direction of different individuals, most of whom have had to operate with insufficient financial support and with inadequate man power. Nonetheless, considerable progress has been made in some areas. Those who are carrying out such studies, and the areas in which they are working, include:

Albert H. Marckwardt of the University of Michigan: the Great Lakes area.

Harold Allen of the University of Minnesota: the upper Midwest.

Marjorie Kimmerle of the University of Colorado and T. M. Pearce of the University of New Mexico: the Rocky Mountain area.

David Reed of the University of California and Carroll Reed of the University of Washington: the Pacific Coast states.

Most of those who are working in the westerly areas are using the Linguistic Atlas questionnaire in one form or another, generally a considerably shorter version than that employed in the East. Moreover, several investigators have found that vocabulary items can be satisfactorily collected by less costly methods than the employment of highly trained fieldworkers. Alva L. Davis[9] was probably the first in this country to demonstrate that a list of items (a "check list") can be mailed out

---

[7] Hans Kurath and others. *Handbook of the Linguistic Geography of New England* (Providence, R. I., Brown University, 1939).

[8] Hans Kurath. *A Word Geography of the Eastern United States* (Ann Arbor, University of Michigan Press, 1949).

[9] Alva L. Davis, "A Word Atlas of the Great Lakes Region" (doctoral dissertation, University of Michigan, 1949—microfilm).

and placed in the hands of the informants themselves, with instructions to mark or write in the words that they themselves employ, and that the results will not be very different from those accomplished by field work. More recently nearly all of those engaged in dialect study have made use of a check list for one purpose or another—usually to supplement the investigations of fieldworkers.[10] As in the case of some of the individuals mentioned above, Gordon R. Wood of the University of Chattanooga is circulating a check list in Tennessee and in adjoining states, particularly those of the Gulf Coast .[11]

THE TEXAS QUESTIONNAIRE AND ITS USE

In the investigation of Texas speech a number of procedures have evolved which are different from those of previous surveys, yet which are akin to all of them. In the first place, a decision was reached to separate vocabulary from pronunciation, since the methods that are applicable to one are not appropriate for the other. No credit for originality is claimed for this division, since among others, Angus McIntosh of the University of Edinburgh[12] had previously adopted the same idea. His investigation of the Scottish vocabulary was carried on by means of a printed questionnaire that was sent out by mail, while plans were being made to use trained fieldworkers for the recording of pronunciation features.

Following this idea, a questionnaire pertaining strictly to vocabulary[13] was prepared for Texas. This was based on the work sheets of the Linguistic Atlas, and contained most of the items that had proved to be highly productive in the East. Because of differences between the rural terrain and economy of the Southwest and those of the East, a number of items were added: for example, those designed to elicit such words as *burro* for a donkey, *mott* for a clump of trees, *morral* for a feed bag, *pilón* for an extra gift with a purchase, and a good many more. Ideas for these additions came from a number of sources besides personal observation; worthy of special mention are Ramon Adam's *Western*

---

[10] David Reed and David De Camp have prepared "A Collation of Check Lists," which is available in mimeographed form.

[11] See Wood, "An Atlas Survey of the Interior South," *Orbis,* IX (1960), 7–12.

[12] See *An Introduction to a Survey of Scottish Dialects* (Edinburgh, Thomas Nelson, 1952).

[13] The questionnaire did, however, contain a sampling of "grammatical" items, such as the past tense forms of *dream, dive,* and other verbs.

Words and *Cowboy Lingo*,[14] and Harold W. Bentley's *Dictionary of Spanish Terms in English*.[15] In its present form (that is, after some years of trial and error), the questionnaire consists of 246 items— considerably more than those included in the check lists that have been mentioned. The approximate content of the questionnaire may be deduced from the Topical Survey (Chapter III), although some of the nonproductive items were omitted from this study.

Since I had been trained in the Gilliéron tradition, I was loath to rely on the mailing out of check lists, and I wanted to use fieldworkers to ask the questions. However, since no funds have ever been available for field work in Texas, things seemed to have reached an impasse.

At this point, about twelve years ago, a number of my senior and graduate students[16] became immensely interested in dialect geography and indicated that they would like to try vocabulary field work in their home communities. Accordingly, several of them took copies of the Texas questionnaire and interviewed older persons of their acquaintance who knew something of rural life. The method was successful from the beginning, although I was not fully aware of this for some time. Meanwhile, a considerable number of other students had chosen this assignment,[17] and had interviewed kinsmen, or friends, or neighbors in various parts of the state.

These student fieldworkers were not, for the most part, highly trained in phonetics (which is hardly necessary for observation of vocabulary); but they were instructed to some extent as to how to use indirect questioning, and they were also "educated" as to the nature of certain things, such as buggy shafts and singletrees.

Some time elapsed before I became fully aware that I had on hand a valuable collection of field records. As a result of the traditional views which I held, I was slow to realize that the professional fieldworker is not the only competent one, or even necessarily the best one, so far as vocabulary investigation is concerned. I should have known better, in view of the excellent and substantial work done by advanced

[14] Ramon Adams, *Western Words* (Norman, University of Oklahoma, 1944); *Cowboy Lingo* (Boston, Houghton Mifflin Company, 1936).

[15] Harold W. Bentley, *Dictionary of Spanish Terms in English* (New York, Columbia University Press, 1932).

[16] Originally in a course entitled "The English Language in America"— English 364K at the University of Texas.

[17] The assignment was never compulsory, but was permitted instead of the more conventional "research paper."

students under the direction of Ferdinand Wrede of Marburg and Louis Grootaers of Louvain. Meanwhile, interest in the project had spread to other colleges and universities in the Southwest, and other teachers of advanced English language courses welcomed the opportunity to try the questionnaires with their own students. These colleagues, listed in alphabetical order, are:

Robert N. Burrows, Ouachita Baptist College (Arkansas)
N. M. Caffee, Louisiana State University
Ernest Clifton, North Texas State University
J. L. Dillard, Texas College of Arts and Industries
Rudolph Fiehler, Louisiana Polytechnic Institute
Alan M. F. Gunn, Texas Technological College
Sumner Ives, Tulane University[18] (Louisiana)
Charles B. Martin, East Central State College (Oklahoma)
Elton Miles, Sul Ross State College (Texas)
Ray Past, Texas Western College
W. R. Van Riper, Oklahoma State University
Harold White, New Mexico Western College
L. N. Wright, Arkansas A and M College

The choice of informants presented some difficulties, since parts of Texas have been very recently settled, and the finding of older "natives" was no easy task. Nonetheless, it was usually possible to find long-time residents, and, indeed, in the older parts of Texas, lifelong residence in the same area was usually an absolute requirement;[19] the same is true of Louisiana and Arkansas. Since many of the Linguistic Atlas items, as well as the additions, had to do with rural life, informants were expected to know at least something about it. They were also expected to be old enough to remember nonmechanized days. After a considerable number of records had been gathered from older informants, some were accepted from younger ones; but still, informants in their forties and younger make up only about 15 per cent of the total. The investigation was almost entirely confined to "Anglo-American" informants, to whom English was native; but there is also a fair sampling from speakers of German background.

The interviewers were expected to ask the questions indirectly so far as possible—not to pose questions like "What is your word for clabber?" In most cases, hints as to the framing of questions were given in

[18] Now at Syracuse University (New York).

[19] That is, within a distance of two or three counties. Naturally, short periods of absence would not disqualify an informant.

the wording of the questionnaire; for example, "fancy daytime cover for bed," to which the response might be *counterpin, counterpane, bedspread,* or *spread.* Absolute standardization of the questions was not considered advisable, since some informants need more explanation of an item than others. In some cases there is no doubt that it would be necessary to use a "trigger" word or phrase—that is, one of the possible synonyms that the informant might actually choose. Such words, for example, are *dry creek bed* (which some informants might use alongside *arroyo*) and *ghosts* (which sometimes probably had to be used in order to explain the idea of *hants*). In other instances, if the informant did not grasp the idea, he might be presented with a choice of several words, such as *pop, soda pop, cold drink, soda water,* and so on. Thus the actual amount of "suggestion" is impossible to estimate, but it was held down as far as possible.

The advantages and disadvantages of the method that has been outlined are fairly obvious. The principal advantage is that the fieldworkers were interviewing persons whom they knew well[20]—friends, relatives, or neighbors. This was certainly more conducive to cooperation on the part of the informants than a written or printed questionnaire to be filled out and mailed to an unknown person or agency. It is doubtful that even a professional fieldworker could have obtained more spontaneous replies, and he certainly could not have done so if it became known that he was an "English professor." In this part of the country (and probably elsewhere) the ordinary citizen regards the teacher of English as a kind of linguistic policeman.

The disadvantages stem mostly from the youth and inexperience of the fieldworkers. It often required much instruction to acquaint them with such things as *shivarees, sawbucks,* and *singletrees,* and even then there were sometimes misunderstandings. Errors of the sort were, fortunately, not consistent, so that they were pretty well cancelled out by mere weight of numbers.[21]

[20] This was not true in all cases. For example, Carlo Kilp, a native of Germany, very successfully gathered vocabulary in New Braunfels, and Kjell Johansen, a native of Norway, produced excellent results in the vicinity of Fredericksburg.

[21] For example, there are such absurdities as *hitching post,* which resulted from fieldworkers' attempts to describe a singletree. But there are only 3 occurrences of this as against 232 of *singletree.* Such obvious misunderstandings have been omitted from the Topical Survey. Indeed, terms that occur less than 5 times are usually excluded from consideration, although this does not usually apply to known dialect words from other areas. Incidentally, there is virtually no evidence of the faking of responses, although sometimes informants obligingly improvise a phrase when no word is current for the thing—for ex-

It might be repeated that the method was designed for vocabulary only; it would have no value for the recording of pronunciation features and it will not be used for that purpose.[22]

There are now[23] available some 468 vocabulary field records for the area that has been investigated. These are distributed as follows: Texas, 322; Louisiana, 52; southern Arkansas, 33; Oklahoma, 50; and southern New Mexico, 11. Probably as many as a hundred and fifty others have been rejected. The rejections were made as soon as the records were received, and without any bias as to what words should or should not have been recorded. The most common reason for rejection was the impossibility of assigning the informant to one specific place; he had moved about too much. Sometimes, also, records were rejected because of serious incompleteness, and occasionally simply because there were already on hand more than were needed for a particular county.

The Texas records are fairly evenly distributed over the state from a geographical point of view; that is, the great differences in population density would be reflected on a map only to a limited extent.

For the purpose of making comparisons of the frequencies of certain words in different areas, the state was arbitrarily divided into six segments: Northwest, West, Southwest,[24] North, Central, and East. The boundaries of these divisions were set purely as a matter of convenience, and are not intended to imply any preconceived notion of dialect divisions. The extent of each area is shown on Map 1 (see Chapter VIII). Some of the calculations are made on the basis of other divisions, such as the Panhandle and the Trans-Pecos area.

In addition to the records that have been mentioned, a number have been gathered for special studies of particular counties or small areas. Masters' theses have been prepared for Kerr County by Zelma B. Hardy,[25] for Travis County by Randolph A. Haynes, Jr.,[26] for Dallas

---

ample, *free gift, set 'em up,* or *something to boot,* where no such term as *pilón* is current.

[22] A study of Texas pronunciation is planned to follow the publication of this volume. It is hoped that it will take advantage of modern linguistic theory and modern equipment.

[23] Field records are still coming in.

[24] In deference to history and tradition I refer to this part of the state as "Southwest" rather than "South," although the latter would be more accurate from a strictly geographical point of view.

[25] Zelma B. Hardy, "A Vocabulary Study of Kerr County, Texas" (master's thesis, University of Texas, 1950—typescript).

[26] Randolph A. Haynes, Jr.. "A Vocabulary Study of Travis County, Texas" (master's thesis, University of Texas, 1954—typescript).

County by Sarah Slay Chalk,[27] and for Kendall and Gillespie Counties by Kjell Johansen (in preparation). Another (directed by Alan M. F. Gunn at Texas Technological College), by Anna Sue Carothers Ker, concerns itself with a considerable portion of West Texas centering about Lubbock.[28]

Some doctoral dissertations have also been concerned with Texas vocabulary. One of these, by Arthur M. Z. Norman, was an investigation of the southeastern corner of Texas.[29] Another, by Janet B. Sawyer, deals with the speech of San Antonio.[30] A dissertation on the vocabulary of northeastern Texas has been prepared by Fred A. Tarpley.[31] Before her death in December, 1960, Mima Babington had gathered much valuable data for her proposed dissertation on the Bayou Lafourche area in southern Louisiana. I have frequently made use of the materials in these theses and dissertations.

ANALYSIS OF THE MATERIALS

Most of the Texas field records (273 of them) were put into organized shape by means of IBM machines. Every occurrence of every word was punched on a separate IBM card—a total of over 82,000 cards. On each card was entered, in addition to the word itself, a series of code numbers indicating the following facts: the identification number of the informant, the county in which he lived, and the general section of the state in which the county is located; the age group, sex, "race" or language background, and degree of education of the informant; and the page and item to which the word was a response (see Appendix).

An IBM sorter arranged together all the responses to the same item; and after this a lister reproduced on large sheets all of the responses to every item, together with the code numbers that recorded all of the circumstances of use. The lister also kept a count of the total number

[27] Sarah Slay Chalk, "A Vocabulary Study of Dallas County, Texas" (master's thesis, University of Texas, 1958—typescript).

[28] Anna Sue Carothers Ker, "The Vocabulary of West Texas: A Preliminary Study" (master's thesis, Texas Technological College, 1956—typescript).

[29] Arthur M. Z. Norman, "A Southeast Texas Dialect Study" (doctoral dissertation, University of Texas, 1955—typescript). A summary, under the same title, is found in Orbis, V (1956), 61–79.

[30] Janet B. Sawyer, "A Dialect Study of San Antonio, Texas: A Bilingual Community" (doctoral dissertation, University of Texas, 1957—microfilm). A partial summary is found in the article "Aloofness from Spanish Influence in Texas English," Word, XV (1959), 270–281.

[31] Fred A. Tarpley, "A Word Atlas of Northeast Texas" (doctoral dissertation, Louisiana State University, 1960).

of occurrences of each word, as well as the number in each age group and in each geographical area. The count of occurrences in the different education groups and sexes was made without the lister; this was not difficult, but the machine could have done it just as well.

Of the 273 informants whose records were handled by machine, the subdivisions are as follows:

Sex	Total
Men	136
Women	124

Age	Total
20–49	40
50–59	51
60–69	85
70–79	67
Over 80	25

Education	Total[32]
Elementary school only	159
High School	88
College	21

The trends that are discussed in Chapter VI are based on these total figures. As will be shown, some of the subdivisions are too small to offer any sound basis for generalization.

A few words might be said about the interpretation of the data given in the following chapters. With regard to the meanings of words, I have tried to derive these from the informants' usage, not from dictionaries or other external sources of information. Informants' usage, however, varies widely. Some know no difference between a *hydrant* and a *faucet*, or between a *maverick* and a *dogie*, or, for that matter, between a *burro* and a *burrow*. Others, however, can state very precisely the difference between *bucking* and *pitching*, or between *clabber cheese* and *cottage cheese*. A compromise seems to be the best solution. The fact that several synonyms are grouped under one topic does not imply that they convey the same meaning to all informants.

I have given percentages of occurrence for the sole purpose of describing the "corpus"—not in order to imply that the same percentage of all Texans would use this particular word under the same circumstances. A linguistic survey is not a Gallup Poll. I feel, however, that the informants who were used are representative of a considerably

---

[32] The subdivisions do not add up to 273 because, in a few cases, the information is missing.

larger group. Whether they represent the majority of Texans is open to doubt. For one thing, they are a group that has remained long in one place, and it is not likely that most Texans could meet that requirement. Moreover, they are probably older and more rural in background than the average citizen. A high percentage of occurrence of a word among the informants (for example, *you-all* or *y'all*) probably means a high degree of currency in the state; but one should not go beyond that conclusion.

It should be observed that the evidence which is presented is convincing only in the mass; the presence or absence of a word in the speech of a single individual is of little significance. To take an example, if one observes the word *surly* (for bull) in a single field record, he will be justified in ignoring it or in regarding it as some kind of mistake which will "cancel out" from lack of repetition. But when (as is actually the case) he finds the word no less than thirty-four times, mostly in West Texas and predominantly in the speech of older informants (Map 9), he has adequate evidence of its currency in that area and age group. Similarly, the fact that the informant from Starr County (on the Rio Grande) failed to give the word *frijoles* obviously does not indicate that the word is not current in that county, since it is found everywhere else in the area (Map 17). Individual usage fluctuates, but the trends of collective usage are always observable.

III TOPICAL SURVEY OF THE VOCABULARY

THE WEATHER

Sunrise. The time of day when the sun first appears is, with almost equal frequency, designated as *sun-up* (54)[1] or *sunrise* (40) (Map 92). Other terms exist, such as *daybreak* (3.3), *daylight* (2.2), and *dawn* (1.5), but they lead a precarious existence.

Clearing up. After a storm, the weather is said to be *clearing up* (33), *clearing off* (20), *fairing off* (13), *fairing up* (9), *moderating* (1.8), or *breaking up* (1.8). See Map 90. Phrases containing the term *fairing* are more common in the older groups.[2]

Thunderstorm. A storm with rain, thunder, and lightning is ordinarily called a *thunderstorm* (49) or an *electrical storm* (29). It may, however, be designated simply as a *storm* (8), a *rain storm* (4.4), or a *thundershower* (3.3).

Torrential rain. For an unusually heavy rain that does not last very long, the most frequent expression is *gully washer* (37), followed by *downpour* (30), and *cloudburst* (19) (Map 89). Other less common terms (less than 5 per cent) are *flood, flash flood, pourdown,* and *waterspout.* A good many humorous phrases have a limited currency—from two to ten occurrences each. Among these are *chunk floater, chunk mover, frog strangler, dam buster, stump mover, trash floater,* and *toad strangler.* Many others occur only once each, but may not necessarily be original: *clod roller, cob floater, duck drencher, dumplin mover,* and so on.

---

[1] The numbers in parentheses are percentages of possible occurrences, except when followed by the abbreviation "oc." In this case the numbers mean occurrences, and indicate that, since the item was not included on all the questionnaires, no attempt is made to calculate the proportion of responses to possible responses. Percentages of 5 or over are rounded to the nearest whole number.

[2] Usages that are described as older or newer are discussed in Chapter VI, and details are given in the tables following Chapter VI. Since a Word Index is also provided, no further cross references need be given.

Not blowing so hard.   When a strong wind begins to abate, it is said to be *laying* (26) (Map 96), *calming down* (20), or occasionally *dying down* (9), *easing up* (9), *letting up* (9), or *ceasing* (3.7). Two Negro informants put a *t* in this last word—*ceasting*.

North wind.   The most dramatic weather phenomenon in Texas (aside from an occasional tornado) is the sudden, sharp wind from the north which can reduce temperatures many degrees in a few hours or even minutes. This is universally known as a *norther* (69) (Map 34), although many informants make such distinctions as *blue norther* (37), *wet norther* (11), and *dry norther* (3.3). *Blue norther* may imply rain (as does *wet norther*); however, it ordinarily means an unusually cold or severe norther, often accompanied by dark clouds. *Blizzard,* a well known western term, also occurs, but not commonly (18), and it is less frequently used among younger informants. *Blizzard* is often thought to denote something very devastating, much worse than a *norther* or even a *blue norther.*[3]

Dry period.   For the unreasonable dryness that periodically afflicts portions of the state, the usual word is *drouth* (80), although *dry spell* (23) is also in use, sometimes with the idea of a shorter period. *Drouth* is entirely standard; the form with *t, drought,* is a rarity (1.8).

THE LANDSCAPE

Running stream.   A stream smaller than a river that usually has water in it is ordinarily called a *creek* (75) or a *branch* (50); many of those who use the latter specifically state that it means something smaller than a creek. *Branch,* a General Southern word,[4] is more common among older and less educated informants. *Bayou,* a Louisiana term, is concentrated in southeastern Texas (Map 53), yet there are two contiguous occurrences in Taylor and Callahan Counties in West Texas. For some reason that I do not understand, a draw that runs through that part of the state has the name of *Pecan Bayou.* Usually *bayou* designates a slow-moving and (to a West Texan) almost stagnant body of water such as may be found in the lower Mississippi Valley.

---

[3] The following front-page headline appeared in the *Austin Statesman* for January 5, 1962: "Near-Blizzard Dumps 4-Foot Snow in Nortex [North Texas]."

Notice that in this item (North wind), as in all other cases where percentages add up to more than 100, some informants use more than one term.

[4] The regional aspects of words are discussed more fully in Chapter IV. For the approximate extent of "Northern," "Midland," "South Midland," "Southern," and so on, see also Figure 15.

The Northern *brook* (4.1) and the North Midland *run* (1.1) are almost nonexistent.

Dry creek (bed).   For that familiar feature of the Texas landscape, a stream without water, no single expression has established itself throughout the state. *Dry creek (bed)* (22) is used much more often than *dry branch* (2.9). In parts of West and Northwest Texas, *draw* (9) is the most usual word (Map 11.) The Spanish loanword *arroyo* (19) is well established in West and Southwest Texas, and extends to a limited extent into adjoining parts of the state, but it is unknown in East Texas (Map 15). *Gully* (10) and *ravine* (3.7) also occur with this meaning.

Canyon.   For a very deeply eroded stream bed, *canyon* (33) occurs throughout the state, its frequency ranging from 20 per cent in East Texas to 54 per cent in the Northwest, where there is at least one real, though small, canyon (Map 30). Other terms are *gully* (28), *gulch* (14), *ravine* (12), and *gorge* (10). *Ditch* with this meaning is more common in Arkansas than in Texas (Map 30).

Backwater of a river.   Aside from *backwater* (15), *slough* (9) occurs occasionally, even in areas where such a thing does not exist. A word characteristic of Southwest Texas is *resaca* (7) (Map 2), which still means to some informants the overflow of a river; however, it more often designates a place where water is artificially stored for irrigation or any other purpose.

Grasslands.   The description suggested for this item was simply "flat, grassy country." The wide currency of *prairie* (61) with this meaning (Map 104) indicates that the word is applied to a considerable variety of terrains—from the low-lying, swampy pasture lands of southern Louisiana to the high, dry plains of Northwest Texas. The scarcity of the word in Trans-Pecos Texas probably means that most of the land there is too mountainous and insufficiently grassy to make this designation appropriate. *Plains* (the plural form) (15) is more or less concentrated in Northwest Texas (Map 12), but is known elsewhere. *Llano* (4.4) survives fairly well in Southwest Texas (Map 3), while *flat(s)* (7) and *meadow* (4.8) are very scattered.

High, flat land.   The book word *plateau* (14) is about equally distributed geographically, but it is used more often by younger informants. The more indigenous term *mesa* (28) is mostly concentrated in the western half of the state (Map 21). The translated version of *mesa, table land* (8), is limited largely to older informants. *Plains* (7) is also sometimes used with this meaning, since the Texas areas designated by the plural form are those of higher altitudes.

Bushy terrain. For a brushy, tangled growth of mesquite (or similar bushes), the Spanish loanword *chaparral* (13) is fairly well concentrated in Southwest Texas (Map 5), and occurs only in scattered fashion elsewhere. Several informants state that this word applies to any thick growth; others apply it to the agarita bush or to other specific bushes. Some informants to whom *chaparral* was suggested said that it means only a kind of bird, the chaparral hen, or road runner. *Mesquite thicket* (16) is used along with a few other terms such as *mesquite flat(s)* (6) and *brush (land* or *country)* (6), the latter of which is confined to Southwest and West Texas. There are six Texas occurrences of *mesquital* and three of *bosque* (Map 8), the latter having been observed only in El Paso and Hudspeth Counties—although there is a Bosque County in Central Texas.

Land where scrubby oak grows. The thick growth of small oaks (formerly an excellent hiding place for fugitives) that covers parts of North Central and West Texas is known as the *shinnery* (95 oc.), chiefly in those portions of the state where this type of growth occurs (Map 13). Most of the informants from other areas are unfamiliar with this terrain. The term *blackjacks* occurs a few times in Oklahoma.

Maple. The maple is not very well known in Texas, and is nearly always referred to as *maple* (42) or *sugar maple* (20). The South Midland *sugar tree* (4.8) is rarely found.

Paved road. A considerable variety of words are in use to differentiate a paved road from the old-fashioned dirt or gravel road. Among these are *highway* (19), *pavement* (15), *hard surface road* (18), and *black top* (8). *Pike* (2.6) is only a remnant. For some reason, *tarv(i)ated road* (one informant calls it *tarvey*) is confined to Central Texas in the vicinity of Austin (Map 38). *Pavement* with this meaning shows considerable concentration in the South Plains (Map 10).

Main irrigation ditch. For modern methods of irrigation, *canal* (26) is in frequent use; *(irrigation) ditch* (19), of course, is also used. An older term, *acequia* (3.3), recalling the days of gravity irrigation, is still in occasional use, chiefly in Southwest Texas (Map 4).

Artificial pool of water. A body of water impounded for the watering of livestock and for other purposes is known throughout most of the state as a *tank* (70); this term occurs in all but the easternmost extremities of Texas (Map 26). This sort of pool is occasionally referred to as a *stock tank* (4) or a *dirt tank* (2.6) if it is felt that a modifier is needed. *Pond* (10) is rare except in East Texas, but it is usual in Arkansas and Louisiana. *Pool* (3.7) is mostly confined to Northeast Texas, but it also shows a few occurrences in Arkansas and Louisiana.

Poison ivy.   The plants that cause a severe rash *(Rhus* or *Toxidendron)* are known throughout most of our area as both *poison ivy* (59) and *poison oak* (49) (Map 91). It is doubtful that informants make any useful distinction between the two; the modern dictionaries do not do so.[5] *Poison oak* is apparently the older usage, *poison ivy* the newer, although the change is gradual. There are a few scattered occurrences of *poison vine*.

Sidewalk.   The southern Louisiana *banquette* occurs only once in Texas—in Jefferson County (Map 44). No other variant of *sidewalk* was recorded.

Grove of trees.   A small group of trees together, surrounded by open country, is referred to as a *grove* (75 oc.) or a *clump* (32 oc.). *Mott* (70 oc.) is rather heavily concentrated in South Central and West Texas (Map 6). Of the nine occurrences of *island* with this meaning, eight are found in the southeastern corner of the state.

Plot where cotton is raised.   The usual expression, applicable to cotton acreage on the family farm, is *cotton patch* (133 oc.). *Cotton field* (57 oc.) is usually thought to apply to larger areas.

Second crop.   *Second crop* (109 oc.), *volunteer crop* (46 oc.), *second cutting* (19 oc.), *top crop* (18 oc.), and *second growth* (10 oc.) are all in use to designate a crop produced after the first one is harvested. Naturally, these do not all apply indiscriminately to all crops. *Top crop*, applicable to a second crop of cotton, rather clearly marks the heart of the old cotton country (Map 114).

THE HOUSE

Nice room at the front.   As in other areas, what was called the *parlor* (43) is giving way to the *living room* (54). A good many refer to this as the *front room* (23) or the *sitting room* (14). The latter is

[5] E.g., *American College Dictionary, Webster's New World Dictionary,* and others. *Webster's Third New International* is somewhat better, but still allows for much overlapping in meaning.

current on all age levels except the very youngest, but is probably also obsolescent.

Shelf over the fireplace. *Mantel* (68) is the most frequent word, in all areas and groups; *mantelpiece* (22) is somewhat less common. *Mantelboard* (13) also occurs, as does the South Midland *fireboard* (10), which is scattered through all major areas (Map 73). All of these are obsolescent except *mantel.*

Troughs to carry off rain. For the metal troughs on a roof, *gutters* (76) is in very general use, apparently without any confusion with the gutters of a street. Neither the Northern *eaves troughs* (6) nor the Midland *spouts* (3.3) has established itself.

Place to keep clothing. *Clothes closet* (49) is the most prevalent term for a place to hang up clothes, followed by *closet* (36). *Wardrobe* (15) is also in use, probably pointing to an era when separate rooms for clothing were not as generally used as pieces of furniture made for this purpose. *Clothes press* (2.9), common in some parts of the country, is almost nonexistent in Texas.

Unfinished space at the top of the house. For the part of a house immediately under the roof, *attic* (86) is in almost universal use, but a few informants use *loft* (15), apparently regardless of whether the structure is a barn or a house (Map 110). *Garret* (7), which also occurs, is almost obsolete.

Porch. For the rather broad, roofed-over areas that most houses used to have, *porch* (30) is a common modern word. A good many feel it necessary to specify *front porch* (33) or *back porch* (39). *Gallery* (39), *front gallery* (7), and *back gallery* (8) (Map 57) are still widely current, although they are obsolescent. *Veranda* (13) probably has a suggestion of luxury; although it is not a newer usage, it is more frequent among better-educated informants. The Northern *stoop* (11) is not of general currency, and is usually used to denote a smaller, unroofed variety of porch.

Room for storage. A room where disused articles are stored is generally a *store room* (40), but is also frequently called a *junk room* (25). An older term that is current, particularly in Central Texas, is *plunder room* (8) (Map 38). A few informants use *smoke house* (7) with this meaning, since no doubt many of the old smoke houses now serve no other purpose.

Siding. For the horizontal, overlapping boards on the outside of the house, the traditional words are *weatherboards* (35) and *weatherboarding* (10). However, the commercial term *siding* (37) is being widely adopted. A few informants use *shiplap* (12), although this material is hardly suitable to finish a respectable house. The Northern *clapboards* (11) is not very well known; to most old-timers this would mean vertical boards or slabs, formerly hand-split.

Main ranch house. The main dwelling on a ranch is called by various names, the most common being *headquarters* (20) and the *big house* (14). *Hacienda* (8), meaning the central establishment of a ranch, usually a very luxurious one, is concentrated in Southwest Texas, with West Texas also showing a few occurrences (Map 7). According to one informant, this word should properly apply to an estate in Mexico, and its use in Texas is rather pretentious. The largest establishment of this type in Texas, or anywhere else (the King Ranch), is always known as the *Ranch;* and its headquarters is known as the *Big House.*

Split boards. For the slabs or boards that were formerly split from a straight-grained log with a froe, *clapboards* (42 oc.) is still fairly well known. *Shingles* (40 oc.) and *shakes* (33 oc.) are also in use, but *shingles* no doubt represents something of a shift in meaning, since the old clapboards were used for a number of purposes besides roofing.

GOODS AND CHATTELS

Piece of furniture containing drawers. The most usual responses for this item are *bureau* (40) and *dresser* (40), with *chest of drawers* (28) not far behind. *Chiffonier* (22) and *chifforobe* (14), no doubt formerly elegant terms, still continue in use, the latter being defined as containing not only drawers but a space to hang clothes as well. *Highboy* (12) is also still in use.

Piece of furniture for hanging clothes. *Wardrobe* (131 oc.) is undoubtedly the prevalent term; a few informants, however, use *chifforobe* (18 oc.) with this meaning. The Louisiana *armoire*, which, like *chifforobe*, denotes a combination of wardrobe and chest of drawers, is of rare occurrence in Texas (Map 50).

Piece of furniture for keeping foods. Before the days of universal refrigeration, many of the less perishable foods were kept in a large enclosure with perforated doors known generally as the *safe*

(114 oc.). The obsolescence of the word is quite striking and will be discussed later. *Cupboard* (63 oc.) is by no means unknown, but the chances are that Old Mother Hubbard, had she lived in Texas, would have gone to the *safe*. Some of those who use *cabinet* (33 oc.) may have in mind the modern and now universal type of kitchen equipment.

Window shades.   Informants were supposed to have been asked for words meaning the kind of window coverings that roll up and down on' rollers. For this, most responses were *shades* (44) or *window shades* (32). A number of fieldworkers recorded the Midland *blinds* (23), but twelve informants specifically state that this means wooden shutters outside the window. To others, *blinds* denotes venetian blinds.

Sofa.   The long piece of furniture to sit or stretch out on has been given a variety of modish names. In Texas the predominant words are *couch* (37), *sofa* (30), *divan* (27), and *davenport* (23). *Lounge* (12) and *settee* (11) also continue in use, the latter being most common in Central Texas (Map 43). *Duofold* (2.2) and *studio couch* (1.8) are far behind. *Lounge* and *settee* seem to be older usages; *divan*, possibly a symbol of elegance, is somewhat more current among educated informants.

Household goods (worthless).   For miscellaneous goods not highly esteemed by the owner or others, the very general term *junk* (40) appears frequently. A more precise word is *plunder* (26), probably of German origin.[6]

Irons to hold logs for burning.   The iron devices used in a fireplace are known variously as *andirons* (43), *dog irons* (40), and *fire dogs* (14) (Map 102). All of these are older usages, no doubt because of the decline of the fireplace in favor of gas heating. *Andirons* has a higher frequency among better-educated informants.

Backlog.   The large log that used to hold fire in the fireplace for a long period is almost universally known as the *backlog* (144 oc.). However, there are nine Texas occurrences of *back stick*, a term that shows somewhat more currency in southern Arkansas (Map 109).

Wooden water container.   For the old wooden device used to draw or carry water, *bucket* (67), with its variants *water bucket* (8), *cedar bucket* (7), and *wooden bucket* (6), far outnumber the occurrences of *pail* (13).

[6] Cassell's *German-English Dictionary* defines the German *Plunder* as "lumber [in the British sense, of course], trash, rubbish."

Metal water (or milk) container. *Bucket* (51) is the predominant usage, along with the variants *milk bucket* (11), *tin bucket* (6), and *water bucket* (3.3). However, *pail* and *milk pail* (36) are considerably more frequent than in the preceding item (Map 106).

Dinner or lunch container. Words for the container in which a man carries his noon meal are *lunch box* (26), *lunch pail* (26), *dinner bucket* (22), *lunch bucket* (14), *dinner pail* (10), *lunch kit* (8), *lunch basket* (4.4), and a few miscellaneous expressions. *Dinner bucket* is strikingly archaic; the phrases containing the word *lunch* are undoubtedly gaining ground.

Waste food container. The question was designed to elicit the word for the farmyard container used to save food for pigs. *Slop bucket* (50) is clearly the predominant term, although it is growing old. The urban equivalent, of course, is *garbage can* (33). The Northern *swill* (as in *swill pail*) did not appear.

Coal container. This item was added to the work sheets rather late. It produced 45 occurrences of *(coal) bucket*, 44 of *(coal) scuttle*, 7 of *hod*. All of these are old-fashioned, since natural gas has been available for a long time, replacing both coal and cow-chips.

Cloth for drying dishes. The cloth with which women used to dry and polish dishes is known as a *cup towel* (45), *dish towel* (39), *dish cloth* (11), *tea towel* (10), *drying rag* (7), or *drying cloth* (5). See Map 85.

Heavy pan for frying. *Skillet* (80) is competing very successfully with *frying pan* (41). There is no doubt that differentiation in meaning has set in. A good many informants specifically state that a frying pan is thinner, or lighter, or smaller, or shallower, than a skillet. *Spider* (3.3), which is fairly well known in the North and parts of the Coastal South, is nothing more than a remnant in Texas.

Device to turn on the water. The device that one turns to make water run is a *faucet* (74), or a *hydrant* (59), or both (Map 87). *Faucet* is coming to predominate for the indoor gadget, *hydrant* for a similar device in the yard. Somewhat more rare are *spigot* (4) and *spicket* (3.7), both of which are in general use in the South Atlantic States.

Large jar for drinking water. In most parts of the state it was difficult to find informants who were familiar with the large, porous, earthenware jar which has been so successfully used to cool drinking water in dry climates. Of those who gave the response *olla* (pronounced *oya*) (8), nearly all were in Southwest or West Texas (Map 14). Four informants give *demijohn*, meaning a large jug or bottle.

Cloth cover for a bed pillow. *Pillow case* (47) is now somewhat more frequently used than *pillow slip* (33), yet the latter is by no means rustic. However, *pillow case*, being supported by commercial usage, is rapidly increasing in popularity. There are three scattered occurrences of the archaic *pillow bier*.

Paper container. The paper receptacle for groceries and other lesser property is indiscriminately known as a *(paper) sack* (71) or a *(paper) bag* (35). *Poke* (14), an old Midland word, is scattered through all parts of the state (Map 94). It is disappearing rapidly.

Oil for lamps. The oil formerly much used for lighting, and occasionally heating, is most frequently known as *coal oil* (76), with *kerosene* (42) as a common variant. Both of these are current in all age groups. *Lamp oil* (3.3) is rare and scattered.

Bed on the floor. When there is an excess of visitors, someone must sleep on a *pallet* (92). This is universal usage in all parts of Texas and in neighboring states. The only peculiar feature of usage here is that in most northern portions of the United States there is no word for this type of accommodation.[7] *Bunk* and *shakedown* do not occur in Texas with this meaning. Four informants give *Baptist pallet*, probably in allusion to large religious gatherings and their attendant discomforts.

Topmost covering for the bed. *Bedspread* (51) is steadily replacing the archaic terms *counterpin* (35), *counterpane* (24), *coverlid* (6) and *coverlet* (3.7). *Counterpane* is distinctly an educated form; *counterpin*, its uneducated counterpart. *Spread* is the favored word in southern Louisiana, and this appears occasionally in Texas, particularly in the southeastern portion (Map 51).

Heavy tacked (not quilted) bed cover. *Comfort* (68), which is usual throughout the Midland and South, predominates in all parts of Texas. The Northern form *comforter* (15) appears also, with slightly greater frequency in Southwest Texas than elsewhere. Both of these words are apparently obsolescent. *Quilt* (14) for this item probably reflects a confusion resulting from unfamiliarity with the old art of

[7] Hans Kurath, *A Word Geography of the Eastern United States* (Ann Arbor, University of Michigan Press, 1949), p. 61, and Figure 88.

quilting; at any rate, it is used somewhat more often by younger informants. *Sugan*[8] (4.4), which is confined to West and Northwest Texas, probably carries the idea of a cover used for outdoor sleeping (Map 9).

Wood to start the fire. The small pieces of wood used to kindle a fire are usually referred to as *kindlin(g)* (68) or *kindlin(g) wood* (20). A few prefer *chips* (6), and there are scattered uses of *pine, shavings,* and *splinters.* The Coastal Southern *lightwood* (or *light'ood*) (2.6) is quite rare, and occurrences are scattered through East and Southwest Texas. As a matter of actual reality, wood was usually not available in the western areas, so cow-chips often had to be used instead. Two informants specifically point this out.

TIME AND DISTANCE

Between noon and night. For the period of time extending roughly from the noon meal to twilight (but not ordinarily including the darkness), *evening* (73) is usually used. However, *afternoon* (35) is also quite well known, and is apparently gradually replacing the older usage.

Fifteen minutes before a given hour. The expression *quarter* (or *fifteen*) *till* (54), characteristic of the Midland, is well established in all parts of Texas and to some extent in neighboring states, but it is somewhat uncommon in southern Louisiana (Map 80). It appears to be holding its own if not gaining ground. Also in fairly general use are *quarter to* (24) and *quarter of* (23); the latter is clearly an educated usage.

Period of time of indefinite length. *Spell* (42), in such phrases as *quite a spell, a long spell,* and others, occurs somewhat more often than *while* (33) in similar combinations. *Spell* is about equally common in the various areas of the state, as well as in the age groups and educational types.

A certain distance. The word *piece* (48), in such phrases as a *little piece, a long piece, a far* (or *fur*) *piece, a good piece,* and so on, is well established in all parts of the state except the Trans-Pecos (Map 77).

The farthest one can go. A plurality of speakers use the construction *as far as (he can go)* (35). A number of others use *the farthest*

---

[8] Pronounced something like *soogin.*

(18), or *the furthest* (2.2). The Midland construction *all the further (farther)* (11) is not in general use (Map 76). Of those who use the superlative form, about one-third use a double suffix: *fartherest* or *furtherest.*

Some distance off.   *Yonder (over yonder,* etc.) is prevalent and completely standard throughout the state. More than twice as many informants give *(over) yonder* (136 oc.) as *(over) there* (52 oc.). *Yonder* is neither archaic nor characteristic of the uneducated.

THE PREMISES

Wall (or fence) made of rocks (or stones).   A barrier built of rocks is usually known as a *rock wall* (45) or a *rock fence* (38). *Stone wall* (17) and *stone fence* (7) also occur. None of these expressions are characteristic of any particular area or age group.

Fence made of wooden rails.   For the old-time fence made of split logs, only *rail fence* (70) has any great currency. *Stake and rider fence* (6) is still known to the very oldest informants, who may know something of its construction. *Worm fence* (5) is also extremely archaic, and appears primarily in North and Central Texas (Map 74).

Fence made of upright slats.   *Picket fence* (67) and *paling fence* (38) are, for all practical purposes, synonyms. There is some evidence that *paling fence* is an older usage and that *palings* are a little more likely to be handmade than *pickets* are (Map 81).

Place to enclose cows.   *Cow pen* (47) is slightly more common than *(cow) lot* (40); both, however, are current in all areas and age groups. *Corral* (19) with this meaning is characteristic of Southwest, West, and Northwest Texas (Map 19).

Place to enclose horses.   The usual word for a horse enclosure is *(horse) lot* (69). This seems to be retreating to the eastward as *corral* (38) gains ground. The latter is somewhat concentrated in the western half of the state (Map 20), but occurs in other areas as well. *(Horse) pen* (7) is not a usual term; *(horse) trap* (3.7), which denotes a much larger enclosure than a *lot,* is confined to the western ranch country (Map 12), and occurs most consistently in the Trans-Pecos area.

The western *corral,* being constructed to contain a more enterprising sort of horse than the eastern *lot,* is often very strongly built from poles or rails placed horizontally or upright.

Place to enclose hogs. *Pig pen* (53) and *hog pen* (50) are about equal in every respect; *hog lot* (2.2) is barely current. The term *(pig) sty* (12), which is at home principally in the Northeastern States, occurs a surprising number of times.

General enclosure about the barn. The trouble with this item is that most informants had no conception of a single enclosure for all purposes. When such an idea is intended, *barn lot* (26), *barnyard* (26), and *lot* (21) are the usual responses. In addition, a number of informants used one of the terms in the previous items, such as *cow lot* (15). *Corral* (3.3) with this meaning is rare, and is confined to West and Northwest Texas.

Bag used to feed a horse. The bag attached to a horse's head (to prevent the waste of feed) is known as a *feed bag* (43) in all parts of the state, though not predominantly in the West. In the old ranch country the Spanish loanword *morral* (35) remains in regular use (Map 23). *Nose bag* (15) is still another variant.

The *morral*, as some informants point out, was used more often for the carrying of one's belongings than for the feeding of horses.

Rope used with cattle. Aside from the universal *rope*, the old ranching term *reata* (8) is still current, presumably for a rawhide rope rather than one made of hemp. It is distinctly concentrated in Southwest Texas, although there are a few occurrences in the West (Map 7). If the rope has a loop or noose, another Spanish loanword, *lariat* (57), is in much more frequent use and over a wider area. Still a third Spanish derivative, *lasso* (34), occurs throughout the area (Map 31). A peculiar phenomenon of Central Texas is *ropin(g) rope* (4.8) (Map 40), while *catch rope* (3.7) occurs sporadically in West and Northwest Texas.

Band to hold the saddle on. The band that passes under the horse's belly to keep the saddle tight is very commonly known as the *(saddle) girt* (32) or the *(saddle) girth* (24). The Spanish loan *cinch* (28) is also well known, particularly in the western half of the state (Map 29). *Belly band* (13) with this meaning also occurs, and a few informants in southern Louisiana use *girdle*.

Shed. The crude structure used to house tools or wood is ordinarily called a *shed* (114 oc.), but some twenty-five informants, primarily in Central Texas, speak of it as a *tool house* or *wood house* (Map 39).

Chaps. The articles of apparel worn on the legs, originally for riding through heavy or thorny brush, are known to informants of all ages as *chaps*[9] (68), and this usage occurs in all of the surrounding states (Map 35). Nearly every modern boy has had a pair of these at one time or another, for the purpose of "playing cowboy." A number of informants give *(leather) leggins* (24), but this is often thought to mean something different from *chaps*.

Working clothes. Several kinds of garments are named and described by the informants. Most of them are familiar with *overalls*, or *overhalls* (73), which designates a garment with a "bib" and suspenders. Another style, with sleeves, is termed *coveralls* (18). For the kind of tight duck or denim pants formerly associated with ranch hands, *levis* (14) sometimes occurs in the old ranch country and in part of Central Texas (Map 16). A more general term for this type of attire is *(blue) jeans* (13); this has, of course, been adopted by adolescents the country over to designate their uniform. *Duckins* (5), which can apply to the pants, or the jacket, or both, is more or less limited to West Texas (Map 16).

Flat piece of stone to sharpen knives. The stone on which knives are rubbed to sharpen them is usually known as a *whetrock* (56). This term is used about equally in all parts of the state, and extends into adjoining states as well (Map 88). *Whetstone* (35) is in limited use in all age groups and educational types.

Round, revolving stone. Contrary to the general tendency to prefer *rock* to *stone* in various contexts (for example, *whetrock, rock wall*), the usual word for the large revolving device for sharpening axes and similar implements is *grindstone* (72). The rather rare *grindrock* (7) is characteristic of older informants.

Support used to saw boards. *Sawhorse* (84) is the general Texas term in all areas and categories of informants. *Trestle* (6) is characteristic of the oldest informants. The fact that *sawbuck* (7) also occurs with this meaning may reflect some confusion with the next item.

Support used to saw logs. The x-shaped device used to hold logs in place is known by a variety of names, including *sawhorse* (18), *sawbuck* (13), *wood rack* (7), *saw rack* (6), and *saw jack* (2.2). All of these tend to be infrequent in the younger groups. For the distribution of *rack*, see Map 108.

Amount of wood one can carry. *Armload* (57), *armful* (30), and *load* (11) are all in use, apparently indiscriminately, since the survey

---

[9] Sometimes given as *shaps*.

reveals no trends for any of them. *Turn* (7), an old Coastal Southern word, which occurs in various parts of the state (Map 58), is rare and archaic.

Buggy shafts. Informants who remember a buggy remember the wooden poles that used to extend on each side of the horse. These were the *shavs* (54) or the *shaf(t)s* (31). A Northern equivalent, *thills* (often pronounced *fills*), is just about nonexistent (2.9).[10]

Wooden bar to which a single horse is attached. The wooden bar with a swivel in the middle, to which the traces (or tugs) of a single horse were attached, is ordinarily known (or remembered) as a *single-tree* (85). The Northern equivalents *whiffletree* (4) and *whippletree* (2.9) are confined to the oldest informants in Texas.

Bar for two singletrees. Each horse had his *singletree*, and where there were two horses, the singletrees were in turn attached to a *double-tree* (82). This is the only term in use; the Northern *evener* (1.5) has almost disappeared, if it was ever current. A few informants volunteered terms for a longer bar in case there were three or more horses; these are *tripletree* (4), *trebletree* (3.3), *thribbletree* (2.2), and *fourbletree* (2.2).

Halter. For various devices, formerly made of rope, used to control an unruly horse, the prevalent word is *hackamore* (51), which is most common in the old ranch country (Map 27). This hardly occurs in the states to the east of Texas, but is apparently known in New Mexico. The alternate responses, *halter* (34) and *rope halter* (6), probably reflect less familiarity with ranching practice. A historical Spanish borrowing, *bosal*[11] (2.2) occasionally appears with this meaning or a similar one (Map 8).

Waste food for pigs. The food that is saved to be fed to the pigs is universally known as *slop* (96). There are a few occurrences of the Northern *swill* (9); but there is some indication that this has acquired the meaning of a kind of grain mash, specifically mixed for the purpose.[12]

---

[10] "The Wonderful One-Hoss Shay" included a reference to the *thills*, which used to puzzle Southern students, as it no doubt now puzzles all students.

[11] See M. M. Mathews, *Dictionary of Americanisms* (Chicago, University of Chicago Press, 1951).

[12] Five informants mention this distinction between *slop* and *swill*.

Big burlap sack. The multipurpose sack made of brown burlap is known to most Texans as a *tow sack* (78). *Gunny sack* (33) is also familiar through all major areas. *Croker sack* (10) is principally concentrated in East Texas (but not Louisiana, where a considerable variety of expressions are in use). It is clearly archaic. *Grass sack* (9) has a certain currency, particularly in Central and Southwest Texas (Map 39), and a few other designations, such as *feed sack* (7), *burlap sack* (6), and others, occur in a scattered way. The geography of all of these terms is very complex, and some of them will be discussed in Chapter IV (see also Map 69).

Ranch employee. The ordinary hired hand on a ranch is generally known as a *cowhand* (39), particularly in the areas of the early ranches.[13] *Cowboy* (28) is likewise more frequent in the west. *Cowpuncher* (8) and *cowpoke* (3.3) are also in occasional use, the latter particularly in the Northwest. Various designations for specialized jobs are recorded *(bronc buster, cook, foreman)*, but the only one of interest here is *(horse) wrangler* (22), from Spanish *caballerango*. This is also somewhat uncommon in East Texas, but is fairly well known elsewhere (Map 24). *Buckaroo* (4), supposedly a widely used western term, has never caught on in Texas. *Vaquero* (4.4), preserving a "purer" Spanish form, is confined to Southwest and Central Texas (Map 2).

Boat used on a river. This item was tried on only part of the informants and without much success in Texas. In southern Louisiana, *pirogue*, for a kind of canoe, has considerable currency (Map 48); but it occurs only four times in Texas, three of these occurrences being in Jefferson and Orange Counties.

Outdoor toilet. The old-style comfort station outside of the house is generally known as the *privy* (133 oc.). *Outhouse* (53 oc.), *toilet* (42 oc.), *backhouse* (14 oc.), and *closet* (13 oc.) just about complete the list of common and respectable words, although a number of local, individualistic, and imaginative terms occur occasionally.[14]

VARIOUS FAUNA

Animal with the bad odor. For the familiar black-and-white animals *(Mephitis, Spilogale,* etc.) that secrete musk, or worse, the most widely

---

[13] Southwest Texas shows 56 per cent, East Texas only 23 per cent.

[14] For example, *Chic Sale, Congress, Federal Building* (no doubt from unreconstructed Confederates), *crapper, escusada* (two occurrences, both from Anglos), *john, johnnie, one-* (or more) *holer, post office, shit-house, sugar bowl,* and so on.

known word is *polecat* (69); but *skunk* (52), which is in general characteristic of the Northern part of the country, is gaining ground. A few informants use *civet cat* (6) and *civvy cat* (2.2), although some state that this means a different kind of varmint.

Terrestrial squirrel. For the many small squirrel-like rodents that run along the ground, *ground squirrel* (69) is most prevalent. However, *chipmunk* (13) is also known, particularly to the better-educated informants. Some seven informants state that a *ground squirrel* is different from a *chipmunk*. There are eleven occurrences of *prairie dog*, a confusion presumably due to the fact that the chipmunk was unknown in the area.

Dry-land froglike animal. The terrestrial creature which everyone is sure causes warts *(Bufo vulgaris*, etc.) is most generally known as a *toadfrog* (61) (Map 113); a fair number simply use *frog* (18). The dictionary word *toad* (22) is considerably more frequent in the usage of the educated.

Call to horses. The use of a particular call to induce horses to come in from the pasture is apparently not an extremely common Texas practice. Most informants state that they either whistle (46) or shout the name of the horse (17). The only horse call that is current can best be rendered by *cope!* (29).

Call to cows. Texans usually call the cattle home by yelling *sook!* (78), sometimes followed by the word *cow*, sometimes by the name of a particular cow. This call is usually rendered in a high and elongated falsetto, and conventional letters can hardly do justice to it. The call *sook!* is, in the Eastern States, characteristic of the Midland. The Northern call, *co boss!* (3.3), is very scattered in Texas. A few modernistic farmers and ranchers have apparently trained their cows to react to the sounding of a car horn[15]—which should work reasonably well if a busy highway does not invade their domain.

Command to a cow to stand still. When a cow begins to stomp her feet or slap her tail full of cockleburrs into the face of the milker, the latter calls *saw!* (66), or sometimes *so!* (10). In rural southern Louisiana a few bilinguals carry over the French *là!* (Map 45).

Call to chickens. All of the chicken calls recorded in Texas involve *chick* and *chickee*, repeated in various patterns.

---

[15] Five informants state that this is their practice.

Call to turkeys. Of those who know how to call turkeys, most use *turk(ee)* (33) in some form or other. Some others use *pee(p)* (9), while still others think that the way to get a turkey to come is to say *gobble-(gobble)* (8).[16]

The noise a horse makes.—For the rather gentle sound made by a horse when he wants to call attention to himself (perhaps at feeding time), the most common Texas word is *nicker* (41) which is also prevalent in Virginia and the South Midland. *Whinny* (25) and *neigh* (24) are also current. Although these show no regional distribution in Texas (Map 67), *nicker* is distinctly an older term. Some informants feel that *nicker* and *whinny* have different meanings, the latter perhaps indicating a louder or more frightened sound.

The noise a cow makes. The Midland *moo* (61) prevails in all areas and age groups. However, the old Coastal Southern *low* (34) (Map 61) is also known and used in all parts of the state, with least frequency in the Northwest. It is apparently obsolescent. *Bawl* (11) is also scattered through the state, with the exception of East Texas, where there is but one occurrence.

Band of saddle horses. For a band of saddle horses, still much used on ranches, the most popular specific word is *remuda* (30). This is current mainly in the old ranch country (Map 22). *Cavvy* (6) and *caviard* (3.3), both of which derive from the Spanish *caballada*, are given by a few informants, almost without exception in the older groups. Four informants actually give the Spanish form *caballada*. *String* (4) is also in use, but to a ranchman means something like an allotment of horses to a single hand. *Herd* (16), *bunch* (5), and other such words probably reflect unfamiliarity with ranching.

Little horse with big spots. The familiar western pony is usually referred to as a *paint* (47), although *pinto* (37) is also in fairly frequent use. *Paint* is general throughout the state, whereas *pinto* is more concentrated in the Southwest and West (Map 37). Neither word is at all usual in Louisiana. *Calico* for this sort of horse occurs at only five points in Texas, but at about twenty in Southern Arkansas (Map 37).

Horse on the left. Attempts to distinguish the two horses in a team resulted in some confusion, since fieldworkers were usually unfamiliar with the driving of teams. *Haw (horse)* (8) usually means the left-

---

[16] I seem to remember from childhood a combination call *pee, turk!* This was in Deaf Smith County, if I am not mistaken.

hand horse—*gee (horse)* (6), the one on the right; some informants could not remember which was which. Other terms for the left-hand horse are *near horse* (33) and *lead horse* (6). *Nigh horse* (3.3) is only a remnant. The other horse is most commonly the *off horse* (13).

Unbroken horse.   A horse that has not been broken for riding may vary from the tame colt of the Eastern farm to the completely un-domesticated animal of the Western prairies. The most usual Texas word for an unbroken horse is *bronc* (50), which occurs throughout the state, but with highest frequency in the West and Northwest. It has also penetrated into southern Arkansas. *Bronco* (16), the alternate form, is rather scattered but shows somewhat more concentration in Southwest and Central Texas than elsewhere (Map 28). *Wild horse* (23) occurs in all areas. Six informants in Southwest Texas give *potro* with this mean-ing (Map 8).

For the entirely undomesticated horse, *mustang* (18) is still known to a fair number of informants,[17] chiefly in Southwest and Central Texas. Almost without exception these speakers specify that the word means a particular type, or "breed," of horse that used to run wild, not an ordinary *bronc.*

To try to throw the rider.   When a bronc wants to dislodge the rider, he is usually said to *pitch* (61) or to *buck* (56). Only an occasional informant speaks specifically of *goating, crowhopping, sunfishing,* and so on—terms that are probably familiar in rodeo circles. *Pitch* and *buck* are probably interchangeable; only a very few informants try to distinguish on the basis of whether the front or the hind feet are in-volved. The informants do not agree even on this.

In Arkansas and Louisiana, *pitch* is of rare occurrence; only *buck* is widely current.

Lonesome calf.   For a calf, particularly a "range" calf, unaccom-panied by a parent, the usual Texas term is *dogie* (62). This word be-comes gradually less frequent as one moves eastward; it is rare in Arkansas and Louisiana (Map 32). A dogie, according to various informants, is "small," "undernourished," "starved," "stunted," "pot-bellied," or of "inferior breed."

---

[17] For a learned and fascinating account of the wild horses of the Southwest, see J. Frank Dobie, *The Mustangs* (Boston, Little, Brown and Company, 1952). The nickname of the Southern Methodist University (Dallas) football team, "the Mustangs," has no doubt made the term familiar to many moderns, who may or may not know what a mustang is.

Another word with a similar meaning is *maverick* (29), which occurs in all parts of Texas except the Northeast and the Trans-Pecos. It does not occur in states to the east (Map 25). No less than thirty-one informants specify that a *maverick* is an unbranded animal; a few others state or intimate that it is a stray. One defines it as a "stolen dogie"—which is quite in keeping with the origin of the word (Chapter VII).

Orphan (calf) (15) is rather scattered in Texas, but is more common in Arkansas and Louisiana.

Male horse. The only words in wide use are *stallion* (51), *stud* (42), and *stud-horse* (10). There are no euphemisms, but *stud (horse)* is slightly more frequent in the usage of men.

Male bovine (with original equipment). The plain term *bull* was given by 77 per cent of the Texas informants, with a steadily increasing frequency in the younger groups. Among the euphemisms that still survive are *male* (6) and *surly* (9). The latter is distinctly concentrated in the South Plains and a portion of Central Texas (Map 9); it is definitely archaic. A Southwest Texas word which still has a limited currency is *toro* (Map 4).

Equus asinus. Because of homonymic conflict (see Chapter VI), the dictionary word *ass* has become unusable for the beast of burden. There is only one Texas occurrence of this word—from a woman in her eighties—and one Louisiana occurrence—from a Negro who is a constant reader of the Bible.[18] Even *jackass* was given infrequently (5), but *jack* (10) is used a little more often.

The most common term for this animal is *donkey* (58), which occurs throughout the area surveyed. However, the Spanish *burro* (42) is almost as popular; it has clearly spread from the western portions, as is seen in the frequencies ranging from over 55 per cent in the Northwest, West, and Southwest to only 22 per cent in the East. There are also scattered occurrences in Oklahoma, Arkansas, and Louisiana (Map 33).

Setting hen. Although not on all work sheets, this item, in addition to *settin(g) hen*, produced some 64 instances of a form spelled *clook*, *cluck*, *glook*, and occasionally *clucker*. This usage is concentrated in Central Texas (Map 40), and is characteristic of, but not confined to, informants of German language background. Not one Texas informant uses the form *sitting*.

---

[18] In fact, he explains his usage by saying, "That's what the Bible calls it."

Woodpecker. Most Texas informants use the standard *woodpecker* (73), although this is somewhat less frequent in the three older groups. An alternate term, with reversal of the elements, is *peckerwood* (28), which occurs in most parts of the state except the Trans-Pecos area. This usage is shared with southern Arkansas and northern Louisiana (Map 93). Another word with this meaning is *woodchuck* (6). The latter two are characteristic of older informants.

Dragon fly. The large insect with transparent wings that is often seen hovering over water is usually known as *snake doctor* (49) or *mosquito (skeeter) hawk* (20). *Mosquito hawk*, uniformly used in Louisiana, is also solidly established in Southeast Texas. It also extends into Central and Southwest Texas, where it competes with the variant *snake doctor*, which strongly predominates in the western half of the state (Map 66). Neither the Northern *darning needle* (4 oc.) nor the Midland *snake feeder* (3 oc.) has any currency. Some informants have no regional term and give the dictionary word *dragon fly* (16). These tend to be persons of better education.

Mud daubers. The type of wasps that build mud cells are generally known as *dirt daubers* (66).[19] This term is universal in East Texas and is the majority form in all other areas, where *mud daubers* (27) also occurs. Only in southern Louisiana is the latter predominant.

Flying insect that glows. *Lightning bug* (89) is very heavily favored; the alternate *firefly* (15) is distinctly an educated variant.

Earthworm. As in the coastal area of the Carolinas, *earthworm* (58) is the most usual word for the annelid used for fish bait (Map 68). There is some rivalry, however, from *fish worm* (17), *fishin(g) worm* (13), *angleworm* (10), and *redworm* (9). The last of these, a South Midland usage, occurs with some frequency in southern Arkansas, and in a more scattered way in the northern portions of Texas (Map 68). The simple *worm*, which has some popularity in southern Louisiana, occurs only ten times in Texas, where no doubt a distinction is felt to be necessary.[20] *Rainworm*, which was recorded occasionally in German-speaking areas of the East, also occurs in Texas, but rarely. Nine of the ten users

---

[19] The word *daub* is pronounced *dob*, and is often so written.

[20] In any case, several other worms are mentioned as usable for fish bait: *catawba worms, grubworms, sawyers, stingin' worms, tobacco worms, tomato worms,* and so on.

are of German-speaking background. It is no doubt, as Kurath suggests,[21] a loan-translation of German *Regenwurm*.

Chigger.   The minute but maddening larvae that get under one's skin are known, throughout most of Texas, both as *chiggers* (70) and *redbugs* (50). *Redbug* is clearly characteristic of the Gulf Coast, and it strongly predominates in southern Louisiana[22] (Map 83). In Texas, its occurrences stop short of the Panhandle and the Trans-Pecos area, but elsewhere it is well established. Southern Arkansas also shows *redbugs* about half the time.

Horned toad.   The small flat lizard with horns on its head and back is known in Texas as a *horn, horned,* or *horny toad* (135 oc.) or a *horn, horned,* or *horny frog* (108 oc.). All of these are somewhat more frequent in the western portion of the state, where the creature is native (Map 105). North Texas prefers the forms with *frog*,[23] the Trans-Pecos leans strongly to *toad*. Otherwise the forms are geographically pretty well mixed, although educated informants show a fairly clear preference for *toad*. The form *horned* occasionally appears as *hornet*.

SOMETHING TO EAT

Fresh corn.   For the ears of fresh corn to be served at the table, all of Texas strongly prefers *roastin(g) ears* (85). *Corn on the cob* (18) is a newer phrase, and is somewhat more frequent among better-educated informants. *Sweet corn* (5) is the only other term with any currency.

Beans served in the pods.   The usual terms for fresh beans in the pods are *snap beans* (or *snaps*) (52), *green beans* (36), and *string beans* (30). *Snap beans*, a Coastal Southern usage, is strongly favored in Louisiana, and it extends to all parts of Texas (Map 63). It is becoming less common. *Green beans*, a Midland term, is used in competition with *snap beans* in all parts of the state. *String beans* occurs everywhere, along with the other variants, with the greatest currency in East Texas (50). *Green beans* is most frequent in the younger groups.

[21] Kurath, *Word Geography*, p. 75.
[22] Only one informant in southern Louisiana uses *chigger* alone. Of those who use it interchangeably with *redbug*, almost all are urban. One Louisiana informant remarks that these insects were never called *chiggers* "until the Yankees got there."
[23] Notice that the football team of Texas Christian University (Fort Worth) is called the "Horned Frogs," not the "Horned Toads."

Large flat beans. For the large flat beans, dried or fresh, the favorite Texas term is *butter beans* (87). This is very frequent in all areas and in all age groups, but it is losing some ground. The alternate, *lima beans* (27), occurs in all geographical areas; it is a newer usage and is somewhat more characteristic of educated informants. Since *lima beans* is the usual commercial usage and can hardly be eliminated, and since most speakers are loath to give up *butter beans,* a fairly consistent attempt is made to differentiate the meanings of the two terms. The usual explanations are that *butter beans* are larger and lighter in color than *lima beans;* some state that *butter beans* are dried while *lima beans* are served green. There are some who reverse these distinctions and others who make no distinction at all.

Mexican brown beans. Those who have been influenced by Mexican cookery are very familiar with the western spotted beans (brown when cooked), which are usually marketed in dried form. The commercial term *pinto beans,* or *pintos* (63), is current all through the state, but with somewhat less frequency in Southwest Texas (45). The older regional word is the Spanish *frijoles* (25), which shows the highest frequency in Southwest Texas (62), but which is also well known in the West and part of the Central area. It is nonoccurrent in East Texas, Arkansas, and Louisiana (Map 17). A number of informants use *red beans* (17), presumably because a good deal of chili often goes with the beans; a few others use *brown beans* (4.4) or *chili beans* (3.3). A jocular kenning given by a few informants is *Mexican strawberries.*

Clingstone peach. The only words that have any currency are *clingstone (peach)* (51) and *cling (peach)* (30). Neither the Virginia *plum peach* (4) nor the Carolina *press peach* (1.8) can be said to have established itself; both usages are confined to informants over sixty.

Freestone peach. A considerable majority of Texas informants in all areas speak of a *freestone peach* (72). *Clearseed* (15), which is rather concentrated in southern Arkansas, has invaded certain of the northern portions of Texas (Map 107). It is clearly archaic.

Seed of a peach. The usual Texas term in all areas is *(peach) seed* (76). *Stone* (18) is somewhat scattered and is more popular among the educated. *Pit* (10) is even less current, with some tendency to concentration in the Northwest and West.

Seed of a cherry. *(Cherry) seed* (58) is the predominant term; however, *pit* (34) is much more frequent than in the preceding item. The latter, apparently of Dutch origin,[24] is, in the Eastern states, characteristic of the North. *(Cherry) stone* (12) is even more limited. Both *pit* and *stone* are slightly more current among educated informants.

Small cake. A rather unsystematic, and in general unsuccessful, attempt was made to elicit words for various small pastries. *Cookie* (25) was the most common response followed by *muffin* (20), *teacake* (19), and *cupcake* (18). Of course, these do not all mean the same thing. *Teacake* is archaic; it shows its greatest concentration in North and Central Texas (Map 103).

Something between meals. Food consumed between the regular three meals is generally called a *snack* (77); the next most popular word is *lunch* (14). The latter has its greatest concentration in Central Texas (Map 42). Other informants use *bite* (12) or, rarely, *piece* (2.9).

Flat pecan candy. The Louisiana *praline*[25] (43) has penetrated to all parts of Texas (Map 55), where it is replacing the older *(pecan) patty* (25).

Homemade curd cheese. The type of cheese made simply by draining the whey from clabber and using the curd is perennially popular. In Texas, as elsewhere, the creamery term *cottage cheese* (51) has gone far toward replacing the older regional usages. The most widespread of these is *clabber cheese* (26), which occurs in all parts of the state, but which is strikingly characteristic of older informants. A few informants, also predominantly older, use *curd* (12). A word evidently borrowed from the German colonists is *smearcase* (8), which shows most concentration in Central Texas and among informants of German-speaking background[26] (Map 41). Some thirteen informants, all of German extraction, give *kochcase*, while eight others give the translated form *cook-cheese*. These two terms designate a different type of homemade cheese, which involves the cooking of the curd.

The southern Louisiana *cream cheese* (also meaning cottage cheese) has penetrated into, but not much beyond, the southeastern counties of Texas (Map 52).

[24] Cf. Dutch *pit*, meaning a seed or kernel.

[25] In Texas generally pronounced *pray-*, in Louisiana *prah-*. But Mima Babington has recorded a few instances of metathesis, with *plarine*.

[26] Since *smearcase* is also Pennsylvania German, and since it has spread over the entire North Midland, some of the Texas occurrences may be importations from farther north rather than independent borrowings from Texas German. See Kurath, *Word Geography*, Figure 125.

Curdled milk. To designate milk that has turned sour and thick, the almost universal Texas word is *clabber* (85), while only a few informants give *clabber(ed) milk* (8). *Sour milk* (5) and *curds* (4) occur very sporadically. None of the Northern terms, such as *bonny-clabber* or *lobbered milk,* are current; and the Pennsylvania German *thick milk* occurs but five times.

Milk that is turning. Milk that has not yet become clabber but that is too sour to drink is usually described by the adjective *blinky* (65). This is used somewhat less often in the youngest groups. A noun with a similar meaning is *bluejohn* (23), which may also imply poor milk, although only one informant specifically says so. The term is decidedly archaic. Very few Texas informants give the word *sour* (5), which is usual in Louisiana (Map 86).

Salt pork. For the sides of pork preserved in salt, usually at home, *salt pork* is most frequent (93 oc.), while *sowbelly* (Map 75) is reasonably common (85 oc.). The North Midland *side meat* is also current (23 oc.), as is *middlin(s)* (17 oc.). For the Louisiana usage *salt meat,* see Map 47. Other terms in occasional use in Texas include *bacon, side bacon, dry salt (bacon), fatback,* and *sowbosom.* Two informants convert *sowbelly* into *sourbelly,* by a kind of folk etymology.

Griddle cake. The flat cake made of wheat flour and cooked on a griddle is most often termed *pancake* (133 oc.), *hotcake* (79 oc.), *flapjack* (65 oc.), *battercake* (39 oc.), or *griddle cake* (18 oc.). Of these, *battercake* and *flapjack* are obsolescent; *hotcake* and *pancake* are both gaining ground.

Pressed pork. For the pressed, jellied loaf made of hogs' jowls and other parts, the most popular term is *souse (meat)* (64). *Head cheese* (22) appears throughout all areas, while *hog('s)-head cheese* (17), the Louisiana usage, is more or less concentrated in the Southeast, the Southwest, and part of the Central area (Map 54). There are seven occurrences of *silze*[27] from German-speaking informants of Kerr, Kendall, Gillespie, and Comal Counties.

"Soft" bottled drink. The omnipresent nonalcoholic beverages that are served cold in bottles go by a variety of names, the most frequent of which is *soda* (or *sody*) *pop* (38). This expression occurs everywhere, but is more common in the western and northern portions of the

---

[27] Cassell's *German-English Dictionary* gives both *Sülze* and *Sulze,* meaning "jelly; meat covered with a jelly."

state. A more regional term which occurs with some frequency is *soda* (or *sody*) *water* (34). This is most prevalent in the eastern and southern portions, as also in southern Arkansas (Map 99). *Cold drink* (16) is also in use, as is the simple *pop* (14). *Soft drink* (4.4) is rare in Texas but somewhat more usual in southern Louisiana.

Doughnut. For the sweetish, doughy, fried pastry with a hole, *doughnut* (75) is the only word of wide currency, and it seems to apply to all varieties, as long as they have a hole. The Northern *fried cake* (5) is rare and scattered. *Cruller* (7) is also in limited use, but informants are in agreement that this is different from a *doughnut*—it has no hole, it is long, the dough is twisted, and so on. Some five informants of German-speaking background use *krebbel*, while a few of French origin in southern Louisiana give *baignet*.

The corn bread family. Without any specific list of recipes, fieldworkers gathered as many expressions as possible for breads and breadlike foods made of corn meal. These might well be mentioned in alphabetical order, with no attempt at exact description other than brief summaries of informants' comments.

Batter bread (4.4)— same as *spoon bread* (refer to following list).
Corn bread (76).
Corn dodger (8)—fried in a skillet.
Corn muffin (3.7).
Corn pone (29)—inferior to corn bread, with only meal and water— no eggs, etc.
Corn stick (5)—long individual piece of corn bread.
Cracklin(g) bread (9)—contains "cracklins": ground-up pork skins from which the fat has been rendered.
Egg bread (9)—a better variety of corn bread, made with meal and eggs; occasionally a synonym of *spoon bread* (Map 84).
Hoecake (10)—simple meal and water—fried or "baked" in a skillet or on the top of a stove.
Hot water (corn) bread (5)—apparently the same as *pone*.
Hush puppy (7)—lump of fried meal.
Johnny cake (4)—meaning not clear.
Mush (38)—This is the closest thing to spoon bread for many Texas informants, but the resemblance is slight.
Spoon bread (33)—soft, contains eggs, baked like a pudding and served with a spoon. Well known in some Texas families, not known at all in others (Map 84).

The southern Louisiana *cush-cush*, which designates some kind of mushy preparation with meal, shows up only twice in Texas (Jefferson and Orange Counties); four other informants use the simple form *cush* (Map 45).

White wheat bread. The ordinary bread made of white flour and baked in loaves is known throughout Texas as *light bread* (79). Only a small number use *white bread* (10), and even fewer seem content with the simple word *bread* (2.9). *Light bread* is almost universal in the South and South Midland, but *white bread* is making a little progress in Texas.

Chicken's furculum. The forked bone of a chicken, commonly served with some of the best "white meat" attached to it, is traditionally broken apart by two children as a sort of wishing charm. As in the rest of the South, this bone is most generally known in Texas as the *pully bone* (78). *Wishbone* (37) is also fairly widespread, with somewhat more frequency among younger informants; it is the only word used in southern Louisiana (Map 72).

"The bracts investing an ear of Indian corn."[28]   The outer leafy coverings of ears of corn are almost always referred to as *shucks* (91), but a few informants use *husks* (13) with this meaning. *Husks* is characteristic of the North and North Midland, *shucks* of the South and South Midland.

Gumbo. The thick soup containing okra (and many other appealing ingredients, both animal and vegetable) is known throughout Louisiana as *gumbo*, and this usage has spread to most of Texas (145 oc.)—but it is doubtful that the dish itself is comparable to that of the "Creoles." In any case, Louisiana usage requires that *gumbo* be used if okra is included; in southern Arkansas, however, *(vegetable) soup* is usually employed whether okra is present or not (Map 56).

Hogs' intestines. The practice of eating the small intestines of hogs (boiled and afterward fried) is very widespread in the coastal South, where the universal word is *chittlin(g)s*.[29] This word-and-thing combination is well known throughout Texas (145 oc.), except in the Trans-Pecos area (Map 64).

---

[28] This gem is from *Webster's New Collegiate Dictionary* (1949). See the definition for *husk*.

[29] The dictionaries usually enter this word as *chitterlings*.

Peanuts. A common Southern word for peanuts is *goobers*, and this was used by 143 Texas informants, although the item was not on all of the worksheets.

FAMILY MATTERS

Resemble. When a boy is like his father, he is said to *favor* him (34) if the resemblance is primarily in appearance, or to *take after* him (46) if the likeness is in other traits as well.

Relatives. Those related to someone (to one's wife, for instance) are predominantly termed *kinfolks* (71), less often *folks* (14) or *relatives* (11). *Relations* (7) is less current, while *kin* (5) is both rare and archaic.

Parents. For the mother and father of someone (for example, of one's wife), *folks* (55) is usually regarded as sufficient. *Parents* (22) is, of course, in use, but is more characteristic of educated informants.

Brought up (children). If a woman has brought children to maturity, most Texas informants would say that she *raised* them (75). This usage predominates in all age and educational groups. *Reared* (23) is clearly an educated form.

Grandmother. The usual family term for one's grandmother is *Gran(d)ma* (66),[30] along with a further assimilated form *Gramma* (7). *Granny* (26) is also in use; it is slightly more common in the older groups, but by no means confined to them. A number of informants give *Grandmother* (18), but it is to be suspected that some of these would not have used the term in speaking *to* her. Of course, many private nicknames show up, most of them only once or twice each: *Ganny, Gram, Grammie, Mammaw, Nanita, Nanna, Nannie,* and so on. Fourteen informants of German background give *Oma*, while another uses *Grossmama*.

Grandfather. Familiar appellations for one's grandfather are *Gran-(d)pa* (70), *Grampa* (5), *Gramp* (3.3), *Gramps* (2.6), *Granddad* (10), and *Granddaddy* (8). *Grandfather* (11), like *Grandmother* above, may not always be "familiar." Miscellaneous nicknames recorded for this item include: *Big Papa, Gompy, Grandpap, Grandpappy* (only

---

[30] Of course, in this area -*pa* and -*ma* would be pronounced -*paw* and -*maw*, whether so spelled or not.

one), *Grandpop, Papaw, Poppaw,* and so on. Fourteen informants of German origin give *Opa;* another *Grosspapa.*[31]

Mother. The majority call their mother *Mama* (63),[32] which is favored in all age and educational groups. The older word *Ma* (27), which is used by nearly half of the oldest group, is rapidly becoming obsolete. *Mom* (15) is perhaps not so often used as in other parts of the country, and does not seem to be making any progress. *Mother* (25) is a newer term. *Mammy* (3.3) is only a relic in this context. There are also very scattered occurrences of *Mater, Mommy, Mummy, Mumsy,* and a few other idiosyncratic forms.

Father. As a familiar and affectionate term for one's father, the most prevalent is *Papa* (50), and this shows only a slight decline in the youngest groups. At the same time, however, *Daddy* (28) is coming into use rather rapidly. *Dad* (27) is about equally popular. *Pa* (24) is strikingly obsolescent. *Pop* (7) is not very common at any age level, while *Pappy* (4) is only a remnant. It is somewhat doubtful that *Father* (9) is often used in real family situations.

Illegitimate child. There is no widely accepted euphemism for *bastard* (62); even *illegitimate child* (11) is not often used. *Woods colt* (6), a South Midland usage, has not established itself. Uncommon and perhaps sometimes improvised terms, occurring from one to six times each, include *brat, bush child, fatherless child, foundling, love child, outside child, scallawag, sidehill baby, sooner babe, stray,* and *unwanted child.*

Woman who helps at childbirth. The woman with only practical training (if any) who delivers babies in the absence of a doctor is ordinarily known as a *midwife* (69). A term still current particularly among older informants is *granny (woman)* (19). At several points along the Rio Grande and in Bexar County the Spanish word *partera* is given with this meaning[33] (Map 8).

[31] These are the same informants who gave *Oma* and *Grossmama* (see *Grand-mother*).

[32] I interpret such spellings as *momma* as the same "word."

[33] One of Mrs. Janet Sawyer's San Antonio informants, a Negro woman, was a "partera," as she herself expressed it. See "A Dialect Study of San Antonio, Texas—A Bilingual Community" (doctoral dissertation, University of Texas, 1957—microfilm).

SOCIAL AND DAILY LIFE

Beads. The beads worn about the neck are known in Texas as a *string (of beads)* (40), a *strand* (31), or a *pair* (13)—the last being most often found in the older groups, while *necklace* (20) is very clearly a newer usage.

Courting. A man who (with more or less serious intentions) keeps company with a lady is said to be *courting* (44), a word which shows most frequency in the middle age groups, but which can certainly be classed as obsolescent. Other terms, also declining in frequency, are *sparking* (23) (Map 111), *wooing* (11), *waiting on* (3.3), and *keeping company (with)* (2.2). *Going with* (9) and *going steady with* (4.4) show up most strikingly in the younger groups.

Kissing. A majority of the informants give no word other than *kissing* (54); a few, however, still use the old euphemisms *bussing* (13) or *spooning* (4.4). Other synonyms, serious or otherwise, are *smacking* (6), *smooching* (8), and *necking* (4.4). The last two are newer usages.

Burlesque serenade. Throughout Texas, as elsewhere in the United States,[34] most rural adults are familiar with a kind of raucous mockserenade, with much beating of pans and blowing of horns, inflicted on newly married couples, usually on the evening of the wedding. Details of this custom vary considerably, but, when known at all, it is invariably designated in this area as a *shivaree* (76). The word, and no doubt the custom, is declining in frequency. There is no indication in Texas that the *shivaree* implies dislike of the wedded couple or that it is restricted to any particular type of wedding. In rural southern Louisiana, however, a considerable number of informants state that the custom is restricted to weddings in which one of the couple has been married before (Map 46). In this area the French form *charivari* is used fairly often.

Harmonica. For the harmonica, the prevailing southwestern term is *French harp* (74). Apparently of South Midland origin, this is very popular in all of Texas and surrounding areas. The Coastal Southern *harp* (11) and *mouth harp* (6) are scattered, but show somewhat more concentration in the southeastern corner of Texas than elsewhere (Map 59). *Mouth organ* (10) is not well established in any area. *Harmonica*

---

[34] See A. L. Davis and R. I. McDavid, Jr., " 'Shivaree': An Example of Cultural Diffusion," *American Speech*, XXIV (1949), 249–255.

(7) seems especially characteristic of informants of foreign-language background.[35]

Boy's weapon. The familiar piece of boys' artillery made of a forked stick and rubber strips is almost always referred to as a *nigger shooter* (88).[36] This usage is not shared with Arkansas, but extends at least to the Mississippi River in Louisiana (Map 101). *Sling shot* (26) has a limited incidence, but no doubt generally means a sling rather than the type of weapon designated by *nigger shooter*.[37] *Bean shooter* and *bean flip*, which are very rare in Texas, appear fairly often in southern Arkansas and eastern Oklahoma.

Christmas greeting. As a greeting early on Christmas morning, a majority of Texas informants in all age groups still know and use the exclamation *Christmas gift!* (59) (Map 71). This phrase is still frequently used throughout the South and a considerable part of the Midland. Several persons associated this greeting with Negroes specifically begging for, or demanding gifts; and this may indeed be its origin.[38] Of course, the more formal *Merry Christmas!* (34) is also in use.

Something to boot. The custom of giving something extra with a purchase (or when a bill is paid) is firmly established in the United States, although it now usually takes the form of trading stamps or "bonus offers." Most areas lack a specific word for this sort of gift. In the Southwest, the West, and part of Central Texas *pilón* (33) is very well known and widely used; it reaches a frequency of 86 per cent in Southwest Texas (Map 18). The Louisiana word *lagniappe* has invaded Southeast Texas, particularly the Beaumont and Galveston areas.

To take someone home. The Southern use of *carry* (43) to apply to a person is fairly frequent in all parts of the state except the Trans-

[35] Of twenty-seven Texas occurrences, sixteen are from informants of German, Latin, or Czech origin; three others are from the college-educated. In the French-speaking area of southern Louisiana, *harmonica* also predominates and *French harp* is rare. Note that among the modern college generation *harmonica* is much more common. See Chapter VI, Table E.

[36] This is somewhat more frequent than the use of *nigger* itself.

[37] Eighteen informants specifically mention this distinction in meaning.

[38] See, for example, Joel Chandler Harris, *Uncle Remus, His Songs and His Sayings* (New York and London, D. Appleton Company, 1911), p. 36: "Honey, you mus' git up soon Chris'mus mawnin' en open de do'; kase I'm gwineter bounce in on Marse John en Miss Sally, en holler Chris'mus gif' des like I useter endurin' de farmin' days fo' de war, w'en ole Miss wuz 'live. I boun' dey don't fergit de ole nigger, nudder."

Pecos and the northern Panhandle (Map 62). Most informants believe that a vehicle must be involved before the word is applicable, but six indicate that it is used even when one goes on foot. *Take (you home)* (32) and *walk (you home)* (26) are also in use. *See you home* (15) is steadily declining in frequency, while *escort* (7) is preserved as a more formal term.

To carry bodily.   Since so large a number of informants use *carry* with the meaning stated above, it is not surprising that only 34 per cent indicate that they would use it to apply to a bundle or a sack of potatoes transported by hand. The Southern *tote* (49) is in general use in all areas except the Trans-Pecos, where it is rare (Map 65). *Pack* (28) has about the same distribution, but it is rare in the records gathered in the states to the east of Texas. *Lug* (10) is not well established in any area.

General or variety store.   A store that sells various kinds of cheap merchandise goes by a number of names, the most frequent of which is *racket store* (47), although this is steadily losing ground. To take its place, among other designations, *variety store* (30) is gradually increasing in frequency. Other synonyms include *five-and-ten (store)* (19), *dime store* (13), *ten-cent-store* (3.3), and *nickel store* (2.6), all of which serenely ignore the realities of inflation. (See Map 115.)

Preacher, trained, or untrained.   The survey item requesting the usual appellation for the preacher was not very successful in its results, since it was badly phrased and included more than one concept. We may, however, conclude that *preacher*, *pastor*, and *parson* are all fairly frequent—the last being more current in the older groups. A minister completely lacking in professional training, who usually preaches "on the side," is fairly often referred to as a *jackleg preacher* (20).

You (plural).   When addressing more than one person,[39] the usual pronoun forms are *you-all* or *y'all*. Since the former spelling usually implies at least some phonetic reduction, the two may be grouped together, with a frequency of 86 per cent. As this usage extends beyond Texas in every direction, it is not possible to determine its limits within the framework of the present survey (see Chapter IV and Map 70).

The old Midland form *you-uns* (6) is of very infrequent occurrence, and is confined to old and uneducated informants. *You folks* (15) is

---

[39] The other person or persons need not always be present, but they are always meant to be included, as far as I can determine. If anything is likely to lead to another Civil War, it is the Northerners' accusation that Southerners use *you-all* to refer to only one person.

more common, but shows no geographical concentration, while *you people* occurs but four times. Only a few informants were content with the simple *you* (7) in this situation.

Familiar greeting.   When a Texas informant meets a close friend, he is nowadays most likely to address him with *hi!* (47), which is to some extent replacing the older *howdy!* (29). Since the informants were not trained in dramatics, not one of them used *howdy, pardner!* (although one gave *hi, pardner!*).

Hello! was apparently often used as a "trigger" word, with the assumption that it is universal. Other greetings infrequently recorded are *good morning, howdy do* (old) and *hidy*, probably a blend of the old and the new. *Hey* is rare in Texas but appears somewhat more often in southern Louisiana (Map 82).

Haunches.   It was sometimes difficult to elicit a word to designate "what you squat down on." The most common single term is *hunkers* (30) (Map 78), followed by *haunches* (22) and *calves* (16). Other words are very scattered, and include *ass, bohunkus, butt, hocks, hunks, rump,* and *thighs.*

Very tired.   When one is practically exhausted, he is usually said to be *worn* (or *wore*) *out* (40). However, a number of older terms are still in fairly frequent use: *tuckered (out)* (22), *give out* (10), *played out* (7), and *petered out* (6). A newer usage that has come in rather rapidly is *pooped (out)* (14).

Very angry.   By far the most popular adjective to denote ire is *mad* (69); only a very small group use *angry* (3.7) in this connection. Older synonyms are *riled (up)* (23) and *het up* (12).

Exclamations of disgust.   Informants were asked for mild terms, and in any case it is doubtful that many would have produced much profanity or obscenity under the conditions. Out of a very large assortment, the most popular interjection seems to be *dad gum (it)* (22) (Map 100). Following this come *darn (it)* (16), *durn (it)* (15), *doggone (it)* (10), *shucks* (7), and *damn (it)* (7). Some of those of less frequency might be of interest; they all occur more than once, and probably show no originality: *chihuahua, consarn it, dad blame (it), dad burn (it), dad rat it, dang, drat it, fiddlesticks, gee whiz, gol darn, golly, gosh, heck, hell, lordy mercy, phooey, plague take it, pshaw, rats, shit,* and *shoot.*

Children's board.   The balanced board that children play on is almost always called a *seesaw* (87). The Northern *teeter totter* (8) is barely current in Texas, but is apparently regular in northern Oklahoma (Map 112). Other regional words may be said not to exist.

To leave in a rush. The most common single expression for hurried departure is *light a shuck* (22) (Map 98), but this item produced a large variety of verb phrases and similes. Some of these are *ball the jack, beat it, blare (his) brownie, high-tail it, light out, skedaddle, skin out, tear out, take off,* and *vamoose.* Or one may *leave like: a bat out of hell, a streak of (greased) lightning, a scared coyote, a turpentined cat, a ruptured duck,* and so on.

Rinse (dishes.) Although a considerable number of informants give the standard form *rinse* (46), almost as many use *rench* (42), which is somewhat more frequent among older and less-educated informants. *Scald* (15) is also in use with this meaning.

Diagonally. When one does not walk straight across an area, the most usual expression is *catty-cornered* (59). Somewhat less current in this context is *antigodlin* (21), with a variant *antigoglin* (3.3) (Map 97). *Catty-wampus* (7) and *anglin(g)* (5) are the only other words of any currency.

Local prison. Although informants were encouraged to give jocular expressions for the jail, a fair number could think of no term other than *jail* (16), and possibly some of the other usages are not entirely humorous. The most prevalent is *calaboose* (45), followed by *hoosegow* (22), *jug* (18), and *clink* (8). Others of less frequency are *jailhouse, cooler, pokey, lock-up, brig,* and *can. Hoosegow,* of Spanish origin (Chapter VII), is most frequent in Southwest and South Central Texas; it is rare outside the borders of the state (Map 36).

The Evil One. Informants were asked to give synonyms for the Devil, but the results were not extremely productive. *The Bad Man* (15) is in restricted use, and appears to be archaic. Also of limited occurrence are *Satan* (11), *Old Scratch* (4), and *Old Nick* (3.7). Another evil being (not, to most people, the Devil), formerly much used to frighten children into being good, is generally known as the *Boogerman* (49), occasionally as the *Boogieman* (11).

Ghost. As a variant of *ghost* (27), which presumably is known everywhere, by far the most frequent is *spook* (49), which is well established in all groups and areas. The Southern *hant* (or *haint*) (21) is scattered over all areas except the three extremities of the Northwest, West, and South (Map 60). *Booger* (16), *sperit* (or *spirit*) (11), and *goblin* (5) are the only other words in use. All of these last four are characteristic of older informants. Naturally, it is impossible to determine the informants' degree of belief or disbelief in the supernatural.

Fairly good. The exact context of this item was not specified, which was a mistake; presumably it most often refers to the state of one's health. One may be *pretty good* (31) or *tol(er)able* (31); the latter term is obsolescent. Other synonyms are *right good* (10) and *fair (to middling)* (7).

OTHER PEOPLE

Stingy. For one who is unusually penurious, the adjective *tight* (41) is most popular. *Chinchy* (20) is also still in use, principally among older informants. Such a person may also be referred to as *close* (6), *short* (2.6), or *close-fisted* (2.2). The corresponding nouns are *tightwad* (51), *miser* (11), *skinflint* (4.4), and *penny pincher* (3.3).

Lively (old person). An unusually active old person is usually said to be *spry* (70), but *peart* (18) is still fairly current in the older groups.

In bad taste. When a person is badly or grotesquely dressed he is most frequently said to look *tacky* (47), although *slouchy* (45) was (to me) surprisingly common. *Sloppy* (12) is also occasionally used with this meaning.

Easily offended. A person who is too easily upset or moved to anger is referred to by most informants as *touchy* (52), less often as *sensitive* (13). An almost obsolete word for this trait is *touchous* (5).

Worthless or lazy. When a person lacks energy, ambition, and probably other traits valued by his community, he is referred to as *no (ac)count* (37), *o(r)nery* (25),[40] *trifling* (14), *lazy* (13), *sorry* (9), *good-for-nothing* (7), *no-good* (7), *shiftless* (4.4), or *worthless* (3.3).

Woman whose husband is dead. A woman bereft of her husband is known by the majority of informants as a *widow* or *widder* (68), but especially among the older and less-educated groups *widow woman* (30) is in fairly regular use.

Italian. In this and the items that follow, an attempt was made to determine the contemptuous and humorous nicknames in use for various

---

[40] This often implies other traits, such as stubbornness or contrariness.

"minority groups." In the case of the Italian, the only terms with any currency are *Dago* (36) and *Wop* (30). Both of these are declining in frequency.

Irishman. An older nickname for an Irishman is *Paddy* or *Patty* (20),[41] which is infrequent among the younger informants. Other terms are very scattered: *Mick* (7) and *Mike* (3.3).

Jew. Very few Texas informants gave a nickname for a Jew; only *Kike* (13) and *Sheeney* (2.9) were recorded.

Acadian French. For a person of Acadian French origin the Louisiana word *Cajun* (31) is fairly frequent in East and South Texas, but becomes rare in the other areas. In keeping with their tendency to avoid "bad words," only five Texas informants gave *Coonass*, a term that I have personally heard many more times than that.

Person of Mexican origin. The word *Mexican* (often shortened to *Mescan*) (20), may or may not be contemptuous; others, which undoubtedly are, include *Greaser* (38), *Pepper-belly* (13), and *Spick* (11). *Pelado* (7)[42] is concentrated in Southwest and South Central Texas (Map 3); the others are more general, but usually less common in East Texas than elsewhere. Other nouns of less frequency are *Peon, Wetback, Hombre,* and *Bracero,* with different shades of meaning. All such appelations tend to be less popular in the younger groups; *Greaser* shows the clearest decline.

Negro. Although informants were asked to distinguish between neutral, polite, and derogatory words, it is impossible to differentiate the shades of feeling and meaning that attach to each term. Certainly the predominant polite usage is *colored (man, person)* (44).[43] *Darky* (17) is said by some to be polite, and is probably intended to give no offense. *Negro* (21) is felt by most to be polite rather than neutral.[44] *Nigger* (80) is sometimes said to be neutral, but more often to be derogatory.[45] It declines in frequency in the youngest groups. Terms that are undoubtedly derogatory are *coon* (14) and *burrhead* (4.4). Other words that occur more than once include *African, black man,* and *chocolate*

[41] These spellings almost certainly represent the same "word," since *t* is usually not distinguishable from *d* in this position.

[42] Pronounced *pee-low.*

[43] Forty-six informants say it is polite; only two say neutral.

[44] Ten say it is polite, six say neutral.

[45] Twenty say neutral—thirty, derogatory.

drop. The presumably Northern words *jigaboo* and *jig* show only nine occurrences between them. A rather large number of insulting appellations *(black devil* is a sufficient example) are offered by individual informants but are probably not of general currency.

White person of low repute. Reflecting consciousness of an old Southern social caste, a number of informants allude to poor, usually ignorant and irresponsible, folk as *(poor) white trash* (36); a few others simply refer to them as *trash* (7).

Rustic person. The urbanized person, perhaps especially the recently urbanized, has a tendency to look with amused contempt on his country cousins. This attitude is reflected by the rather frequent occurrence of such words as *hick* (32) and *hillbilly* (28). The latter of these may not be derogatory in all cases, but probably at least reflects the user's feeling of superiority.[46] Other terms for the rustic type of person are *hayseed* (17) and *yokel* (8), as well as such local usages as *cedar ·chopper* and *charcoal burner,* both of which are recorded only in Travis County.

VERB FORMS AND SYNTAX

Instances of nonstandard "grammar" are probably considerably more prevalent in unguarded conversation than during an interview. Nonetheless, those that follow at least give an indication of comparative frequency of the different dialectal variants.

Dragged (a log). The past tense of *drag* is preponderantly *drug* (66), which is favored in all areas and in all age and education groups. *Dragged* (19) is clearly an educated form.

It wasn't me. The pronoun usually chosen in this phrase is *me* (66). The use of *I* (9) is more characteristic of the educated groups, but constitutes a small minority even here.

The verb form most often employed is *wasn't* (59), with phonetic variations. In eight instances, *u* is written for *a* *(wuzn't)*; in sixteen *d* is written for *s* *(wadn't* or *wudn't)*. A trained phonetician using a phonetic alphabet would probably have recorded more instances of /ə/ for /a/ and /d/ for /z/, since these phenomena are likely to escape the ear in rapid speech. Two other forms recorded—*weren't* (10) and

---

[46] As we know from observation, the "hillbilly" is often glorified in song, story, and comic strip.

warn't (5)—are both archaic. The common Coastal Southern form *wan't*[47] was recorded only three times.

Threw (a rock). Since a considerable number of informants substitute the word *chunked* (39), instances of *throwed* (29) are probably more limited than they would otherwise be. *Threw* (24) is an educated form.

Dived. The most usual past form of *dive* is *dove* (50). This is not an uneducated form; in fact, it is slightly more prevalent among the educated. *Dived* (38) is also in use at all levels. *Div* (6) is only a remnant and is confined to the least-educated informants.

Climbed. A majority of informants give *climbed* (59), but *clum* (33) has considerable currency among the uneducated. *Clim* (4.4) occurs only occasionally.

Dreamed. The two past tense forms of *dream*, *drempt* (46) and *dreamed* (43), are about equally common, and there is no doubt that both are standard. Individual communities differ in their preference of one or the other; but, in the state as a whole, *dreamed* is gaining ground. The form without *t*, *dremp* (8), is characteristic of uneducated informants.

Woke up. As the past form of *wake*, *woke* (64) is predominant; *waked* (21) is passing out of use. Other forms (such as *awakened*) are negligible.

Helped. The past form of *help* was usually given as *helped* (59). The old Southern form[48] *holp* (10) does not occur very often; a little more frequently it appears with *-ed* added: *holped* (11)—a form that occurs very rarely in the South Atlantic states.[49] Both of the latter are characteristic of the old and uneducated.

Saw. Most informants gave the form *saw* (54) as the past of *see*; the most prevalent nonstandard form is *seen* (37). *Seed* (4.4) occurs only occasionally.

Sweated. Both *sweated* (45) and *sweat* (29) are in general use, and there is no significant difference in the age or education of the users. A few informants, predominantly women, substitute *perspired* (11).

[47] See E. Bagby Atwood, *A Survey of Verb Forms in the Eastern United States* (Ann Arbor, University of Michigan Press, 1953), Figure 24. *Wan't* is also used, to a lesser extent, in the North (but not the Midland).

[48] *Ibid.*, Figure 13.

[49] *Ibid.*, p. 17.

The sun rose. Those who use the verb *rise* usually form the past with *rose* (47). The Southern form[50] *riz* (9) is rare, archaic, and uneducated; *rised* (2.9) is of negligible occurrence. The use of the base form *raise* with the past *raised* (normal in the South Midland)[51] is hardly current (1.5). However, a number of informants use *come up* (25) as a past form, while others use *came up* (15).

Want to get off. The Midland idiom *want off* (44) was recorded in all parts of Texas (Map 49), usually in the context of wanting to leave a bus. Various other phrases were elicited, such as *want to get off* (18) and *let me off* (12). The expression *want to get down* is very scattered in Texas, but in rural southern Louisiana becomes quite regular (Map 49).

Wait for (someone). The idea of waiting until someone else is ready is expressed by *wait on* (48) and *wait for* (42) with almost equal frequency. The former is primarily a Midland phrase.[52] *Wait on*, of course, also means to serve; apparently there is no conflict in the two meanings (see Map 79).

Ought not. *Oughtn't* (23) is slightly more prevalent than *hadn't ought* (20), but both of these forms seem to be giving way to *shouldn't* (27).

Might be able. A phrase conveying the possible ability to do a thing was somewhat difficult to elicit; still, there seems to be sufficient evidence of the wide currency of *might could* (33) as against that of *might be able* (23), the latter being an educated phrase.

MISCELLANEOUS TERMS

All of the words and phrases previously discussed were given in answer to a question of some type, and were thus a result of systematic investigation. There is, however, a considerable residue of terms that came out spontaneously in conversation, some of which might well have been included in the questionnaire if one had been able to foresee informants' responses. Others are mere samples of the sort of thing that is sure to show up in an investigation of this kind. Only a very brief sampling will be given here.

All of the following are recorded more than once except those marked

[50] *Ibid.*, p. 19 and Figure 16.
[51] *Ibid.*, Figure 16.
[52] From the Linguistic Atlas field records rather than from Kurath.

with *, and these few I myself can vouch for as a "native speaker." The definitions and quotations are from the informants or the fieldworkers.

Bolster. A long pillow.

Car house. A garage.

Chamber. A chamber pot.

*Clean your plow.** "Give a good whipping."

Devil's horse, devil's walking stick. A praying mantis.

Duster, black duster. A heavy sandstorm. Recorded in the Panhandle.

Fetch. To bring.

*Freeze the horns off a billy goat.** (Cold enough to—).

Gee. Call for a horse to go right (one informant says left).

Haw. Call for a horse to go left (one informant says right).

*Hog-killing weather.** Cool or cold weather.

*House** *(in the).* "Excludes the kitchen."

*Laws.** "Police officers."

*Lobo.** A wolf.

*Loco.** "Foolish or crazy."

Peaked. A little sick looking.

Play-party. Games, etc.

Pounding. A party, for the new preacher, to which everyone brings a pound of something.

*Prairie coal.** "Cow-chips."

Puncheon floor. A floor made of "logs split in the middle."

Sad iron. Used "to iron clothes."

Slop jar. "A bedchamber." (What this means is a chamber pot. See *chamber.*)

Son-of-a-gun. A stew made at beef-killing time. Informants are vague about its ingredients. "Sweetbreads," "brains," "liver," and "heart" are mentioned. Recorded only in West Texas and New Mexico. One informant gives *son-of-a-bitch,* probably the original term.

Square-dab. Exactly in the middle, as "*square-dab on the nose.*"

Trundle bed. A bed that slides under a larger bed.

Varmint. "Any small wild animal." Those specifically mentioned are "skunks," "possums," "foxes," "raccoons," "bobcats."

Vinegarone. One informant says a "lizard"—another, a "large type of scorpion."

Vittles. "All kinds of food."

Wutzi. A call to pigs. Comal, Kendall, and Gillespie Counties.

IV GEOGRAPHICAL ASPECTS OF USAGE

EASTERN WORDS

Undoubtedly the major portion of the regional vocabulary observable in Texas was brought into the area from various parts of the eastern United States. Since most of this territory has been covered by the Linguistic Atlas,[1] we are in position to determine with some accuracy the vocabulary features of the eastern dialect areas. A very thorough summary of the Atlas data may be found in Hans Kurath's *Word Geography of the Eastern United States*,[2] which will be referred to frequently in the ensuing discussion.

Kurath divides the Eastern States, with regard to vocabulary, into three major dialect areas: the North, the Midland, and the South, each of which is divisible into various subdialects.[3]

The North consists of all of New England, New York, northern New Jersey, and approximately the northern one-third of Pennsylvania.[4] Kurath's six dialectal subdivisions may conveniently be reduced to three: Eastern New England; New York City and the Lower Hudson Valley; and Inland Northern.

The Midland is made up of the southern two-thirds of Pennsylvania, southern New Jersey, northern and western Maryland, West Virginia, and the western portions of Virginia and North Carolina. We may conveniently refer to the North Midland and the South Midland, the two being divided approximately by the Kanawha River in West Virginia. Within the North Midland is contained the Pennsylvania

[1] The Linguistic Atlas has been further explained in Chapter II.

[2] Hans Kurath, *A Word Geography of the Eastern United States* (Ann Arbor, University of Michigan Press, 1949).

[3] See Figure 15.

[4] The survey of the Great Lakes region by A. H. Marckwardt indicates that we may justifiably include Michigan and Wisconsin, as well as the northern portions of Ohio, Indiana, and Illinois, in the Northern dialect area. See Marckwardt, "Principal and Subsidiary Dialect Areas in the North-Central States," *Publication of the American Dialect Society*, No. 27 (1957), 3–15.

German area, which extends some distance on both sides of the Susquehanna.

The South, as Kurath delineates it, is made up of southern Delaware, southern Maryland, and the eastern portions of Virginia, North Carolina, and South Carolina. The most striking subdivision is Eastern Virginia (the Virginia Piedmont), extending approximately from the Blue Ridge eastward to the Fall Line or beyond. McDavid,[5] more recently, has cited enough lexical items from the South Carolina Low Country to enable us to establish this area as a clear-cut subdivision of Southern (see Fig. 15).

A very large number of Southern words extend also into the South Midland; Kurath cites about three times as many of these as he does words that are confined to the area east of the Blue Ridge.[6] In the ensuing discussion I refer to these words of wider distribution as *General Southern*, and use the term *Coastal Southern* for words that are limited to the South as it is defined by Kurath.[7]

NORTH

As one might expect from the settlement history of Texas (as given in Chapter I), words that are characteristic of the North or of major portions of it occur with very little frequency among the Texas survey informants. Northern words for which questions appeared on the work sheets include the following, with percentages of occurrence given in each case:

pail (37)   *hadn't ought*[9] (20)
(cherry) pit[8] (34)   *comforter* (15)

[5] Raven I. McDavid, Jr., "The Dialects of American English," in W. Nelson Francis, *The Structure of American English* (New York, The Ronald Press Company, 1958), pp. 480–543.

[6] Kurath, *Word Geography*, pp. 38 ff.

[7] This is partly in order to avoid the awkwardness of such phrases as "South-and-South-Midland words"; but it also implies some reinterpretation of Kurath's materials. That is, I am inclined to think that the South Midland is more Southern than Midland.

[8] The eastern distribution of this word was derived directly from the Atlas records, rather than from Kurath. The same is true of several of the others that are mentioned in this chapter, including *clapboards, wait on, French harp, pack, mouth harp,* and *jackleg.* For the meanings of all words discussed in this chapter, see Chapter III and the Word Index.

[9] Not discussed in Kurath. See E. B. Atwood, *A Survey of Verb Forms in the Eastern United States* (Ann Arbor, University of Michigan Press, 1953), Figure 26.

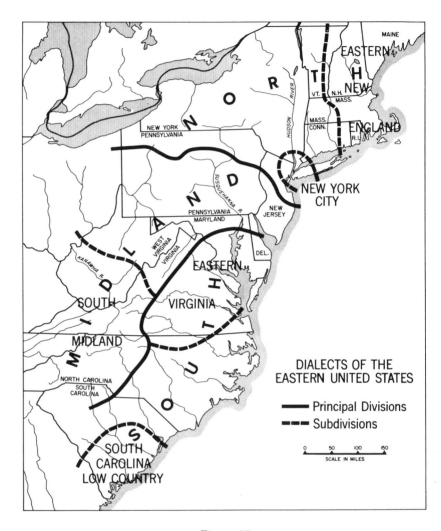

Figure 15

Data from Hans Kurath, *A Word Geography of the Eastern United States*
(Ann Arbor, University of Michigan Press, 1949).

stoop (11)   *brook* (4)
clapboards (11)   *johnny cake* (4)
angleworm (10)   *spider* (skillet) (3.3)
swill (9)   *co, boss!* (cow call) (3.3)
teeter totter (8)   *thills* or *fills* (of a buggy) (2.9)
whiffletree (7)   *darning needle* (1.5)
eaves troughs (6)   *lobbered milk* (1.1)
fried cake (5)   *Dutch cheese* (0.4)

Of those words that show the highest percentages, *pail* is probably
not a Northern importation; it occurs with some frequency in Louisiana
(about 35 per cent) and may be characteristic of the Gulf States as
well as of the North.[10] *Hadn't ought* might also be current in other parts
of the South, although in the South Atlantic States it shows up only
in eastern North Carolina.[11] Commercial reasons probably lie behind
the rather high frequency of *(cherry) pit* and *comforter*.[12] Most cherries
consumed in Texas are imported, and they are often described as "pit-
ted." Those purchasers who bought bed covers from mail-order
catalogues had to order them under the name *comforters*.[13]

The composite frequency[14] of these Northern words is 9.6 per cent.
Their geographical distribution in Texas is very spotty, because of their
rarity; as a group they show no tendency to concentration in any one
part of the state.[15]

Of words characteristic of Eastern New England, only *(pig) sty*
shows any currency (12 per cent) in Texas. *Bonny-clabber* (0),[16] *sour
milk cheese* (3.7), and *buttonwood* (2.2) are barely current. Hudson
Valley words are likewise almost nonexistent; those on our questionnaire include *dominie* (preacher) (0), *olicook* (doughnut) (0), *pot
cheese* (0.4), and *thick milk* (1.8).

[10] Of five stray informants in Alabama and Georgia, four gave the word
pail.
[11] Atwood, *Verb Forms*, Figure 26.
[12] The traditional Midland and Southern term is *comfort*.
[13] For example, in the Sears, Roebuck and Co. General Catalogues of 1910,
1928–1929, and 1956–1957. The current catalogue still carries the item, but
only for babies' beds.
[14] This is derived by the simple formula: total occurrences × 100 ÷ number of informants × number of items. In other words, it shows the extent of
actual occurrence in comparison with maximum possible occurrence.
[15] They vary only from 8.3 per cent in West Texas to 10.7 in East Texas.
[16] One informant (Lubbock County) claims to have heard this from "Irish
people."

MIDLAND

Words characteristic of the Midland, and their frequencies in the Texas records, are as follows:

sook! (78)	*blinds* (25)
(quarter) till (55)	*poke* (sack) (14)
wait on (48)	*all the further* (11)
piece (distance) (47)	*you-uns* (6)
want off (44)	*spouts* (3.3)
green beans (36)	*snake feeder* (1.1)

The composite frequency of this group of words is 30.3 per cent. It should be carefully noted that the words as a group show no striking differences in frequency in the separate areas of the state: Northwest, 33.5; West, 25.2; Southwest, 27.4; North, 36.7; Central, 32; East, 28.3. Some of the individual words, to be sure, show slight tendencies to concentration; and the nonoccurrence of some of them in Louisiana will be commented on later. In any case, no one major area of Texas appears to be more strongly characterized by Midland terms than another.

A few words may be cited as characteristic of the North Midland, although some of these occur in the North as well. These, together with their frequencies in the Texas records, are:

string beans (30)	*smearcase* (7)
whinny (25)	*worm fence* (5)
sheaf (of wheat) (17)	*clothes press* (2.9)
(corn) husks (13)	*piece* (snack) (2.9)
side meat (8)	*run* (stream) (1.1)

The composite frequency of this group is 11.2 per cent. There is no concentration of these terms in any geographical region; their frequency varies only from 9.7 in North Texas to 12.5 in East Texas.

As Kurath has pointed out, there are not a great many words specifically characteristic of the South Midland. Those for which Texas records are available are limited to:

French harp (74)	*woods colt* (6)
pack (carry) (28)	*sugar tree* (5)
fireboard (10)	*ridy horse* (seesaw) (0.4)
redworm (9)	*milk gap* (cow pen) (0)

Only the first of these is a predominant usage, and it brings the composite frequency of the group up to 16.3. North Texas shows the highest frequency of South Midland words (21), East Texas the lowest (13.4).

Terms of Pennsylvania German origin[17] have not, as a rule, reached Texas at all. There are no occurrences of *saddle horse*, *(paper) toot* (bag), or *fossnocks* (doughnuts); only two of *fat-cakes* and five of *thick milk* (clabber).[18] *Ponhaws*[19] (a pork mixture) occurs only among informants of German background in Kerr, Kendall, and Bexar Counties, in the recorded form *panas*. *Clook* (setting hen) and *smearcase* would appear, from their concentration in Central Texas (Maps 40 and 41), to be independent contributions of the Texas Germans rather than importations from Pennsylvania.

SOUTH

Words that are characteristic of the Coastal South—that is, those which in the Eastern States do not penetrate to the west of the mountains—are not numerous. In the Texas materials we have only the following:

chittlins (62)	*low* (verb) (34)
snap beans (52)	*(mouth) harp* (16)
tote (49)	*croker sack*[20] (10)
carry (take) (43)	*turn (of wood)* (7)

The composite frequency of this group is 31.7 per cent. The lowest frequency occurs in Southwest Texas (25.5), the highest in East Texas (43). However, the only item that shows anything like concentration in East Texas is *croker sack*, and even this is a minority term (Map 69). The possible outer limits of Southern words will be discussed later.

General Southern words which occur in the Texas materials are the following:

pallet (92)	*light bread* (78)
(corn) shucks (91)	*(horse) lot* (69)
you-all (86)	*Christmas gift!* (greeting) (59)
pully bone (78)	*whetrock* (56)

[17] Kurath, *Word Geography*, p. 35.

[18] Mentioned also in the section on the "North" in this chapter. *Thick milk* is characteristic of the Hudson Valley as well as of the Pennsylvania German area.

[19] Probably from a Low German equivalent of German *Pfannhase*, literally "pan rabbit." Kurath, *Word Geography*, p. 32.

[20] This predominates in eastern Virginia and in South Carolina, not in the whole of the Coastal South. In most of North Carolina, *tow sack* is used. Kurath, *Word Geography*, Figure 71.

branch (stream) (50)   *hants* (21)

clabber cheese (26)   *jackleg (preacher)* (20)

The composite frequency of this group of words is 59.8 per cent, by far the highest of any set of regional terms. There is no major area that does not show a preponderance of these words; the lowest percentage is 52.5 in Southwest Texas, the highest is 70 in North Texas. As will be shown later, most of them extend beyond the borders of Texas.

There are, of course, a good many words that are characteristic of specific portions of the South. Not many of these show any currency in Texas. Words from Eastern Virginia include *batter bread* (4.3), *hoppergrass* (grasshopper) (2.9), and *corn house* (0.7). *Lumber room* (store room) and *cuppin* (cow pen) do not occur at all.

Words of the South Carolina-Georgia Low Country are *pinders* (peanuts) (1.8), *cooter* (turtle) (1.1), *ground nuts* (peanuts) (0.4), *fatwood* (kindling) (0), *savannah* (prairie) (0), and *yard-ax* (untrained preacher) (0).

Of the terms that are current in Virginia and the South Midland, two are rather frequent in the Texas records: *nicker* (41) and *snake doctor* (49). The latter is rare in East Texas but becomes increasingly prevalent to the westward (Map 66).

From the coastal areas of Virginia and the Carolinas come two words that occur in Texas, *earthworm* (58) and *mosquito hawk* (20). The former is equally common in all parts of Texas (Map 68); the latter is concentrated in the southeastern part, and becomes rare in the northern and western portions. It is regular in Louisiana (Map 66).

We might here sum up the degrees of currency of words from the various Eastern dialect areas:

Area	Percentage
Northern	9.6
Midland	30.3
North Midland	11.2
South Midland	16.3
Coastal Southern	31.7
General Southern	59.8
All Southern	48.5

It is clear that, on the basis of actual proportion of occurrence, the regional vocabulary of Texas is basically Southern, with some admixture of Midland words and a considerably smaller proportion of Northern ones. Of the Midland words that occur, those that extend into the South Midland—that is, into areas adjacent to the South—are distinctly more common than those confined to northern portions of the Midland.

It remains to consider the question of whether one portion of Texas may be predominantly Southern while another portion is basically Midland. The assumption has been made for some time that only the eastern one-fourth to one-third of the state can be considered Southern; the rest has been termed "General American," or "Western," or (more recently) "Midland." This idea goes back at least to the publication of Kurath's pamphlet *American Pronunciation*[21] in 1928, and it appears as recently as the second edition of A. C. Baugh's *History of the English Language*.[22] C. K. Thomas formerly drew such a line, but in the latest edition of his *Introduction to the Phonetics of American English*[23] he has moved it considerably farther to the west, to indicate that of the major parts of Texas only the Panhandle and the Trans-Pecos region lie outside the Southern dialect area. Most of the previous attempts to arrive at a major dialect division have been based on pronunciation features, although Kurath conjectured that the Southern vocabulary items extend "probably to the valley of the Brazos River" in East Texas.[24]

Now, of the Southern words that have been examined, very few show any sign of coming to an end in the eastern half of Texas.[25] One of these is *croker sack* (Map 69), which shows a frequency of 30 per cent in East Texas but which hardly occurs to the west of Austin. Another is *mosquito hawk* (Map 66), which is almost universal in Southeast Texas and Louisiana, but which seldom occurs in the North, Northwest, and West. On the maps of Southern items one may perhaps perceive the somewhat higher frequency of *low* (Map 61) and *mouth harp* (Map 59) in East Texas, but it is not possible to regard either word as being really concentrated.

Clearly, in order to determine the possible limits of Southern words, it will be necessary to move farther to the west. Following this idea, I have calculated separately the frequency of the Southern words in the northern and western extremities of the state. These areas are the Panhandle, made up of all the counties to the north of Plainview (Hale County), represented by eighteen informants; and the Trans-Pecos

[21] Hans Kurath, *American Pronunciation,* Society for Pure English Tract No. 30 (Oxford. Clarendon Press, 1928).
[22] A. C. Baugh, *History of the English Language* (New York, Appleton-Century-Crofts. Inc., 1957), p. 438.
[23] C. K. Thomas, *Introduction to the Phonetics of American English* (New York. The Ronald Press Company, 1958), p. 232.
[24] Kurath, *Word Geography,* p. 37.
[25] This does not apply to the Louisiana words that will be discussed.

region, consisting of the nine counties[26] lying to the west of the Pecos, represented by twenty informants. I have also been able to examine the materials gathered for another survey, that of T. M. Pearce for New Mexico. This survey covers all parts of the state and embodies responses from fifty informants. Pearce very kindly entered the occurrences of the Southern words on outline maps for me.

We may dismiss the Panhandle briefly by stating that it shows almost precisely the same frequency of Southern words as the state as a whole. The Coastal Southern group has a frequency of 35.4 per cent, the General Southern group 54.2 (as against 31.7 and 59.8 for all of Texas). Whether the northernmost portion would show a difference in usage I am not able to determine at present, since the number of informants is insufficient.

When we come to the Trans-Pecos area and to New Mexico we find some very perceptible differences in frequency, both as to individual words and as to the groups as a whole. These may well be presented in the form of a table:

COASTAL SOUTHERN WORDS—PERCENTAGES IN:

	All Texas	Trans-Pecos	New Mexico
chittlins	62	37	26
snap beans	52	40	8
tote	49	20	6
carry	43	15	4
low	34	25	22
mouth harp	16	10	16
croker sack	10	0	0
turn (of wood)	7	0	4
Composite	31.7	18.9	10.7

GENERAL SOUTHERN WORDS—PERCENTAGES IN:

	All Texas	Trans-Pecos	New Mexico
pallet	92	80	58
shucks	91	70	40
you-all	86	65	8
pully bone	78	60	10
light bread	78	50	48
(horse) lot	69	10	2
Christmas gift!	59	50	8
whetrock	56	45	8
branch	50	20	10
clabber cheese	26	15	10

[26] These counties are El Paso, Hudspeth, Culberson, Reeves, Jeff Davis, Pecos, Presidio, Brewster, and Terrell. At least one informant was available for each of these except Culberson.

GENERAL SOUTHERN WORDS, *continued*

	All Texas	Trans-Pecos	New Mexico
hants	21	5	2
jackleg	20	5	unavailable
Composite	59.8	39.6	19
Both Groups	48.5	30.6	15.3

Even with allowances for differences in method, this consistent decline in frequency is very striking. Moreover, some of the Southern words (e.g., *carry*, *turn of wood*, *you-all*, and *whetrock*) are current only in eastern New Mexico, while nearly all[27] of them show greater frequency in that area. That such words do not extend to the Pacific is shown very clearly in the unpublished material (from over a thousand informants) gathered by David W. Reed for California and neighboring states. Of ten Southern words available for comparison, the composite frequency for the Pacific area is only 4.8 per cent, as against 49 per cent for Texas. Thus we may say with some confidence that, except for sporadic individual penetrations, the Southern vocabulary finally comes to an end somewhere on the slopes of the southern Rockies. We may, if we like, classify the Trans-Pecos as a transitional area, since the drop in Southern words is very consistent, although not so great as to justify the conception of a dialect boundary.[28]

As for the northern limits of Southern words, we cannot, in most cases, determine these within the limits of the present survey. As far north as our records take us in Arkansas (approximately to Hot Springs), the Southern words occur with even greater frequency than in Texas: 38.3 per cent for the Coastal Southern group, 65 for the General Southern group, and 54 for both groups. Except for *turn (of wood)* and *croker sack* (Maps 58 and 69), none of the words can be regarded as nonoccurrent in the area.

In Oklahoma we seem to see a fading out of the Southern vocabulary as we move northward. Some of the Southern words, noticeably *snap beans* (Map 63) and *low* (Map 61), seem to stop short of central Oklahoma, but most of the others are current farther to the north. If we

[27] *Pallet*, *light bread*, and *shucks* seem to be about equally common in all parts of the state.

[28] Moreover, the extreme sparcity of Anglo-American population in the area is a considerable obstacle to the establishment of conventional dialect "boundaries." The relative absence of other words from the area can also be observed on some of the maps—for example, *gallery*, *paling*, *redbug*, and *peckerwood* (Maps 57, 81, 83, and 93 respectively).

arbitrarily divide Oklahoma into northern and southern halves, we find that the entire list of Southern usages shows a frequency of 51.3 per cent in southern Oklahoma, 31.6 per cent in the northern portion. Moreover, a number of other words, which should probably be regarded as Southern, are quite common in Texas but infrequent in Oklahoma, except for the southernmost portion. These include *toadfrog* (Map 113), *redbug* (Map 83), *gallery* (Map 57), and *seesaw* (Map 112).

That Southern usages do not extend much to the northwest of our territory is strongly indicated by Clyde T. Hankey's *Colorado Word Geography*.[29] A composite of sixteen Southern words available for comparison shows a frequency in Colorado of 14.1 per cent as against 53.3 per cent for Texas. The Southern terms tend mostly to be confined to southeastern Colorado.

We have seen that Southern usages extend considerably farther to the west than previously expected. Several reasons might be given for this. First, there is the indubitable fact that the planter class enjoyed an inordinate prestige in early Texas, and exercised an influence far out of proportion to their numbers (see Chapter I). Thus their vocabulary might have been expected to spread to the westward. Moreover, there is some probability that those Texans who came from, or through, the inland South and the "border states" had already acquired many Southernisms before their arrival. Our own survey shows, for example, how prevalent Southern words are in southern Arkansas; the same may have been true of Tennessee and other inland states. Then, too, we must consider that there were no geographical barriers to the advance of a prestige dialect until one reached the mountain and desert country of the Trans-Pecos. Finally, the rapid expansion of agriculture, particularly cotton growing, in the former cattle kingdom may have promoted the spread of rural terms from the Old South.

LOUISIANA WORDS

In addition to the words that have been discussed, which occur in the Eastern States, a good many terms appear in Texas which clearly first gained currency in the southern part of Louisiana.

This area, first settled under French rule in the years following 1700, had a considerable population (French and otherwise) before migration from the east had penetrated into the other Gulf states. The

---

[29] C. T. Hankey, *Colorado Word Geography, Publication of the American Dialect Society*, No. 34 (1960), 10–13 especially.

French element was reinforced by the arrival of the Acadians, who were deported from Nova Scotia in 1755 and who found their way into Louisiana in large numbers two or three decades later. In spite of the presence of speakers of other languages, French was the principal spoken medium; and it still constitutes a very significant substratum, particularly in the rural areas.

The importance of New Orleans as a center of culture and commerce before the Civil War is too well known to require discussion. We will be concerned with it here only as the heart of a "focal area" from which vocabulary items radiated. Even in our limited sampling, and in spite of the fact that most of the items on our questionnaire were designed to elicit Texas usages, we find adequate evidence of the spreading of lexical features from this area.

Some of the words that can be observed remain rather close to the center of the area. One of these is *banquette*, an old word for sidewalk (Map 44); this does not extend far to the north or west. Others are *cush-cush* for a corn meal dish (Map 45), and *pirogue*, for a kind of river boat (Map 48); the latter term extends somewhat farther to the westward. All of these occur in Texas, but only in Orange and Jefferson Counties in the southeast corner. A few rural informants in southern Louisiana use *là!* (French) to a cow to make her stand still (Map 45). Another usage concentrated in the area is *(want to) get down* (from a bus), probably a translation of the French *descendre* (Map 49). A nonlinguistic feature, but one that nevertheless showed up in the survey, is the rather consistent statement, in rural southern Louisiana, that the *shivaree* occurs only when one of the parties at a wedding has been married before (Map 46).[30]

Spreading northward, well into southern Arkansas, but not into Texas, we find *salt meat* for salt pork (Map 47). Another term that shows somewhat more spread to the north than to the west is *armoire* for a wardrobe with drawers (Map 50).

Several of the Louisiana terms have spread into southeastern Texas but are rare farther to the west. Among these is *cream cheese* for cottage cheese (Map 52), which is concentrated in the Houston-Galveston-Beaumont area. Another with a similar distribution is *lagniappe* for something extra (Map 18). I am inclined to think, moreover, that the use of the simple *spread* (rather than *bedspread* or *counterpane*) must

---

[30] *Shivaree* (the thing as well as the word) occurs commonly throughout the Southwest, but nowhere else does it have this implication.

have come at least partly from Louisiana influence (Map 51), since its concentrations are similar to those of the terms just mentioned.

A word showing a still wider distribution is *bayou*, which extends both northward and westward from the focal area (Map 53). Its heavy occurrence in Harris County (Houston) should be observed, as well as its scattered incidence in other parts of Texas. Still more widespread, but of the same general trend, is *hog('s)-head cheese*, which has partly displaced the more common *souse* in Southeast and Central Texas and to some extent in Southwest Texas as well (Map 54).

There are also words of apparent Louisiana origin which have spread into all parts of Texas. One of these is *praline* (Map 55), which is replacing the older *(pecan) patty* throughout our territory. Another is *gumbo* (Map 56), which is familiar throughout Texas, at least to younger informants. The advance of both of these terms must have been aided by commercial distribution of the things themselves (Chapter VI). The currency of *gallery* (Map 57) may also owe something to Louisiana influence, although the word is also in use in the Eastern States.[31]

It is not difficult to find reasons for the occurrence of Louisiana words in Texas. For one thing, their areas of concentration coincide with the areas of heaviest Louisiana settlement in the nineteenth century (see Chapter I). Moreover, in the days before statehood, most of Texas' sea trade was with New Orleans, from which also came most of the military equipment in the war for independence.[32]

It might be pointed out that there is another body of evidence, of a negative type, that also tends to mark off southern Louisiana as an independent dialect area. That is the absence from the area of a considerable number of regional words that prevail in the South Atlantic States, in Texas, and probably throughout the rest of the South. Among these are *Christmas gift!* (Map 71), *whetrock* (Map 88), *branch* (Map 53), and *pully bone* (Map 72). *Low* (Map 61) and *carry* (Map 62) have also failed to penetrate appreciably into this territory, while such other regional terms as *counterpane* (Map 51), *peckerwood* (Map 93), and even *(paper) sack* (Map 94) also seem to skirt the New Orleans focal area. The following section on "Southwestern Words" contains a further discussion of Texas-Louisiana differences.

---

[31] Kurath, *Word Geography*, p. 52, merely states that it occurs, without giving its frequency or its geographical distribution.

[32] R. N. Richardson, *Texas, the Lone Star State*, second edition (New York, Prentice-Hall, 1958), pp. 67, 101.

SOUTHWESTERN WORDS

The most interesting and important words, from the viewpoint of this study, are not those which were imported from other regions, but those which first gained currency within Texas. Many of these have spread for considerable distances.

I believe that it is justifiable to speak of a Southwestern focal area, or at least of an area of radiation, the heart of which is Southwest Texas, the cradle of the range-cattle industry. To be sure, the integrity of the area has been obscured by the influx of a mass of new settlers in the Lower Valley and by the immense advance of agriculture in that region; yet it is quite possible even now to trace a distinctive set of words which have spread to various distances from the same central area. Most of these words pertain either to topography or to the raising of livestock. Since the Spanish-speaking settlers had earlier become familiar with features of the landscape, and since they had learned to raise cattle by methods entirely foreign to the farmers and planters of the East, it is not surprising that most of the distinctively Southwestern words are of Spanish origin.

Not a great many words are now entirely confined to Southwest Texas. Probably the best example is *resaca* (Map 2) for standing or impounded water. No doubt its concentration would have appeared even more clearly if I had had the foresight to frame a better question to elicit it. *Vaquero* (Map 2), no doubt at one time much more general,[33] is now limited to this area, as is *llano*[34] (Map 3). Another remnant is *acequia* (Map 4), which must formerly have been current in other areas with a heavy Latin population.[35] A few other rare terms, such as *potro* and *mesquital*, survive primarily in this area (Map 8).

Other terms that have a noticeable concentration in Southwest Texas are: *hacienda* (Map 7), *pelado* (Map 3), *toro* (Map 4), *reata* (Map 7), *chaparral* (Map 5), and *mott* (Map 6). The last of these seems most concentrated in the Corpus Christi area, but has extended to a considerable portion of South Central and Southwest Texas. *Maverick*

---

[33] J. Frank Dobie quotes John Young as saying: "In Southwest Texas, where sixty years ago and more I was 'running cattle,' cowboys were—and still are—generally referred to as 'vaqueros.'" He adds that "'cowboy' was sometimes used, but not nearly so commonly as now." Dobie, *A Vaquero of the Brush Country* (Dallas, The Southwest Press, 1929), p. 1.

[34] Both a county and a town of Llano exist, but are located somewhat farther north than the present currency of the word extends.

[35] For example, in Albuquerque, where an *acequia* ran through the middle of town during my childhood, we used to call it the "sakey."

(Map 25) also shows some signs of its Southwestern origin,[36] but it has travelled over the state in a rather irregular way.

Other terms are about equally frequent in Southwest and West Texas but show little or no frequency in the Northwest. One of these is *olla* (Map 14); another is *arroyo* (Map 15). Some of these extend also well into Central Texas—specifically *pilón* (Map 18), *frijoles* (Map 17), *remuda* (Map 22), and *morral* (Map 23).

Still other Southwestern words are current not only in the areas mentioned but also in Northwest Texas and no doubt much farther to the northward and westward. Such are *mesa* (Map 21) and *corral* (for a cow pen) (Map 19).

It is clear that there is a very close correspondence between the distribution of the words already mentioned and the extent of the early ranching industry (see Chapter I). In view of the glamour of the "open range" and the prestige which the cattleman must have enjoyed,[37] it is not strange that a good many of the Southwestern words have also spread a considerable distance to the eastward. The adoption of *corral* for an enclosure for horses is possibly the best illustration (Map 20). This word has advanced not only into Oklahoma but also to a limited extent into Louisiana. *Tank* (Map 26) and *hackamore* (Map 27) extend deep into East Texas, but not beyond. *Bronc* (Map 28) is in use in southern Arkansas but is missing from most of Louisiana. The same may be said of *lariat* (Map 31), except that the latter is fairly regular in the northern and western parts of Louisiana. *Dogie* (Map 32) has penetrated into Louisiana to a greater extent than into Arkansas. A considerable number of other ranch-country terms show no exact limits, but gradually decrease in frequency as one moves eastward: *cinch* (Map 29), *canyon* (Map 30), *burro* (Map 33), *norther* (Map 34), *pinto* (horse or pony) (Map 37), and *chaps* (Map 35).

A few words show their greatest frequency in West Texas—specifically the South Plains area—rather than in the old ranch country as a whole. These are apparently not of Southwestern origin, but by some kind of selection acquired concentration in that portion of Texas. One of these is *sugan* (Map 9), which was recorded only in a limited portion

---

[36] Samuel Maverick and his unbranded cattle are the subject of much folklore and fiction. Fact is skillfully unravelled from fancy by J. Frank Dobie, *The Longhorns* (Boston, Little, Brown & Company, 1941), pp. 43–49. See also Chapter VII.

[37] I hold, however, that the phenomenal romanticizing of the area and the era of the "open range" by writers of literature and illiterature had little to do with the geographical spread of the ranching vocabulary. See Chapter VI.

of West Texas. Extending somewhat farther to the eastward, but in a scattered way, are *surly* (euphemism for bull) (Map 9), *pavement* (paved road) (Map 10),[38] *draw* (Map 11), and *shinnery* (Map 13). The distribution of the last term is, of course, partly determined by the presence of the phenomenon itself; Texans in other areas have no need for such a word. *Plains* (the plural) (Map 12) is fairly prevalent in Northwest Texas, and extends into North Texas as well. *Trap* (enclosure for horses or cows) (Map 12) is most common in the Trans-Pecos area but was also recorded farther to the eastward.

A few words find their greatest concentration in Central Texas, even though obviously not all of them had their origin there. *Tarv(i)ated road* (Map 38), from the old commercial firm *Tarvia*, is very much concentrated in the vicinity of Austin, and must have resulted from transactions with that company some time in the past. *Grass sack* (Map 39) was certainly from the East,[39] but it has a distinct concentration in South Central Texas. Another word that shows a slight tendency to the same concentration is *house* for *shed*, in the phrases *wood house* and *tool house* (Map 39). The peculiar formation *roping rope* (Map 40) also shows a good many occurrences in this area, whereas it could not be elicited from informants in other parts of the state.

Some of the Central Texas terms probably owe their origin to the early German settlers, who must have carried over numerous German words into their English. The term *plunder room* (Map 38) would seem by its concentration to owe something to German influence, although the word *plunder* has long been current, and in various parts of the country.[40] *Clook* (Map 40), from German *die Klucke*, is often anglicized to *cluck* or even *clucker*, but it shows its greatest frequency in the areas of heaviest German settlement. *Smearcase* and *kochcase* (Map 41) also show a concentration in the Texas German areas. The former, to be sure, was also introduced by the Pennsylvania Germans and has spread to most of the North Midland, but the distribution of the term in Texas would indicate an independent adoption of it from the Germans of the area. Another usage that probably indicates German influence is that of the word *lunch* to mean a snack (Map 42). The

---

[38] An Edwards County informant speaks of "a ranch on the pavement."

[39] It is most common, according to Kurath (*Word Geography*, Fig. 71), in the Chesapeake Bay area.

[40] M. M. Mathews, *Dictionary of Americanisms* (Chicago, University of Chicago Press, 1951); Harold Wentworth, *American Dialect Dictionary* (New York, Thomas Y. Crowell Company, 1944). *Plunder room* also occurs in the East, primarily in North Carolina (Kurath, *Word Geography*, Fig. 52).

Germans had, and still have, the practice of eating a light meal in mid-morning and midafternoon, to which they applied the term *lunch*, and this usage has spread to some extent into neighboring areas. A specialized questionnaire would probably uncover a good many other examples of German influence; and even in the present general survey a few other German usages creep in from time to time: for example, *Opa* and *Oma* for grandfather and grandmother, *krebbel* for doughnut, and *silze* for pork loaf.

MISCELLANEOUS DISTRIBUTIONS

A few words show signs of having been imported specifically from Arkansas, although it is very doubtful that any of them had their origin there. In any case, they show some concentration in the southern Arkansas records, and they tend to follow the lines of heaviest Arkansas settlement—across North Texas and into the central part of the state. Most of these words also show an extension directly westward into the South Plains area. Fairly clear examples are *redworm* (Map 68) and *(saw* or *wood) rack* (Map 108); the latter also has some currency in East Texas. *Loft* (of a house) (Map 110) is somewhat similar in distribution, as are *back stick* (Map 109) and *ditch* (for a gully) (Map 30), but the last two are very widely scattered in Texas. *Clearseed (peach)* (Map 107) is fairly heavily concentrated in Arkansas and northern Louisiana, but its Texas occurrences do not show a very close correspondence to the Arkansas settlements.

Some of the words that have been mapped, even though their Eastern distributions are unknown, seem to be characteristic of the Gulf Coast. One of these is *redbug* (Map 83), which is almost universal in Louisiana and which covers all of Texas except the Panhandle and the Trans-Pecos area. Another is *hey!* as a simple greeting (Map 82), but this is of much less frequency, particularly in Texas. *Spoon bread* (Map 84), which is infrequent in the East,[41] is the only term known in the Texas communities in which the thing itself is known. The word must have been current in some of the other Gulf states, if not elsewhere.[42]

Many other words of unknown distribution in the Eastern States are common in all or most of Texas; as will appear later, many of them

[41] Kurath, *Word Geography*, p. 68.
[42] All three of the informants available from Georgia give this word, as do three of the four from Mississippi.

are missing from southern Louisiana. Some of these are *blinky* (Map 86), *hydrant* (Map 87), *gully washer* (Map 89), *counterpane* (Map 51), *peckerwood* (Map 93), *(wind is) laying* (Map 96), *antigodlin* (Map 97), *light a shuck* (Map 98), *soda water* (Map 99), *dad gum!* (Map 100), and *nigger shooter* (Map 101). The last of these, unlike most of the others, is missing from Arkansas but is current throughout Louisiana. *Cup towel* (Map 85), as far as the Southwest is concerned, seems to be a distinctively Texas term and extends little beyond, in any direction.

EASTERN LIMITS

It has been shown previously that it is hardly possible in most cases to trace the western limits of the Southern words which might be expected to come to an end within our territory, since most of these extend farther to the westward than had hitherto been believed. On the other hand, there are a number of words whose spread to the eastward is limited and whose limits can be clearly perceived on the maps. Some of these diminish in frequency so gradually that it is impossible to draw lines for them; but others have such clear limits that it is possible to present them by means of *isoglosses*. An *isogloss* as used in this study may be defined as a line marking the outer limit of a lexical feature— never as a dividing line between two features. Lines were drawn halfway between communities where the word occurs and those where it does not occur. Stray occurrences of a word that lie outside the line are always entered on the maps; moreover, no isogloss was drawn if more than four such scattered occurrences would fall beyond it.

Not many of the ranch-country terms show completely clear eastern limits, as pointed out earlier. The spread of these is rather gradual, from Southwest Texas into West and Central Texas and beyond. Some of them, however, permit the drawing of isoglosses, as for example *pilón* and *frijoles* (Map 116), which cover the Southwest and West but do not extend into the Northwest. Somewhat similar lines may be drawn for *mesa, remuda,* and *morral* (Map 117). These also occur in the Northwest, and occasionally in Oklahoma, but in a rather scattered way; no attempt is made to extend the isoglosses beyond the Red River. Most of these Southwestern terms, and several others (Maps 14 to 18), reach their eastern limits in the vicinity of Refugio and De Witt Counties, and thus show a striking correspondence to the area of heaviest Latin population (Chapter I and Figure 5).

Some of the common Texas words come to an end in the vicinity of the Texas-Louisiana border, and do not occur farther to the eastward. These are *tank, cup towel,*[43] *hackamore,* and *gully washer* (Maps 118-119).

The isoglosses of another group of words come very near to separating Texas and Arkansas on the west and north from almost the whole of Louisiana. These are *bronc, want off, blinky, snake doctor,* and *paling* (Maps 119-120). Some of these penetrate noticeably to the eastward in the vicinity of Beauregard and Vernon Parishes.

A considerably larger number of isoglosses tend to throw northern and western Louisiana with Texas and Arkansas—that is, to set off southern Louisiana from the remainder of the territory that has been surveyed. This group of words, arranged more or less in the order of their eastward penetrations, includes *souse, lariat, dogie, counterpane, Christmas gift!, soda water, whetrock, fairing, sun-up, tow sack, branch, pully bone, peckerwood, (paper) sack, French harp,* and *nicker* (Maps 121 to 125).

Now, an actual count of the lines that have been mentioned shows that most of them pass just to the eastward of Jefferson and Hardin Counties, setting these off from Orange County and the Louisiana parishes of Calcasieu, Acadia, and St. Martin, as well as from all the other points lying closer to New Orleans. As the accompanying sketch (Fig. 16) will show, most of the lines to the northward branch out in an irregular way, but still reveal very clear bundles setting off southern Louisiana. Moreover, no less than a dozen other words, whose incidence is somewhat too scattered to permit the drawing of isoglosses, have a very similar general trend: *hant* (Map 60), *hunkers* (Map 78), *quarter till* (Map 80), *howdy* (Map 82), *chigger* (Map 83), *antigodlin* (Map 97), *light a shuck* (Map 98), *wait on* (Map 79), *dad gum(!)* (Map 100), *hydrant* (Map 87), *poison oak* (Map 91), and *racket store* (Map 115). It will be observed that some of the terms that fail to penetrate to southern Louisiana are Southwestern words such as *bronc* and *dogie;* others are Midland terms such as *want off* and *quarter till;* still others are common throughout the rest of the South (as far as evidence goes); *branch, whetrock, pully bone,* and *Christmas gift!*

The evidence just presented, plus a consideration of the Louisiana terms mentioned previously in this chapter, leaves no doubt that a major dialect boundary exists, although its exact limits may be less clear than those of some of the areas in the Eastern States. The presence

---

[43] Note also a small patch where *cup towel* occurs in southern Arkansas.

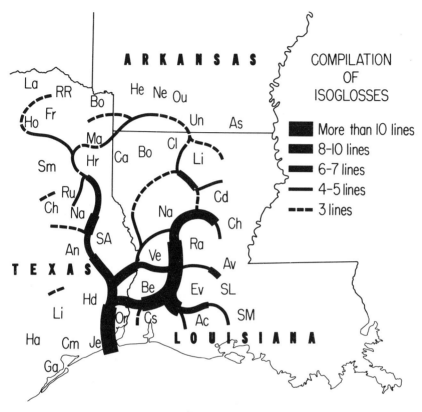

Figure 16

The Texas counties represented on this map, and their abbreviations, are: An, Angelina; Bo, Bowie; Ch, Cherokee; Cm, Chambers; Fr, Franklin; Ga, Galveston; Ha, Harris; Hd, Hardin; Ho, Hopkins; Hr, Harrison; Je, Jefferson; La, Lamar; Li, Liberty; Ma, Marion; Na, Nacogdoches; Or, Orange, Ru, Rusk; RR, Red River; Sm, Smith; SA, San Augustine.

The Arkansas counties are: As, Ashley; He, Hempstead; Ne, Nevada; Ou, Ouachita; Un, Union.

The Louisiana parishes are: Ac, Ascension; Av, Avoyelles; Be, Beauregard; Bo, Bossier; Ca, Caddo; Cd, Caldwell; Ch, Catahoula; Cl, Claiborne; Cs, Calcasieu; Ev, Evangeline; Li, Lincoln; Na, Natchitoches; Ra, Rapides; SL, St. Landry; SM, St. Martin; Ve, Vernon.

Counties and parishes that lie well beyond the lines in question are not entered on the map.

of a good many of the Louisiana terms in southeastern Texas—
particularly in the counties from Galveston to the eastward—prevents
us from regarding the division as being quite as sharp as the sketch
of eastern limits would imply. It is probably safer to consider this
corner of Texas as being a transition zone; certainly in some respects
it shows the same usages as southern Louisiana.

The classification of Texas with reference to the country as a whole
must be very tentative, since little material on vocabulary has been
published from the states to the eastward and northeastward, particularly
Mississippi, Alabama, Arkansas, Tennessee, and western Georgia.[44]
Nevertheless, I have no hesitation in classing virtually all of Texas
and an indeterminate portion of the surrounding states as a major
branch of General Southern, which I will label *Southwestern*. The
characteristics of Southwestern are: (1) the presence of a large number of Southern usages, which are current in the Eastern States from
the Potomac to eastern Georgia, and probably in the Gulf States as
well; (2) the admixture of a somewhat lesser proportion of Midland
words; and (3) the presence of many words that first gained currency
in the Southwest. The last criterion clearly distinguishes the vocabulary
of Texas from that of the South Midland or any other area that has
been demarcated in the East. The first, on the other hand, sets it off
from other portions of the West which may share the Southwestern
usages, either as borrowings from Texas or as independent acquisi-
tions from Spanish-speaking settlers. The second and third of these
features, and even to some extent the first, are missing from Southern
Louisiana.

It is possible to set off the old ranch country from the territory to the
eastward, but only as a subdivision of Southwestern, based on a greater
frequency of cattle-raising (principally Spanish) terms in this portion
of the State—certainly not on an absence of Southernisms in the area.
The push of cattle raising to the eastward and that of cotton growing to
the westward have probably obscured what may at one time have constituted a major division. Southwest Texas may also be regarded as a
subdivision, based on a greater survival of some of the earlier Southwestern vocabulary, while Central Texas also shows a certain in-
dividuality resulting to some extent from the presence of German settlers in the days before statehood.

I will not draw lines showing the limits of Southwestern or of any

[44] As mentioned in Chapter II, material has been gathered in these areas
by Gordon R. Wood of the University of Chattanooga, and it is to be hoped
that the publication of this material will occur at a not too far distant date.

of its subareas. Far too many lines have been drawn already, probably by popular demand and certainly on insufficient evidence, purporting to show the limits of speech areas in the West. In any case, we must await evidence on pronunciation and grammar before even our principal classifications can be regarded as final.

It is rare to find, within a widely spoken language, a single feature in a given area that is unique and that appears in no other dialect. Yet there is always some combination of features that marks an area, or sometimes (if we search far enough) even a community, as distinct from every other. In this sense the vocabulary of the Southwest has a character that sets it apart from all others.

V DIALECT MIXTURE AND MEANING

It must have become evident that there have often come into Texas usage more than one word for the same thing. These words were in many cases characteristic of different regional dialects in the East, but in Texas they exist side by side: *pail* and *bucket, green beans* and *snap beans, low* and *moo*, and many others.

BLENDING

When such a situation exists, a number of processes may take place. One of these is *blending*, to which the late Edgar H. Sturtevant paid much attention as a type of linguistic change.[1] Briefly stated, this means beginning with one word or phrase and ending up with another, as in Sturtevant's example *upcry*, from *uproar* and *outcry*. Some of the examples from the Texas materials show only one occurrence each, and may be only "slips," or "lapses" as Sturtevant terms them, but at any rate they demonstrate the sort of thing that is likely to happen when two synonyms are about equally prominent in the speaker's mind.[2] These are: *flapcakes (flapjacks* + *pancakes* or *battercakes); teeter saw (teeter totter* + *seesaw); freeseed (freestone* + *clearseed); blinky john (blinky milk* + *bluejohn); firemantel (fireboard* + *mantel); weather siding (weather-boards* or *boarding* + *siding)*; and *slingshooter (slingshot* + *nigger shooter)*. A few others occur from two to six times each and may have a limited currency: *firebug (firefly* + *lightning bug), head souse (head cheese* + *souse), hoghead souse (hoghead cheese* + *souse), chitlets (chittlins* + *giblets), parlor room (parlor* + *living* or *sitting room), hunches* and *honkers (haunches* + *hunkers), clinker* (jail) *(clink* + *cooler)*, and *horse doctor (horse fly* + *snake doctor)*.

[1] E. H. Sturtevant, *Introduction to Linguistic Science* (New Haven, Yale University Press, 1947), Chapter XI.
[2] The explanations are conjectural, since there is no way of being sure what is in another person's mind. Two of the examples cited here, *freeseed* and *firebug*, were also occasionally observed by Kurath in the Eastern States (*Word Geography*, Figs. 129 and 142).

Still more current are *mantelboard* (*mantel* or *mantelpiece* + *fire-board*), and *hidy* (*hi* + *howdy*). The former shows thirty-four occurrences, the latter fourteen. One such formation must be touched by folk etymology: of three informants who use *swingletree* (*swing* + *single-tree*), one states that it is "because they swing."

DEVELOPMENT OF DISTINCTIONS

Blending, it seems, is only an occasional phenomenon; usually the presence of more than one word for the same thing has different and more far-reaching results. Since every self-respecting dialect abhors exact synonymy, the speakers usually take steps either (1) to abandon (gradually, of course) one of the words and use the other, or (2) to develop some kind of distinction in meaning that makes both words useful. Both processes may sometimes occur; that is, a word while on its way out may have acquired a meaning different from that of the word which is replacing it. This is true of *branch*, for example.

The matter of obsolescence will be discussed in the next chapter, and a few speculations will be presented regarding the reasons for the loss of certain words. We might here look briefly at some of the attempts to resolve the problem of synonymy by the development of distinctions in meaning.

In many cases we find hardly more than a groping for some kind of difference between synonyms. For example, an informant in southern Arkansas, where *snake doctor* and *mosquito hawk* are about equally frequent, says that the former term applies to the insect when over the water, the latter when over the land. Two informants state that a *(paper) bag* is larger than a *(paper) sack*, but certainly no such distinction is of general currency.

Other distinctions that are given by only a few informants probably also reflect nothing but the feeling that different words should have different meanings;[3] that, for example, in a *rock wall* cement is used whereas in a *rock fence* it is not;[4] that a horse *bucks* by using his back feet and *pitches* with all four (or vice versa); that a *mouth organ* is smaller than a *harmonica*; and that when a horse *whinnies* he makes a

---

[3] Reactions to this idea, as well as to some of the examples, are likely to be quite indignant. Many people have the feeling that anyone but a fool knows the difference between a *doodad* and a *doohickey*—that the difference always existed and always will. Moreover, persons with a special knowledge of a subject (for example, horsebreaking) often develop certain distinctions in terminology that are not familiar to the general public.

[4] One informant states the opposite.

louder noise than when he *nickers*. Perhaps in the same category should be put an informant's comment that one *waits on* a person when he is present but *waits for* him when he is not present but is expected.

Even in cases where there is some scientific reason to make distinctions, informants often can not agree on the criteria. Several kinds of skunks are native to Texas,[5] and certainly some of the rural informants have observed differences between them; yet the assignment of the terms *polecat* and *skunk* seems to lack general agreement. Three informants think a *polecat* is smaller than a *skunk*, one that it is larger. Two state that a *polecat* has spots rather than stripes, one that it has stripes rather than spots. A similar observation probably holds for *poison oak* and *poison ivy*, yet there is evidence that the former is consistently used by some informants for the varieties that are of more bushy habit. Since *poison oak* is obsolescent, it is probable that the modern urbanized generation feels no need of a distinction, if one was ever generally current.

When things change with the times, often a word is associated only with the older form of the thing. Of those who use the word *banquette* in southern Louisiana, two state that it is applicable only to a sidewalk made of brick or of boards; presumably *sidewalk* would be used for the modern concrete type of walk. Similarly, *gallery*, which to some speakers is synonymous with *porch*, is felt by others to be applicable only to the old-time structure, larger than a porch, which went all around the house. A few informants hold that *snap beans* and *light bread* apply only to the home-produced product, not to the same thing when bought in stores. *Corn pone* is often associated with times when only meal and water were available for its preparation, whereas *corn bread* refers to bread made by more sumptuous recipes. A similar attempt is made to differentiate older and newer styles of furniture, but usually with much less success. For example, twenty-two informants state that a *bureau* has a mirror, seven that it does not. With regard to a *chiffonier*, five vote for a mirror, eight against.[6]

It goes without saying that distinctions in meaning may spread from one speaker to another until some of them become general. These may represent a satisfactory resolution of the annoyance of synonymy. Quite a number of informants state that a metal container is a *bucket* if for water, a *pail* if for milk; moreover, there are eighteen occurrences of *milk pail*, only three of *water pail*. (This does not represent

---

[5] Seven species are described in the *Texas Almanac 1958–1959* (Dallas, A. H. Belo Corporation), p. 211.

[6] Of course, both types went under the name of *chiffonier*.

majority usage, in which *bucket* is used for both.) A *frying pan* is very generally thought to be lighter, or thinner, or smaller, or shallower than a *skillet*, and there is no reason why both terms should not survive. A very large majority of informants hold that a *branch* is smaller than a *creek*, but in this case the former term is nevertheless becoming obsolete, probably because in parts of Texas anything smaller than a creek would not be a stream at all. Both *hydrant* and *faucet* are current throughout Texas, and there is no doubt that they are to some extent interchangeable; yet there is a striking trend toward confining *hydrant* to the device outside the house, *faucet* to its indoor equivalent. Another distinction which is fairly consistent is that which has developed between *lima beans* and *butter beans*, formerly, no doubt, undistinguished[7] synonyms. This distinction has been exploited by the food packers, who in general use *lima beans* for the small greenish beans, *butter beans* for the large yellow variety (see Chapter VI).

As a corollary to the idea that has been presented, there is no doubt that distinctions which were once observed may be lost or blurred. *Maverick*, which once meant an unbranded or unclaimed cow or calf, has in the minds of many Texans come so close to the meaning of *dogie* that it may become an unnecessary synonym. In any case, increased watchfulness over valuable livestock has made mavericks much less usual. Fortunately the term has acquired some figurative meanings which assure its survival in literature for a long time.

It is certainly not to be inferred that synonymy, in a general sense, is invariably a destructive force. For example, as long as a speaker has a sense of time and place and situation, as long as he has a feeling for style, there is no reason why he should confine himself to *downpour* or *cloudburst;* he may also have at his disposal *gully washer,* or *chunk floater,* or *clod roller,* or *duck drencher,* or *frog strangler,* or any number of other terms. But when two words exist, either of which might convey precisely the same meaning and feeling in the same situation, he is likely to feel that the best thing to do is to abandon one of them.

---

[7] In this and similar cases, I refer only to lexical denotation. No doubt there are usually vague differences in "tone" or "style" or "connotation" between two words.

VI OBSOLESCENCE AND REPLACEMENT

As has been pointed out in Chapter II, the original idea of this vocabulary survey was to sample the usage of mature (middle-aged and older) residents of Texas who knew at least something of rural life. An overwhelming majority of the informants fall between the ages of 40 and 85, with the heavier concentrations in the 60's and 70's. As part of the processing of the materials, a count was kept of the occurrences of each word in each age group: under 50, 50–59, 60–69, 70–79, and over 80. Numbers were reduced to percentages, and in cases where there seemed to be consistent increases or decreases in frequency corresponding to age, the figures were entered on tables. In view of the small number of informants in the subdivisions, the figures were usually unconvincing in themselves. Since I was virtually certain, from years of unsystematic observation, that the usage of the younger (mostly urban, high-school educated) generation would show very noticeable differences from that of the survey informants, I took written samplings of the usage of a group of university students in a number of different classes. One hundred questionnaires were filled out for some of the items, two hundred for others. The results were not at all surprising save in a very few instances,[1] and tended to confirm the impression of obsolescence or of innovation suggested by the usage of the survey informants. Although the method of collection was different, and the results, strictly speaking, not comparable,[2] these student usages have been added to the tables for whatever they may be worth.

[1] For example, one sampling of 100 students produced 55 occurrences of *spooks*, meaning ghosts. A second set of 100, made two or three years later, gave only 11 occurrences. Apparently the word has recently acquired certain slang meanings that make it inappropriate for use with its original meaning.

[2] That is, the questionnaires presented each item as a group of words, usually followed by the entry "no term," from which the students were to encircle the appropriate one. This might have led to a slightly higher frequency of all words, since students have long been conditioned to give *some* kind of answer on a "quiz"—although in this instance they were earnestly requested not to encircle a word that they did not actually use.

The tables of words showing increasing and decreasing frequencies are presented at the end of this chapter. The words are arranged approximately in the order of their frequency among the survey informants. The reader is warned against these tables and the figures they contain, particularly with regard to the interpretation of the figures. The only claim to accuracy that is made is that they are a description of the actual data that was collected. It would be absurd to assert, for example, that exactly 45.9 per cent of all Texans in their sixties use the term *gallery*, whereas 0.5 per cent of all students do so; the figures apply only to the groups of informants actually surveyed. Indeed, toward the end of each table some of the words are so rare that a numerical presentation is unconvincing and not very appropriate. In short, no conclusive mathematical "proof" is contained in any of the tables.

In spite of the warnings that have been given, I am going to assume that the informants whose usage was examined are representative of a considerably larger group, and that in that larger group (however large it is) certain usages are clearly dying out while others are coming in. This assumption is based on various reasons in addition to percentages of usage. One is the obvious disappearance of certain *things*, such as buggy shavs and kitchen safes. Another is the body of statements from the informants that certain usages are older or newer in their own communities.[3] Then there are the easily observable labels in stores and catalogues,[4] some of which will be discussed later. Finally, the trends that appear usually coincide with my own experience and observation as a "native speaker" of Southwestern English.

REASONS FOR VOCABULARY CHANGE

In general, vocabulary changes are attributable to the following reasons. The first of these is the very existence of synonymy, which usually comes about through some historical accident. This was discussed in Chapter V. Another very obvious reason is the disappearance or rarity of things themselves. When we read of *ash-hoppers* and *shot-towers* in Mark Twain we may be in need of a glossary in order to know what these were and what they were for. Similarly, in the Texas materials, *singletree*, *(kitchen) safe*, *stake and rider fence*,

[3] For example, 22 informants state that *counterpane* is older, none say that it is newer. Similar statements for other "older" words are *parlor*, 25 to 1; *gallery*, 22 to 1; *(kitchen) safe*, 15 to 0; *holp(ed)*, 12 to 0; *racket store*, 11 to 0; *dog irons*, 9 to 0.

[4] For example, *green beans*, *pillow case* (rather than *snap beans*, *pillow slip*.)

and other such terms[5] designate things that to most moderns are only a memory, if indeed they are familiar at all.

Again, things may change in nature to such an extent that the older terms hardly seem applicable. The once-fashionable *gallery*, which extended across the front and sides of a house—and sometimes across the back as well—has been replaced by the less commodious *porch*; and this in turn may in the future become unfamiliar as the *patio* and the *terrace* come into fashion.

Vocabulary may also be expected to change when things are differently distributed or marketed. When an item formerly produced at home (such as what used to be called *clabber cheese*) is available at stores under another name *(cottage cheese)*, we may expect the trade term to prevail, since that which is homemade (in spite of the lip service paid to it) seldom carries the prestige of that which is bought. If the article is brought from a considerable distance, the appeal of the new term is probably even greater—for example, the Louisiana *praline*, which is replacing the indigenous Southwestern *pecan patty*.

Another reason for change is certainly to be found in education and increasing familiarity with such books as dictionaries. Terms like *pully bone*, *rench* (for *rinse*), and *widow woman*,[6] not being sanctioned by the arbiters of usage, are therefore less likely to survive than their approved equivalents.[7]

In some areas, vocabulary may change because of the adoption of words from a neighboring dialect of greater prestige.[8] Such a process does not seem to be operative in Texas to any great extent; Midland words do not seem to be consistently replacing Southern words, or vice versa (see Table F, following this chapter). However, it seems clear that a few South Louisiana words were adopted in Texas for this reason (Chapter IV).

A reason for obsolescence that operates in some instances is homonym-

---

[5] All of the words classed as "older" in this chapter (except certain ones mentioned in footnotes) are entered in Tables A to C following this chapter; those classed as "newer" appear in Tables D and E. Since a word index is provided, no further cross-references need be given.

[6] None of these are entered in the *American College Dictionary* (1948), *Webster's New Collegiate*, or *Webster's New World* (1957).

[7] A further discussion of the influence of education is included in the following section: "Social and Economic Factors Involved."

[8] Parisian French has exercised such an influence on its neighbors for centuries. The late Louis Grootaers of Louvain told me of a Walloon informant who spoke of his own hat as a *capyá* (Walloon) but of his wife's hat as a *chapeau* (Parisian).

ic conflict. That is, when words with the same pronunciation but with entirely different meanings share many of the same distributions in utterances, one of the words is very likely to become unusable.[9] The most striking example of this process in the Texas materials is to be found in the word *ass*, which has become obsolete as a term for the animal *equus asinus* because of the wide currency of its homonym with the meaning of posterior, or rump. Possibly similar reasons may contribute to the obsolescence of other terms, as occasionally intimated in the results of this survey.

The most intangible reason for vocabulary change is fashion. An example may be found in the various familiar terms for one's father: *pappy, pa, papa, daddy*, and so on. I am unable to explain such changes on a rational basis; but there is no doubt that, quite apart from slang usages, many vocabulary items simply go out of fashion, even among the "kinship terms," which are usually regarded as the most stable.

It is often said that radio, television, and movies are bringing about or will bring about considerable changes in vocabulary usage. I am unable to confirm or deny this, since the first two are relatively recent so far as general use is concerned. With regard to commercial announcements, probably the same terms are used for products as those displayed in stores; so it is hardly possible to determine where the influence really comes from. As for the adoption of "Western" terms from various forms of popular entertainment, I am somewhat skeptical; the material covered in Chapter IV (and the maps) tended to show that the principal medium for the spread of such terms is still "surface" communication. For example, Arkansas and Louisiana have had the same chance as Texas to hear *maverick* and *corral* on Western radio or television programs, but neither term has made much progress in the former areas. There is no doubt, however, that because of greatly improved facilities for travel and communication, words of national currency are likely to replace regional and local words in all parts of the country.

SOCIAL AND ECONOMIC FACTORS INVOLVED

For the remainder of this chapter we might look more closely at some of the features of social and domestic life in the Southwest that have resulted in specific vocabulary changes.

[9] This idea was first given currency by the French linguistic geographer Jules Gilliéron. For a discussion of the operation of this principle in English, see Edna R. Williams, *The Conflict of Homonyms in English* (New Haven, Yale University Press, 1944).

It is well known to everyone that the Industrial Revolution brought about very drastic and far-reaching changes in the material features of domestic life. Indeed we might be justified in speaking of a "Domestic Revolution" if the phrase did not have questionable semantic overtones. There has probably never been a period in history when (without the violence of conquest or captivity) an individual might have observed more changes in everyday living than those that have been seen by a person born in the 1870's or 1880's in one of the frontier states and still living there in the 1960's. Texas is very typical in this respect.

First there is the matter of urbanization. In 1880 the population of Texas was 9.2 per cent urban, 90.8 per cent rural. The urban element has increased steadily; in 1900 it constituted 17.1 per cent; in 1940, 45.4 per cent. In 1960 the urban population had risen to no less than 75 per cent.[10] This change was brought about not only by the moving of country people to town but also by the rapid increase in the population of most parts of the state. Many an inhabitant found himself transformed from a rural to an urban citizen without moving from his property.

Moreover, the farm itself has been transformed by the increasing use of motors and electric power to replace the work of horses and men. In the United States as a whole the number of horses on farms decreased between 1920 and 1957 by a ratio of about 7 to 1;[11] in Texas the decrease was almost as striking, 5 to 1,[12] in spite of the continued usefulness of horses on some of the ranches. Tractors, meanwhile, have come into general use; in 1954 about 60 per cent of the Texas farms were provided with at least one tractor.[13] The use of horses in the cities and on the highways has, of course, diminished to practically nothing as motor vehicles have become universal.[14]

Decreasing familiarity with rural life and with premechanized days is most clearly evident in the waning knowledge of the horse and his uses. This is reflected in the obsolescence of the terms *nicker, near*

[10] *Texas Almanac 1961–1962* (Dallas. A. H. Belo Corporation), p. 196.

[11] *Agricultural Statistics 1957* (U.S. Department of Agriculture, Washington, U.S. Gov't. Printing Office, 1958), p. 441.

[12] *Texas Almanac 1956–1957* (Dallas, A. H. Belo Corporation), p. 278. The period covered was 1920–1955.

[13] *Ibid.*, p. 252.

[14] In 1917, motor vehicles in Texas averaged about one to every 225 persons. *Ibid.*, p. 352. In 1959 a total of over 4,600,000 such vehicles were registered, or about one to every two persons. Information from D. L. Mills of the Motor Vehicle Division of the Texas Department of Public Safety, Austin.

horse, off horse, lead horse, whiffletree, singletree, doubletree, shavs (of a buggy), and *horse lot.* Even the romantic term *remuda* is becoming unfamiliar to the youngest generation,[15] and fewer people know how to call a horse in from the pasture; the disappearance of *cope!* is not surprising.

Growing unfamiliarity with cows is also apparent. Younger informants are less familiar with *sook!*; with *low*; and with both *dogie*[16] and *maverick,* as terms for a calf.

Lack of direct acquaintance with the rural scene probably also accounts for the increasing use of such book words as *firefly, dragon fly,*[17] *skunk,* and *barnyard*[18] for the traditional regional terms *lightning bug, snake doctor* (or *mosquito hawk*), *polecat,* and *(cow) lot.* The decline of *worm fence, stake and rider fence,* and *paling fence* reflects the replacement of the old handmade materials by manufactured products. The upright slats used for fencing, although still common, seem always to be marketed under the name *pickets* rather than *palings.*[19]

With regard to topography, the term *branch* may be dying out simply because it is unnecessary; there are not enough kinds and sizes of streams to justify all of the terms originally current. Homonymic conflict may also play a small part. For an elevated area, the book word *plateau* seems to be gaining ground at the expense of *table land* and probably other words and phrases. The diminishing currency of *poison oak* is very likely a result mainly of less familiarity with the countryside—although it is doubtful that the term ever conveyed a useful distinction from *poison ivy.*

In connection with urbanization as a factor in obsolescence, we should observe that the terms from the cattle country, specifically those of Spanish origin, do not show the same decline in frequency as the terms from the farm vocabulary. Consider the following twenty-six words, all of which are derived from Spanish: *arroyo, canyon, resaca, llano, mesa, chaparral, mott, acequia, hacienda, olla, corral, morral, lariat, lasso, reata, hackamore, vaquero, remuda, pinto (horse), bronc(o), burro, frijoles, partera, pilón, hoosegow,* and *cinch.* Although some of these are becoming rare, others (for example, *corral*) are probably gaining in currency. The composite frequency of the

[15] Students, 6 per cent; survey informants, 30 per cent.
[16] Students, 20 per cent; survey informants, 62 per cent.
[17] Students, 81 per cent; survey informants, 16 per cent.
[18] Students, 73.5 per cent; survey informants, 25.6 per cent.
[19] For example, in the Sears catalogue of 1928 and later numbers, I have never found *paling* listed.

whole list in the different age groups in percentages is: 20–49, 25.6; 50–59, 24.6; 60–69, 22.6; 70–79, 27; over 80, 21.2.[20] Since ranching has always carried more prestige than "dirt farming," informants seem less likely to lose the vocabulary of the ranch country, and probably, at least in some instances, they feel a certain pride in their usages.

With regard to the house and its furnishings, a considerable list of older and newer terms may be examined (some of the older terms, of course, have no modern equivalents):[21]

Older	Newer
weatherboards	*siding*
clapboards	——
gallery	*(porch)*[22]
parlor	*living room*
garret, loft	*attic*
privy, backhouse	*outhouse*
turn (of wood)	——
dog irons, fire dogs	——
mantelboard, mantelpiece, fireboard	*mantel*[23]
lounge, settee,[24] *davenport*	*(sofa, couch)*[25]
bureau, chiffonier,[26] *chifforobe*[27]	*chest of drawers*

[20] Frequencies from the student generation are not available, and in any case the number of students from the ranch country is not proportionate to that of the survey informants. One student made the interesting comment that when on the ranch he called a certain enclosure the *horse lot*, but since he has come to the University he calls it the *corral*.

[21] Naturally, it is often not possible to pair off older and newer usages. Frequently a thing itself goes out of use, so that no new word is needed. In other cases, an older word may be replaced by several newer ones, or several older ones by a newer word. Again, an older word may linger during the time when a newer one is establishing itself.

[22] *Porch* is not a newer usage, but has been long in use, side by side with *gallery*. The same is true of other words enclosed in parentheses; they show no striking increase in frequency among the survey informants. although they are in a sense "replacements" of the older terms.

[23] Students, 87.5 per cent; survey informants, 67.8 per cent.

[24] Students, 1 per cent; survey informants, 22.8 per cent.

[25] One or the other is used by 66.5 per cent of the survey informants. as against 87 per cent of the students.

[26] Students, 2 per cent; survey informants, 22.4 per cent.

[27] Students, 1 per cent; survey informants, 13.9 per cent.

Older	Newer
safe	*cabinet*[28]
counterpane	*bedspread*
pillow slip	*pillow case*
poke	*(bag, sack)*
dinner bucket	*lunch (kit,* etc.)
slop bucket	*garbage can*[29]

The increasing use of milled lumber is reflected in the obsolescence of the terms *clapboards* and *weatherboards*. The former applied to slabs split by hand from a log, the latter to simple boards that were nailed on so as to lap one over the other. Ready-prepared lumber for this purpose has been marketed under the name *siding* for decades.[30]

Few modern home builders feel that they can afford the space for the broad, roofed-over area known as the *gallery;* hence the word often has an application only to the older structures that may still be in use. The room where guests might be entertained was termed the *parlor* for a generation or two, and there is no doubt that the word connoted great elegance.[31] *Living room* has also been in use for a century at least, but earlier probably implied that the family had only one room to live in.[32] Very likely the elevation in the meaning of *living room* came about through real estate agents and builders, who sought some means of avoiding the suggestion of overformality conveyed by the older word *parlor.*

The obsolescence of the terms *turn (of wood)*, *dog irons*, *fire dogs, mantelboard, mantelpiece,* and *fireboard* reflect the far-reaching changes in domestic heating that have taken place in the last generation. The use of gas for this purpose increased strikingly in the 1920's; in 1933 Texas was consuming over one-seventh of the utility gas of the nation.[33] By 1950, over 75 per cent of the dwellings in Texas were heated by either utility gas or butane; only 11.5 per cent used wood and 0.7 per

[28] Students, 79 per cent; survey informants, 18.1 per cent.

[29] Students, 72 per cent; survey informants, 33.4 per cent.

[30] *Siding* is the main listing in the 1910 Sears catalogue. Cross-references to *weatherboards* and *clapboards* were given in the indexes as late as 1928–1929, but were no longer included by the time the 1960 edition appeared.

[31] The 1910 Sears catalogue offers "parlor desks," "parlor tables," and "parlor and music cabinets."

[32] Note the following 1860 quotation given in M. M. Mathews' *Dictionary of Americanisms* (Chicago, University of Chicago Press, 1951): "The interior consisted of one large 'living-room,' and a 'lean-to,' used as a kitchen."

[33] *Historical Statistics of the Gas Industry* (New York, American Gas Association, 1956), pp. 186–187.

cent coal. Even the majority of farm dwellings used either gas or liquid fuel, while only 37 per cent used wood and 1.2 per cent coal.[34] No doubt rural consumption of gas is still increasing,[35] and the fireplace, once the primary source of heat and the symbol of family unity, will survive only as a luxury.

The obsolescent terms *lounge, settee, davenport, bureau, chiffonier,* and *chifforobe* reflect changing fashions in furniture, as well as the purchase of items from large distributors rather than from local makers. For a good many years, *davenport* was the favorite term in the catalogues, and no doubt in the stores, for the piece with arms and a back— *couch* for the flat type with an elevation at the head.[36] *Settee* designated a smaller, stiff-backed bench mainly for porches or lawns, but it is probable that the word was also in use for a sofa.[37] Some wonderful combinations must have appeared from time to time; the 1910 Sears, Roebuck and Co. General Catalogue pictures and describes a combination of "Roman divan, sofa, davenport, and couch." By 1956, everything was a *sofa* or *sectional sofa,* and the term *davenport* has entirely disappeared, even from the index.

Pieces of furniture containing drawers have also suffered a good many changes in nomenclature. The term *chiffonier* was certainly popular for some time; the Sears catalogues of 1910 and of 1928 offer many models, with only a cross-reference for *bureau.* The term *chifforobe,* supposed to be a combination of *chiffonier* and *wardrobe,* was first observed, according to M. M. Mathews' *Dictionary of Americanisms,* in the Sears catalogue of 1908; items under this name were offered as late as 1956, although by this time the term applied only to a piece of nursery furniture for children's clothing.

The item of kitchen furniture known as a *safe,* in which were kept not only dishes but certain kinds of foods as well, has hardly survived as such, since the coming of refrigeration has relieved it of much of its

---

[34] *Census of Housing 1950* (Washington, U.S. Gov't. Printing Office. 1953), Vol. I, Part 6, p. 43–18, Table 12. Compare these figures with those for Virginia, where 62.5 per cent of all dwellings, and 87.4 per cent of farm dwellings, were heated by wood or coal.

[35] Between 1954 and 1959, for example, there were over 100,000 *new* installations for butane. Information from Frank Harvick of the Texas Railroad Commission.

[36] For example, in the Sears catalogues of 1910 and 1928–1929. The former gives *sofa* only in the phrase "davenport bed sofas"; the latter has only a cross-reference for *sofa,* the main entry being *couch.*

[37] In the index of the 1928–1929 Sears catalogue, *settee* is a cross-reference for a section of "davenports."

function. The Sears catalogue of 1910 offered only two models of the *safe;* by 1928 the word was only a cross-listing for *cabinet,* and now no such term is used at all.

Counterpane and *pillow slip* are clearly becoming less frequent because of the merchandising terms *bedspread* and *pillow case.*[38] A similar reason probably applies to *dinner bucket,* which has given way to phrases containing the term *lunch.*[39] As for *poke* (sack), I can give no reason for its obsolescence other than possible homonymic conflict; moreover, the dictionaries give this term no support.[40]

A considerable number of obsolescent terms have to do with food in one form or another. Some of these are:

Older	*Newer*
chittlins	——
middlins	——
souse	——
(corn) pone	*corn bread*[41]
corn dodger	——
hush puppies	——
cracklin' bread	——
egg bread	——
light bread[42]	*white bread*
teacake	——
flapjacks, battercakes	*pancakes, hotcakes*
snap beans	*green beans*
butter beans	*lima beans*[43]
roasting ears	*corn on the cob*
clabber cheese	*(cottage cheese)*
pecan patty	*praline*
clearseed peach	——
plum peach	——
clabber	*sour milk*

[38] I have not found *counterpane* in a catalogue; *pillow slip* occurred in the 1910 Sears catalogue, but only to designate a cover for a sofa pillow.

[39] Sears, which formerly offered *dinner pails* (1910), later changed over to *lunch kits* (1928-1929).

[40] For example, *Webster's New International:* "Now dial., local, or archaic." The *Third New International* (1961), somewhat more tolerantly, simply labels *poke* as "chiefly South and Midland."

[41] This does not increase in frequency except in the student generation: students, 96 per cent; survey informants, 76.2 per cent. The only significant feature is the loss of the other terms.

[42] This is constant among survey informants (78.4 per cent), but drops to 35 per cent among students.

[43] This increases noticeably only in the student generation: students, 70 per cent; survey informants, 27.4 per cent.

Older	Newer
blinky	sour
bluejohn	——
lunch	snack
pully bone	wishbone
——	gumbo

It is plain that the principal cause of change here is the fact that a large number of foods that were formerly produced and prepared at home are now purchased, often in different forms, from stores. The slaughter of hogs, for example, is more and more being left to the packing houses; the number of farm-killed hogs in the United States declined by half between 1930 and 1956.[44] It is not surprising that fewer people are familiar with *chittlins, middlins,* and *souse.*[45]

Breads are now mostly purchased, either ready-baked or in the form of prepared dough; and since corn bread is not offered in stores, many people are no longer familiar with *pone, corn dodgers, hush puppies, cracklin bread,* or *egg bread.* Even meal seems to be giving way to *corn bread mix* and *corn muffin mix.*[46] As for ordinary white baker's bread, I have been unable to find a loaf under the name *light bread;* it is always *white bread* or *enriched bread* or *white enriched bread.* The use of *pancake* has clearly been encouraged by such old-time products as "Aunt Jemima's Pancake Flour" (now "Pancake and Waffle Mix") as well as other "Pancake Mixes."[47] As for *hotcake,* it is probably a restaurant term. In any case, one can hardly expect to purchase anything under the name *battercake* or *flapjack.* Similarly, nothing can be bought (at least, not at the local stores) under the name *teacakes,* which suggests the homemade product and thus lacks prestige.[48]

Although fresh vegetables are still available at most stores, there has been a striking increase in the consumption of the canned and frozen

[44] *Agricultural Statistics 1957,* p. 394.

[45] Swift and Company (and probably others) put out a packaged product known as *souse,* but there are many more exotic concoctions to overshadow it: for example, *Braunschweiger, Pepperoni, Salami, Thuringer, Olive Loaf,* and so on.

[46] Such are the products offered in one of the local Safeway Stores.

[47] For example, Pillsbury, Kitchen Craft, and Betty Crocker, observed at Safeway.

[48] At two local grocery stores I observed, in addition to various kinds of "cookies," the following confections: *jelly juniors, ginger snaps, waffle cremes, fig bars, fig newtons, cream patties, vanilla wafers, sugar wafers, pecan sandies, vanilla sandwiches, coconut bars, butter macaroons, lemon cream sandwiches, sugar tops, griddle wafers,* and several others—but nary a *teacake.*

product,[49] particularly green beans and lima beans.[50] Since *green beans* is invariably the name found on the labels,[51] it is not surprising that this term is superseding the traditional *snap beans*. As to lima beans, the situation is slightly different. Although the use of the formerly rare term *lima beans* has certainly been encouraged by the labels on cans, the canners are also reviving the term *butter beans*, to designate the large yellow variety only. Frozen ears of corn I have observed only under the label *corn on the cob*, and this term is no doubt also suggestive of the more expensive restaurants, which would never serve this old favorite under the name *roasting ears*.

Similar observations apply to the obsolescence of *clabber cheese*, *clearseed peach*, and *plum peach*, as the items in question are never marketed under those labels. Likewise, the term *pecan patty* is giving way to *praline*, which applies to a store-bought and exotic confection of much greater appeal.

As for *clabber*, *blinky*, and *bluejohn*, the loss of these terms simply reflects a decline in the home production of milk; and in any case improved refrigeration[52] would hardly permit so much milk to turn sour.

Pully bone may be declining solely because it is not in "the dictionary." *Lunch*, which is coming into use for the noon meal, can hardly also be expected to survive with the meaning of a snack.

Gumbo, previously unknown, is becoming more familiar no doubt partly because of its commercial distribution; at least two major food companies[53] now use this label on canned soup.

In everyday social intercourse with family and friends a good many words and phrases are obviously changing, among them the following:

Older	Newer
Pappy, Pa, Papa	*Daddy*
Ma, Mama	*Mother*
howdy	*hi*
courting, sparking	*going (steady) with*

[49] From a per capita consumption of 18.5 pounds in 1920 to 51.14 pounds in 1956. *Agricultural Statistics 1957*, pp. 308–314.

[50] About five times as many pounds per capita as in 1920. *Ibid.*, pp. 310–311.

[51] At one store alone I observed ten brands of canned beans labelled *green beans*, none labelled *snap beans*.

[52] Even among farm dwellings, 64 per cent had electric refrigeration in 1950; another 18.2 per cent had ice available. *Census of Housing 1950*, Vol. I, Part 6, 43–18, Table 13.

[53] H. J. Heinz Co. (Pittsburgh, Pa.), and Campbell Soup Company (General Offices, Camden, N.J.).

Older	Newer
bussing, spooning	*necking,*[54] etc.
see you (home)	*walk you*
shivaree	——
widow woman	*widow*
parson	*(pastor)*
Paddy (Irishman)	——
hant	——
hunkers	——
antigodlin	——
light a shuck	——
evening	*afternoon*
racket store	*variety store,* etc.
French harp	*harmonica*
rench	*rinse*
drempt	*dreamed*

Among the most striking of these are the terms for one's parents. Apparently the oldest term for the father is *Pappy,* which has almost been lost in this context; next comes *Pa,* followed by *Papa,* and finally *Daddy.*[55] Sometimes it seems that a new term comes in with each generation.[56] *Ma* shows a similar obsolescence, but *Mama* has not gone out so strikingly as has *Papa.*[57] *Mother,* however, has shown about the same gain as *Daddy.*

Changing mores of courtship are probably reflected in the decreasing frequency of *courting* and *sparking.* That is, *going (steady) with* seems to imply that most wooing is no longer done at anyone's home; one must take a girl somewhere in order to impress her. If he walks with her, this is sufficiently uncommon to need mention *(walk you home).* Petting has no doubt become so familiar as to breed contempt, as reflected by the modern terms for it.

Probably the main reason for the decline of *widow woman, hant, hunkers, evening, antigodlin, rench* and *light a shuck* is that they are not sanctioned by dictionaries. *Shivaree* denoted a primarily rural

[54] Students, 25 per cent; survey informants, 4.4 per cent. Probably *necking* would have been more common a decade ago; newer slang terms, such as *smooching, grubbing,* and *making out* seem to be taking its place.

[55] *Pop* is probably also newer, but it is not very common in Texas.

[56] A study in Eastland County of three generations in the same family, by Mrs. Maureen McElroy, shows the oldest generation using *Pa,* the next *Papa,* and the youngest *Daddy,* with very little overlapping of usages. A similar study in Tom Green County, by Robert E. Mims, shows *Pa* in the oldest generation, *Daddy* and *Father* (with overlapping) in the two younger ones.

[57] *Mama* is still used by 31 per cent of the students (as against 63 per cent of the survey informants).

custom which has given way to more expensive and elaborate celebrations and to such forms of annoyance as sabotaging the groom's car or tying cans and signs to it. In the case of *racket store*, homonymic conflict may have played a part,[58] but in any case many of these stores are now members of national chains, which could hardly be expected to use regional terms. *French harp* is giving way to *harmonica* for the obvious reason that these instruments are marketed under the latter name.[59]

It appears, from many of the preceding examples, that the ultimate reasons for the choice of one synonym over another must often be sought in the fertile minds of the merchandisers. These minds are keenly attuned to the inarticulate desires of the public; so it is very probable that they are merely catering to, or serving, the frantic urge for newness, the uneasy search for prestige, and the aversion to rusticity that prevail in the Southwest and elsewhere. Only occasionally does a producer of merchandise exploit the appeal of old-time things, as in the recent use of *hush puppies* for a kind of cocktail snack—and also as the brand name of a certain type of shoe.

It has been pointed out earlier that one of the factors in the obsolescence of words is education. It is hardly possible in the present survey to isolate the influence of this element, since the informants in the older groups were consistently of less formal education than those in the younger groups.[60] This roughly represents the situation in Texas as a whole; the average amount of schooling has increased considerably since the turn of the century.[61] Thus most of the words classed as obsolescent also show less frequency among better educated informants. Typical examples are *branch, nicker, rench, widow woman, peckerwood, Ma, Pa, flapjack, poke* and *turn (of wood)*. Usually, also, the newer usages are at the same time characteristic of informants of better education: for example, *widow, skunk, bedspread, hi!, dreamed, pillow case, lima beans, Daddy,* and *corn on the cob*.

There are, however, a few instances in which education, rather than age, seems to be the most important consideration. *Veranda*, although by no means new, is considerably more frequent among educated

[58] For example, with the *racket* used in tennis.

[59] The Sears catalogues have consistently listed only *harmonicas*, at least as far back as 1910.

[60] Of informants over sixty, 62.8 per cent were limited to elementary school only; of those in the fifties, 43.1 per cent; of those under fifty, 27.5 per cent.

[61] In 1890, all of the high-school enrollments in Texas amounted to less than 2 per cent of the total population of the state. By 1940, this figure had risen to about 19 per cent. See C. E. Evans, *The Story of Texas Schools* (Austin, Steck Company, 1955), p. 177.

informants. *Counterpin* and *counterpane* are both older usages; the former is an uneducated form, the latter its equivalent among the educated. Other terms that seem to be characteristc of educated speakers are *parents, reared, andirons, divan, quarter of, dragon fly,* and *toad* (rather than *toadfrog*).

Items of nonstandard "grammar" are usually considerably more frequent (or at least easier to elicit) in the less-educated group: for example, *clum* (climbed), *throwed, holp(ed), riz* (rose), *dremp,* and *div* (dived). This to be expected in view of the school drills that used to take place in the "principal parts" of verbs.

When we examine the usage of men as against that of women, with regard to the preservation or loss of lexical features, we find very little difference. It is not true among the Texas informants, as has been alleged for parts of Europe,[62] that women preserve a more archaic usage than men. Although the women informants represent a slightly older group,[63] their use of archaisms is almost exactly equal to that of men. A composite of 63 words judged to be obsolescent shows 28.3 per cent occurrence among women, 29.2 per cent among men.

There is a slight indication in our materials that women informants may be less inclined to use "bad words," including insulting terms for "minority" groups. The most striking example is *damn,* given by seventeen men as against one woman.[64] A composite including *damn, dad gum, bastard, wop, kike, coon,* and *greaser* shows 32.2 per cent occurrence among men, 21 per cent among women.

There is some little evidence that men informants have retained greater familiarity with terms implying close contact with horses. A composite of the ten terms *stud (horse), hackamore, nicker, near horse, off horse, cope!, cinch, feed bag, nose bag,* and *morral* shows 40 per cent occurrence among men, 27.6 per cent among women.

A good many other words show variations between the sexes, but none very strikingly. *Light a shuck* is given more often by men (28

---

[62] See, for example, Sever Pop, *La Dialectologie* (Louvain, The Author, 1950), Vol. I, p. 725.

[63] Of the women informants, 31.4 per cent are in their seventies. as against 18.4 per cent of the men. On the other hand, only 26.6 per cent of the women are in the sixties, as against 34.6 per cent of the men. The other age groups show approximately even distribution.

[64] No attempt was made to elicit real profanity, where no doubt striking differences would have resulted. *Damn* was given as a term of "mild disgust," not intense wrath.

per cent to 15.3), whereas women informants show more occurrences of *perspired* (16.1 per cent to 6.6), *divan* (37.9 per cent to 18.8), and *veranda* (18.5 per cent to 8.1). (None of these figures will be very convincing to anyone who has ever matched coins or played poker.) In general, we might well conclude, with the legendary member of the Chamber of Deputies, that "il y a peu de différence entre les hommes et les femmes."

TABLES SHOWING THE PERCENTAGES OF USAGE
IN THE AGE GROUPS

TABLE A: Greatest Frequency of Usage in the 70's or 80's
(By Percentages)

	Students[65]	20–49	50–59	60–69	70–79	Over 80
roasting ears	20*	62.5	84.2	85.9	95.5	84
evening (afternoon)	12	57.6	64.7	77.6	82	72
shivaree	21	52.4	72.5	73	83.6	88
safe (kitchen)	1	46	52.8	71.2	60.5	92.3
souse (meat)	2	45	51	70.5	65.7	80
drempt	9	40	33.3	45.9	53.7	60
poison oak	19	37.5	43.1	51.8	58.3	48
weatherboards	5	30	33.3	46	52.2	56
shavs (buggy)	0	30	54.9	55.3	61.2	56
racket store	0	30	29.4	48.2	68.6	44
bureau	10	27.5	39.2	44.6	44.8	40
counterpane	0	27.5	56.8	63.5	74.6	60
greaser	——	25	37.2	38.8	40.3	44
gallery	0.5*	22.5	27.4	45.9	41.8	52
low (verb)	10.5*	22.5	33.3	33	38.8	40
dog irons	0	20	31.4	44.7	46.3	56
nicker (a horse)	10	20	39.2	45.9	41.2	56
tol(er)able	3	17.5	27.4	35.3	37.3	24
parlor	2*	17.5	37.3	49.5	55.2	48
laying (the wind)	0	15	21.6	29.4	35.8	20
antigodlin	2	15	17.6	22.4	25.4	24
(corn) pone	4.5*	15	29.4	29.4	35.8	20
clabber cheese	0.5*	15	19.6	24.7	31.4	44
riled	0	12.5	17.6	29.4	19.4	32
chinchy	——	12.5	15.7	23.5	20.9	28
clapboards	1	11.4	15	20.3	23.6	35
Ma	1.5*	12.5	13.7	27.1	32.8	48
hant	0.5*	10	17.3	23.5	20.9	24
holp(ed)	——	10	25.4	25.9	15.4	28
light a shuck	2	10	11.7	25.9	25.4	32

[65] Items marked with an asterisk indicate a sampling of 200; otherwise the sampling is of 100.

TABLE A, *continued*

	Students[65]	20–49	50–59	60–69	70–79	Over 80
hayseed	6	10	13.7	18.6	17.9	28
Pa	1*	7.5	11.5	23.5	32.8	44
see you home	3	7.5	7.8	14.1	19.4	32
trifling	3	7.5	9.8	12.9	19.4	20
peart	1	7.5	13.7	17.6	28.3	28
granny (midwife)	——	7.5	13.7	18.8	25.4	28
bluejohn	4	7.5	11.7	28.2	32.8	36
clearseed (peach)	1	7.5	11.7	11.5	19.4	24
near horse	0	7.5	23.5	36.4	35.8	60
off horse	0	5	9.8	17.7	10.4	20
dinner bucket	2	5	13.7	28.2	31.4	16
waked up	12	5	17.6	23.5	28.3	32
bussing (kissing)	1	2.5	13.7	10.6	16.4	24
swill (slop)	1	2.5	7.8	9.4	11.9	12
teacake	1	2.5	19.6	20	23.9	16
surly (bull)	0	2.5	2	8.2	14.9	20
Bad Man (Devil)	——	2.5	9.8	14.1	11.9	24
battercake	0	2.5	3.9	14.1	20	29.2
the sun riz	——	2.5	5.9	10.1	13.4	12
garret	0	0	5.9	5.9	10.4	12
whiffletree	1	0	3.9	7.5	6	28
poke (sack)	0	0	3.9	16.5	19.4	20
turn (of wood)	0	0	3.9	7.1	8.9	12
you-uns	0	2.5	3.9	7.1	9	8

TABLE B: Greatest Frequency of Usage in the 60's
(By Percentages)

	Students[65]	20–49	50–59	60–69	70–79	Over 80
singletree	15	67.5	86.2	89.5	89.5	76
French harp	18*	62.5	66.6	82.4	79	64
doubletree	11	55	82.4	87	86.5	76
polecat	19	52.5	60.7	74	70.1	72
chittlins	19	42.8	57.2	74.5	64	68.4
courting	3	37.5	49	50.6	46.3	32
carry you	8	37.5	39.2	49.5	40.3	40
tote	7.5*	37.5	49	55.3	43.2	52
slop bucket	27	32.5	52.9	54.1	50.8	44
right smart	2	30	33.3	51.8	41.8	32
widow woman	2	25	21.5	45.9	29.8	20
he seen	——	25	25.4	48.2	43.2	28
pillow slip	19.5*	24.3	38.6	50	41	28.6
maverick (calf)	13	20	23.5	33	31.4	24
howdy	14	20	21.5	36.5	31.3	20
peckerwood	2	17.5	23.5	35.3	34.4	24
(pecan) patty	9	15	27.4	37.6	14.8	20

TABLE B, *continued*

	Students[65]	20–49	50–59	60–69	70–79	Over 80
cope! (to horses)	0	12.5	25.4	44.7	32.8	32
flapjacks	4	12.5	23.5	28.2	27.7	20.8
sparking	1	12.5	11.5	34.1	20.9	24
Paddy (Irishman)	0	5	9.8	32.8	20.9	28
fire dogs	1	5	11.8	17.6	16.4	12

TABLE C: Fluctuating, but Greatest Frequency of Usage in the
Three Upper Age Groups
(By Percentages)

	Students[65]	20–59	Over 60
Sook! (to cows)	11	68.1	80.2
pully bone	53*	68.1	82
(horse) lot	24.5*	58.3	72.9
branch	5.5*	46.1	50.3
Papa	0.5*	45	52
rench (dishes)	6	30.8	45.7
paling (fence)	2	28.6	41.9
mantelpiece	9	19.8	28.2
tuckered out	3	18.7	24.3
fairing (up, off)	1	14.3	24.3
parson	0	12.1	19.8
loft (of a house)	1	11	17
booger (ghost)	7.5*	11	18.1
coon (Negro)	——	8.8	14.7
belly band (of saddle)	1	8.8	15.5
blizzard	1	6.6	22.6
lounge (sofa)	7	6.6	17
settee	1	6.6	11.9
lunch (snack)	0	6.6	18.1
mantelboard	1*	5.5	17
fireboard (mantel)	0	4.4	10.7
plunder room	0	4.4	8.5
cracklin bread	1	3.3	10.7
croker sack	3	3.3	12.4
it weren't me	——	3.3	12.4
table land	0	3.3	10.7
coverlid	0	2.2	7.9
cavvy (horses)	0	2.2	7.3
lead horse	1	2.2	7.3
egg bread	1	2.2	9
played out	0	2.2	9
shiftless	1	2.2	5.7
grindrock	——	2.2	8.5
pillow sham	0	1.1	7.9
worm fence	0	1.1	8.5
Pappy	0*	1.1	5.7

TABLE C, *continued*

	Students[65]	20–59	Over 60
woodchuck (woodpecker)	0	1.1	7.9
spooning	0	1.1	6.2
touchous	0	1.1	5.1
plum peach	0	0	5.1
stake and rider (fence)	0	0	7.9

TABLE D: Gradual Increase; Highest Frequency of Usage in
the Younger Groups
(By Percentages)

	Students[65]	20–49	50–59	60–69	70–79	Over 80
bull	——	92.5	88.2	76.5	67.2	64
attic	99	100	88.2	87	71.6	72
lunch (pail, etc.)	98	92.5	100	83.5	53.7	36
bedspread	86	80	56.8	53	32.8	32
pillow case	93	83.8	56.8	62.5	41.1	33.3
living room	92.5*	75	64.6	56.5	31.4	36
poison ivy	92	75	66.6	57	50.8	44
bucket	——	72.5	51	48.3	49.2	32
hi!	76	72.5	64.7	42.4	28.4	36
woke(up)	81	72.5	64.7	63.5	58	60
skunk	95	65	64.7	49.4	44.7	40
pancakes	78	62.5	54.9	44.7	48.2	33.3
dreamed	93	57.5	56.8	41.2	34.3	36
Daddy	61*	57.5	31.4	20	19.4	12
shouldn't	——	50	31.4	22.4	20.9	20
afternoon	93	47.5	47	34.1	22.4	24
chest of drawers	89	42.5	35.3	32	17.9	32
Mother	64*	42.5	37.2	14.2	20.9	12
going (steady) with	96	42.5	21.5	10.6	7.5	0
wishbone	65*	40	47	42.3	29.8	20
take you home	74	40	45	27.1	26.9	16
variety store	29	40	37.2	29.4	22.4	24
hotcakes	42	40	45	24.7	24.6	16.7
corn on the cob	91*	35	23.5	22.4	3	12
firefly	21.5*	35	23.5	10.6	9	4
pooped (out)	41	27.5	21.5	13	9	0
five–and–ten (store)	23	27.5	21.5	18.8	13.4	4
plateau	70	27.5	17.3	12.9	6	8

TABLE E: Tending to Show Greater Frequency of Usage in Younger Groups
(By Percentages)

	Students[65]	20–59	Over 60
woodpecker	100	84.5	66.5
snack	93	83.5	69.5
norther	86	77	58.2
gumbo	69	51.6	38
praline	77	49.5	40.7

TABLE E, *continued*

	Students[65]	20–59	Over 60
picket (fence)	79	48.3	32.4
green beans	63*	46.1	30.5
siding	48	44	33.9
lima beans	70*	38.4	30
cinch	46	34	25.4
sour (milk)	74	16.5	3.4
relatives	79*	15.4	9.4
white bread	47*	14.3	6.8
harmonica	84.5*	11.6	4

TABLE F: Distribution of Regional Words in the Age Groups
(By Percentages)

	20–49	50–59	60–69	70–79	Over 80
Northern words	5.9	10.7	9.4	9.1	13.8
Midland words	35.6	29.4	31.4	31.4	29.7
North Midland words	10	10.8	10.5	12.8	9.2
South Midland words	12.8	13	19.1	17.9	13.5
Coastal Southern words	23.1	31.1	34.7	31.5	33
General Southern words	52.9	55.5	64.7	59.5	59.3
All Southern words	41	45.8	52.7	48.3	48.8

VII LEXICOGRAPHICAL PILÓN

The present study is not meant as a major contribution to word history or etymology. Another book would be required to trace the origins and the changes in form and meaning of the words that have been discussed. Nevertheless, it might be well to comment further on some of the words, particularly those of Spanish origin. Often these seem to have departed rather far from their usages as given in most of the standard textbooks and school dictionaries, which are usually somewhat too much concerned with European Spanish. "Border" Spanish—that spoken in Southwest Texas and the adjoining portion of Mexico— often shows greater agreement with Texas usage, although not in every case.

AUTHORITIES FOR "BORDER" SPANISH

My principal informants for Border Spanish were Américo Paredes, Associate Professor of English at the University of Texas—a native of Brownsville; and Mrs. Evan S. Reese, Assistant Librarian of the Latin-American Collection at the University of Texas—a native of Monterrey. For the usage of central Mexico, I was fortunately able to interview Wigberto Jiménez-Moreno, Professor of Anthropology at the University of Mexico City—a native of Leon, Guanajuato. For usage in other parts of Latin America, I have on some points questioned a number of graduate students from Central and South America and the West Indies. Of course, Santamaria's new dictionary of Mexican Spanish[1] is very valuable, and will be cited where pertinent, but I believe that our informants often throw more light on the spoken usage closest to Texas English. In the ensuing notes, *B* will mean the Brownsville informant, *M* that of Monterrey, and *G* that of Guanajuato.

---

[1] Francisco J. Santamaria, *Diccionario de Mejicanismos*, first ed. (Mexico City, 1959).

ETYMOLOGIES AND MEANINGS

Acequia. An irrigation ditch *(B, G, M)*. Also a stream or trench *(M)*.

Arroyo. A creek or stream *(B, G, M)*; *B* uses it also for a dry bed. Texas in general agrees with the latter and seldom uses *arroyo* for a running stream.

Bronco. Always or nearly always an adjective, meaning wild in the sense of untamed or unmanageable *(B, G)*. But *M* uses it as a noun, for a "wild horse" (from Texas influence?). Santamaria states that in rural usage the adjective is sometimes applied to a shy or recalcitrant horse.

Caballerango *(wrangler)*. One who goes along with another, more important, horseman *(caballero)* to take care of his horse(s); a kind of squire *(G, M)*. Santamaria does not record this meaning, but applies the word to a groom or stable-boy on a large estate. Texas ranch usage surely preserves no more than a touch of the connotation of servility.

Chaparral. Our informants give no indication that this could mean an oak grove, as in Spain. They apply it to a mass of low-growing, bushy vegetation *(B, G, M)*. It usually also carries the idea of thorns *(B, M)*. Santamaria states that on the southern coast of Mexico *chaparro* (and hence *chaparral*) may apply to some kinds of oak. He also lists *chaparro amargoso* for a certain kind of thorny bush.

Corral. A barnyard, or enclosure for any kind of animals—cows, horses, sheep, poultry *(B, G, M)*. Santamaria states that it is for "ganado mayor"—larger livestock. The specialization to the idea of a pen for horses evidently occurred after the adoption of the word into Texas English.

Frijoles. This is used by *G* for beans in general; by *B* for "cooked beans." Only *M* restricts it to pinto beans (Texas influence?). Santamaria lists some of the "muchas variedades" that exist in Mexico.

Hacienda. A large or fine or important ranch or estate *(B, G, M)*. This is general in Mexico (Santamaria); a smaller establishment would be a *rancho*. *Hacienda* is rarely used with the literary meaning of property in general *(G)*.

Jáquima *(hackamore)*. This term is used by *B* and *M* for a halter —usually of horsehair, according to *B*. However, *G* is entirely unfamiliar with the word.

Juzgado (*hoosegow*). A court of justice *(B, G, M)*; *B* indicates that the word is no longer very common. He adds, however, that *corte* (courthouse) is sometimes used for a jail.

Lagniappe. There is no doubt that, as the major dictionaries state, *lagniappe* is a gallicized version of the Spanish *la ñapa*, and that the latter was introduced into Latin America from Kechuan *yapa*, which, according to Harold H. Key of the Summer Institute of Linguistics, is still in use in Kechuan. The initial consonant varies considerably in Latin America. An informant from Bolivia gives *yapa*; one from Panama, *yapa* alternating with *japa*. Informants from Uruguay and Paraguay use *žapa*.[2] The form with the nasal consonant, *ñapa*, was given by informants from Puerto Rico, Cuba, and Venezuela. This nazalization of an initial palatal is a feature of dialectal Spanish, the extent of which I cannot determine. It has been observed, at least sporadically, in various areas. Navarro Tomás records it for Puerto Rico;[3] others have attested it for Cuba, Argentina, Honduras, and other countries.[4]

No Latin informants from South America or the Caribbean have given *pilón* with this meaning, while *yapa* is apparently unknown in Mexico *(B, G, M*, Santamaria).

Mata (*mott*). M. M. Mathews *(Dictionary of Americanisms)* is clearly correct in deriving *mott(e)* from Spanish rather than from French, as most other dictionaries do.[5] The geographical distribution of *mott* is sufficient evidence of this (Map 6). *Mata* in European Spanish can mean a clump of trees,[6] but the present meaning in Border Spanish is a plant *(B, G, M*, Santamaria). Although *G* also gives the meaning of a clump of trees, *B* and *M* do not. Santamaria lists the latter meaning for southern Mexico.

It is probable that a close study of place names would further con-

---

[2] *Japa* more or less as in English *job;* the *ž* is close to the medial consonant in *vision*—but both sounds are usually true palatals in Spanish rather than pre-palatals as in English.

[3] T. Navarro Tomás, *El Español en Puerto Rico* (Río Piedras, University of Puerto Rico, 1948), p. 102.

[4] For a summary, see Joseph Matluck, *La Pronunciation en el Español del Valle de Mexico* (Mexico City, The Author, 1951), p. 112, fn. 377.

[5] For example, *Webster's New International, American College Dictionary,* etc. Mathews gives no details whatever; merely the abbreviation "[Sp.]."

[6] See for example M. Velázquez, *A New Pronouncing Dictionary of the Spanish and English Languages* (Chicago and New York, Wilcox & Follett Co., 1948). *Mata,* definition 3: "Grove, a cluster of trees of one species; copse."

firm the connection between *mata* and *mott*. For example, Margaret G. Clover, in a study of Atascosa County, recorded *Peeler's Mott* and *Mata Hermosa*, both of which carried the idea of a clump of trees. The latter was in turn syncopated to *Mottamosa (Post Office).*[7] *Matagorda* must also derive from this meaning of *mata*. Among the Texas towns containing the element *mott*, we find *Long Mott* (Calhoun County), *Blue Mott* (Victoria County), and *Elm Mott* (McLennan County).

Maverick. Although the origin and early meanings of the term have been fully explained (refer to Chapter I, fn. 27) by J. Frank Dobie in *The Longhorns*, dictionaries persist in referring to Samuel Maverick in somewhat misleading ways, for example that he was a "19th-c[entury] Texas rancher who did not brand his cattle."[8] In order to clarify the story, I append a few excerpts from a letter written by George M. Maverick (a son of Samuel A. Maverick) to the St. Louis *Republic* on November 16, 1889. A copy of this letter was kindly placed in my hands by Mrs. Mary Lane (a descendant of Samuel Maverick). It represents the version accepted by Dobie as well as by the Maverick family.

Samuel A. Maverick . . . was a lawyer with a strong propensity for speculation in real estate. . . . During [the] year 1845, a neighbor being indebted to Mr. Maverick in the sum of $1200 paid the debt in cattle, transferring 400 animals at $3.00 per head. . . . Mr. Maverick did not want the cattle, but as it was a case of cattle or nothing, he passively received them and left them in charge of a colored family [near Matagorda Bay], nominally slave but essentially free. . . . Under the distinguished management of the colored family, who really were not to blame, as they had no interest in the outcome, the cattle were left to graze, to fatten, to multiply, and to wander away. . . .

About one-third of the calves were branded, and the branding iron was kept so cold and rusty that in 1856 the entire plant or "brand" was estimated at only 400 head, the original number. . . .

Now the neighbors shrewdly surmised [the unbranded] calves to be Maverick's, and they called them 'mavericks'—but did they continue to recognize them as such? Ah, no; they hastened to burn into their tender hides their own brands and the beasts were Maverick's ('mavericks') no longer. . . .

Mr. Maverick, all statements to the contrary notwithstanding, was never a cattle king, for with the exception of the herd mentioned, and a few necessary cow ponies, he never owned any cattle or horses.

Mesa. In addition to a table, *mesa* may mean a flat-topped hill—that is, a flat, elevated area with fairly steep sides *(M, G)*. In Texas English

---

[7] "The Place Names of Atascosa County, Texas" (M. A. Thesis, University of Texas, 1952—typescript).

[8] *Webster's New World Dictionary* (1957).

the word more often means any plateau, as it seems to mean in European Spanish.

Morral. In Mexico, a small, narrow bag formerly woven from the fibers of a plant. According to *M*, these are *lechuguilla* fibers; *G* assumes that they were from agave and knows the term *ixtli* for them. Only *B* uses *morral* with its Texas meaning, the feed bag of a horse, although this is an old application of the term in Spanish.

Olla. In Mexico, usually a cooking pot of any material *(B, G)*. In this case, *M* specifies a clay pot, which may have a wide mouth—certainly an approach to the Texas meaning.

Pelado. Commonly used in Spanish with a derogatory meaning, implying that a person is ill-bred, unmannerly, or vulgar *(B, G, M, Santamaria)*—a bum or ruffian *(B)*. However, *B* states that in the familiar speech of men it may often imply no more than a guy or fellow. It may have been the frequency of this latter usage that led to the adoption of the word in Southwest Texas.

Pilón. This has a considerable variety of meanings, but few of them concern us. To *G* it may mean a very large conical sugarloaf, from which sugar was chopped as needed. In addition, *B* states that *pilón* could mean one of the conical weights used in Roman-type scales. All *(B, G, M)* are very familiar with the meaning of an extra gift with a purchase; but *G* states that modern stores are becoming less and less inclined to give *pilón*. Santamaria of course lists the meaning of extra gift; also the meaning of a small, usually cone-shaped, piece of brown-sugar candy (more often called *piloncillo*). Perhaps it was this last meaning, and the giving of such morsels by storekeepers, that led to the common Texas and Mexican application of the word *pilón*.

Reata. A rope of any kind *(B, G, M)*.

Remuda. Here *G* and *M* give only the meaning of a change or relay of horses, mules, or oxen, as does Santamaria. However, *B* says that *remuda* means any sort of band or group of saddle horses—an idea more in accordance with the usage of the word in Texas English.

Resaca. The course of the development in meaning is not clear. While *M* is familiar with the word with the meaning of surf, *G* has the idea that it means any kind of debris left after the ebbing of the tide—shells, weeds, driftwood, and so on (although he is careful to state that, having been brought up far from the sea, he is not sure of this meaning). Both *B* and *M* agree that it can also mean some kind of pool of standing water—any kind of accumulation according to *B*, an artificial one according to *M*.

Vaquero. All agree that this means the kind of cowboy who does the work—a cowhand. In this connection *B* states that the dudish, fancily dressed type would be known as a *charro* instead. Santamaria lists both words with approximately the meanings mentioned.

VIII WORD ATLAS

EXPLANATION OF THE MAPS

All of the maps which follow should be interpreted in terms of the Base Map (Map 1), which indicates the points from which data might have been expected. The symbol + which follows certain numbers on this map means that a good many additional records were gathered for special projects—usually masters' theses or doctoral dissertations.

The purpose of the word maps is to indicate the geographical distributions of a selected group of words (not to duplicate the statistical information given in Chapter III). Each symbol on these maps represents one occurrence of the word in question. However, since there was often not room on the maps for the entry of all occurrences, a systematic reduction was usually made. In the case of words of state-wide prevalence, only the first two occurrences at a given point were entered, except at points representing a large population, or a large area, or both. Even where the intention was to show the local or regional concentration of a word, it was often impossible to enter all occurrences on the maps. Thus, although the incidence of a word in a given community is never suppressed, the actual number of occurrences should not necessarily be regarded as exact.

Naturally, not all responses to all items are presented on maps; many of them would have been of little interest from a geographical point of view, and their inclusion would have extended the Atlas to an intolerable length. For example, *snap beans* and *green beans* are mapped, but *string beans*, which is current in all areas, is not.

Maps 116–125, which present outer limits in the form of lines (isoglosses), are fully explained in Chapter IV.

The titles of the maps are meant to indicate, very roughly, the meanings of the words (see also the list of Illustrations).

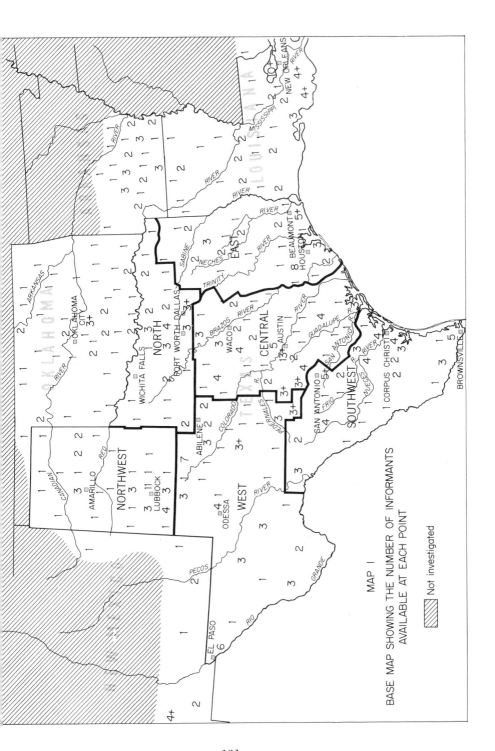

MAP I

BASE MAP SHOWING THE NUMBER OF INFORMANTS
AVAILABLE AT EACH POINT

▨ Not investigated

131

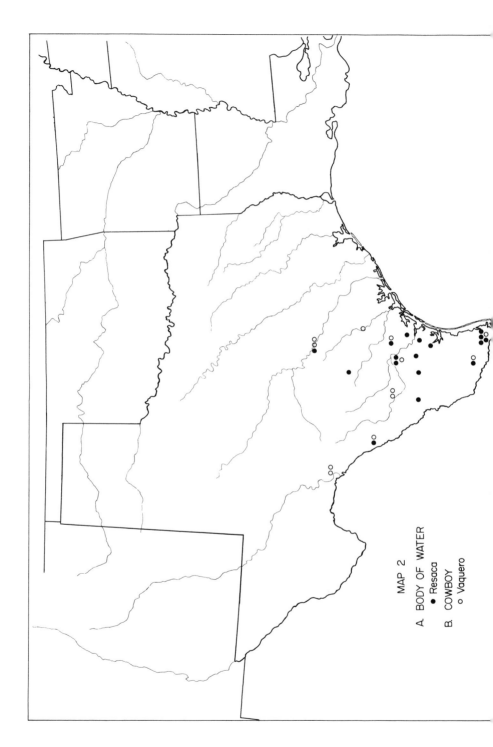

MAP 2

A. BODY OF WATER
   ● Resaca

B. COWBOY
   ○ Vaquero

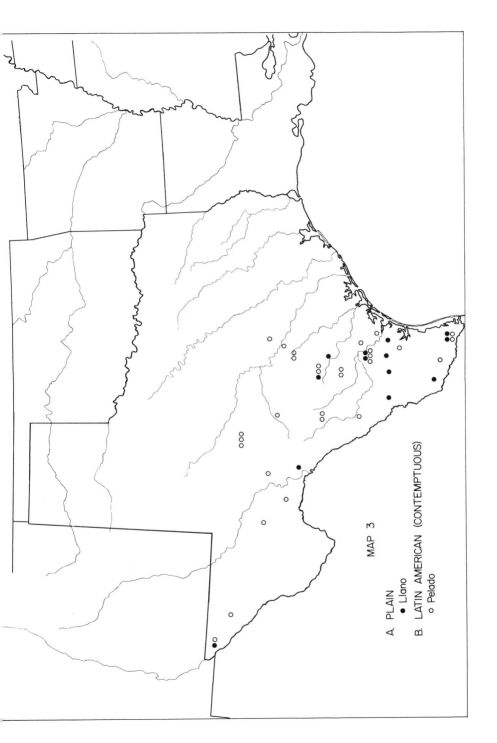

MAP 3

A. PLAIN
   ● Llano
B. LATIN AMERICAN (CONTEMPTUOUS)
   o Pelado

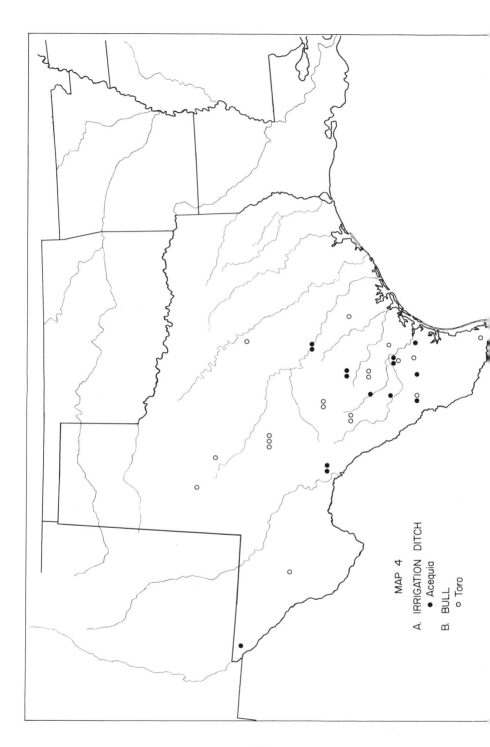

MAP 4

A. IRRIGATION DITCH
   ● Acequia

B. BULL
   ○ Toro

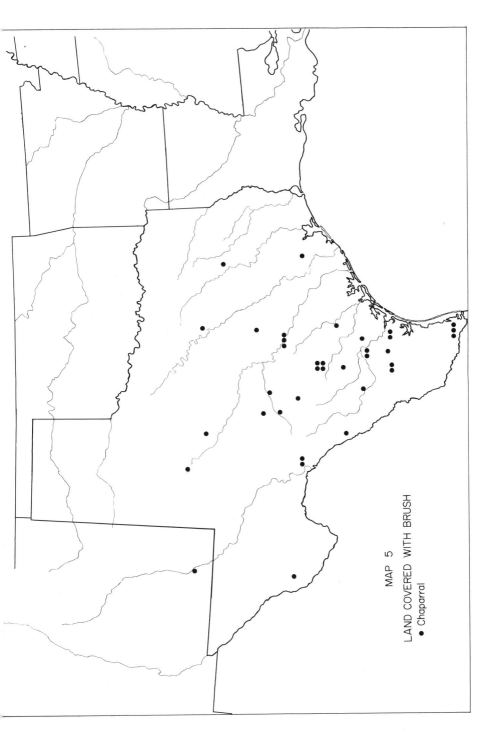

MAP 5
LAND COVERED WITH BRUSH
● Chaparral

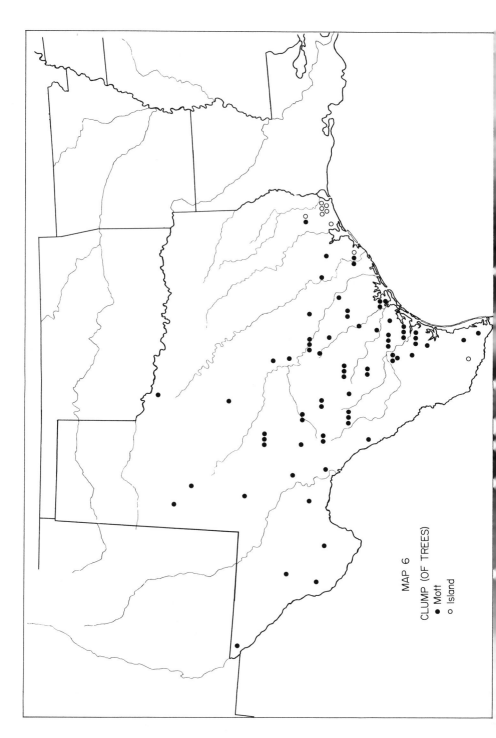

MAP 6

CLUMP (OF TREES)

- Mott
- ○ Island

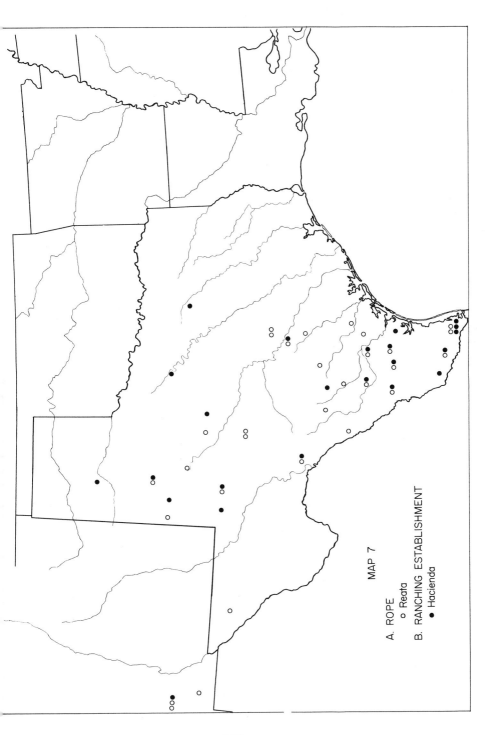

MAP 7

A. ROPE
   o Reata

B. RANCHING ESTABLISHMENT
   ● Hacienda

137

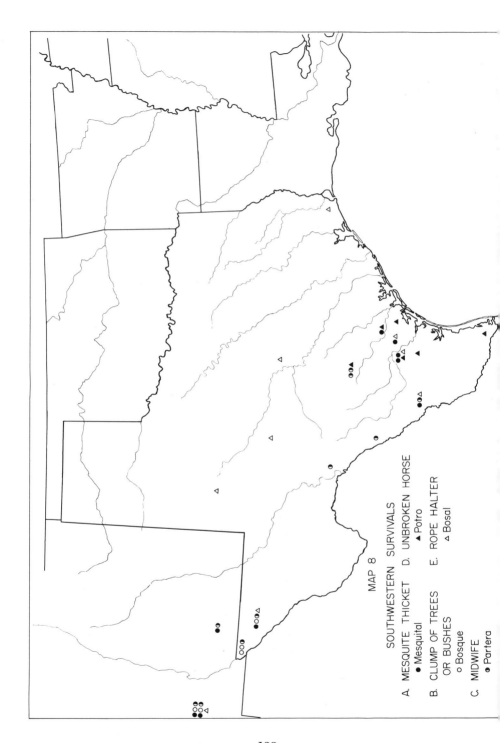

MAP 8

SOUTHWESTERN SURVIVALS

A. MESQUITE THICKET   D. UNBROKEN HORSE
   ● Mesquital   ▲ Potro

B. CLUMP OF TREES   E. ROPE HALTER
   OR BUSHES   ◁ Bosal
   ○ Bosque

C. MIDWIFE
   ◉ Partera

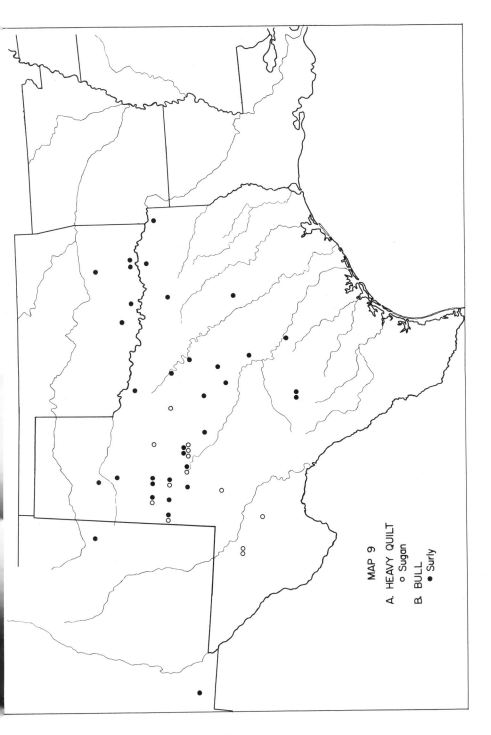

MAP 9

A. HEAVY QUILT
    o Sugan

B. BULL
    ● Surly

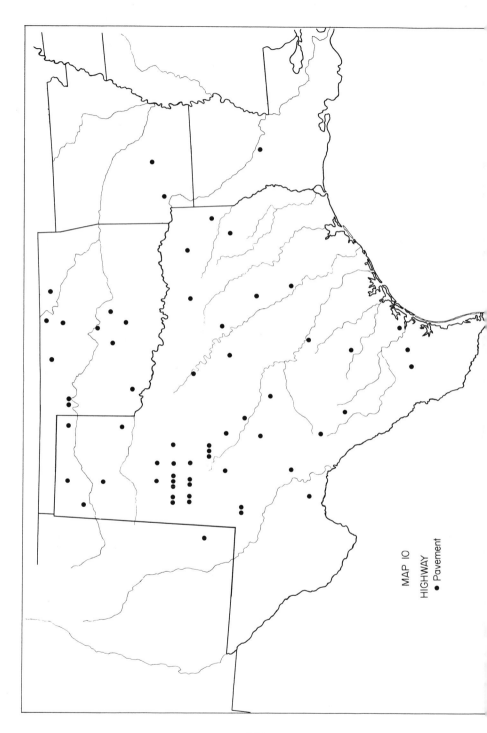

MAP 10

HIGHWAY
• Pavement

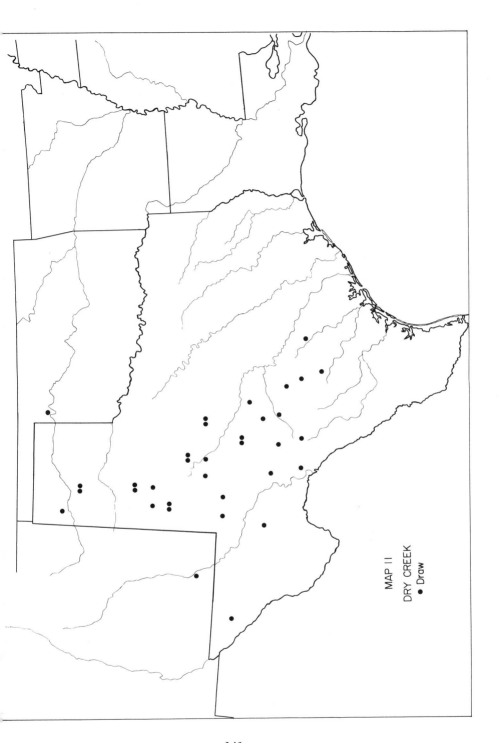

MAP II

DRY CREEK

• Draw

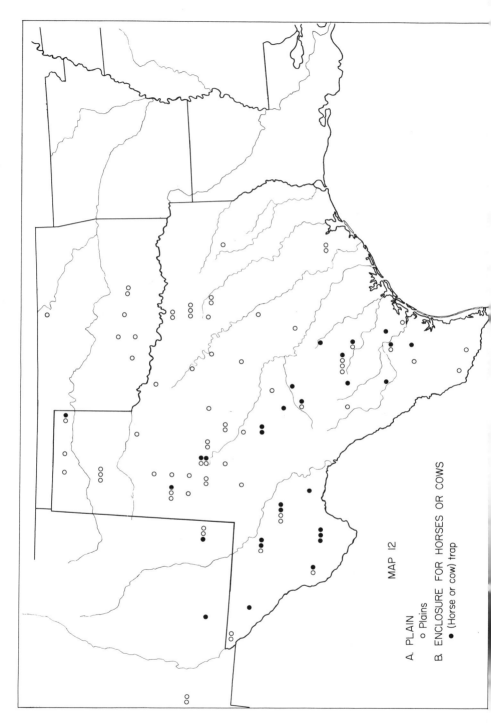

MAP 12

A. PLAIN
   o Plains

B. ENCLOSURE FOR HORSES OR COWS
   ● (Horse or cow) trap

142

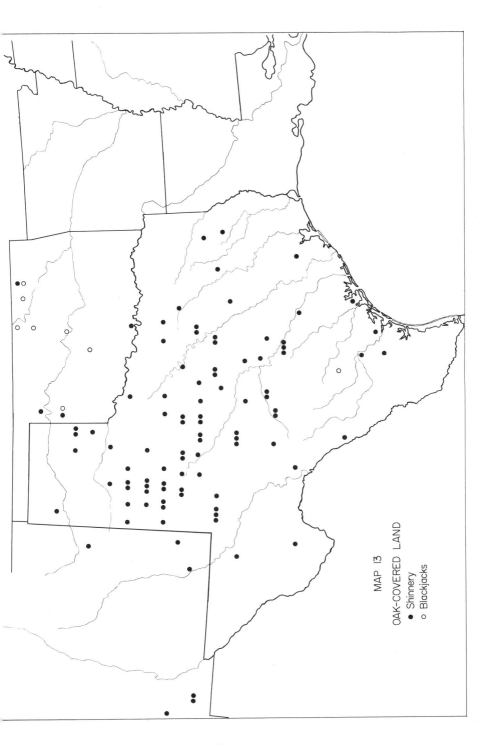

MAP 13

OAK-COVERED LAND

• Shinnery
○ Blackjacks

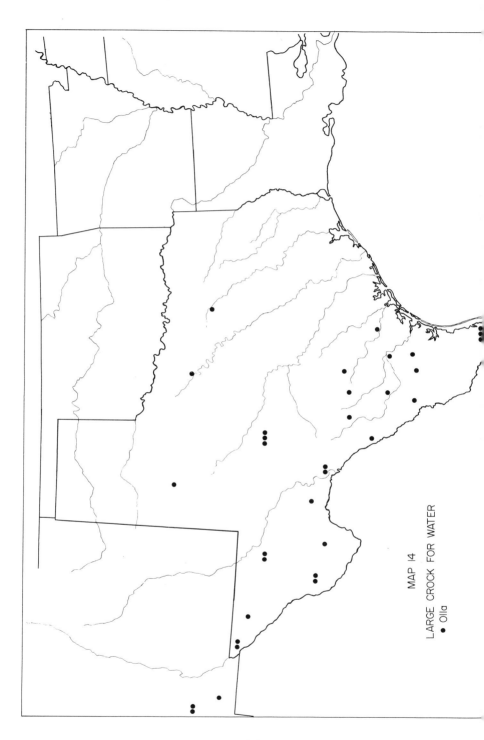

MAP 14

LARGE CROCK FOR WATER

● Olla

144

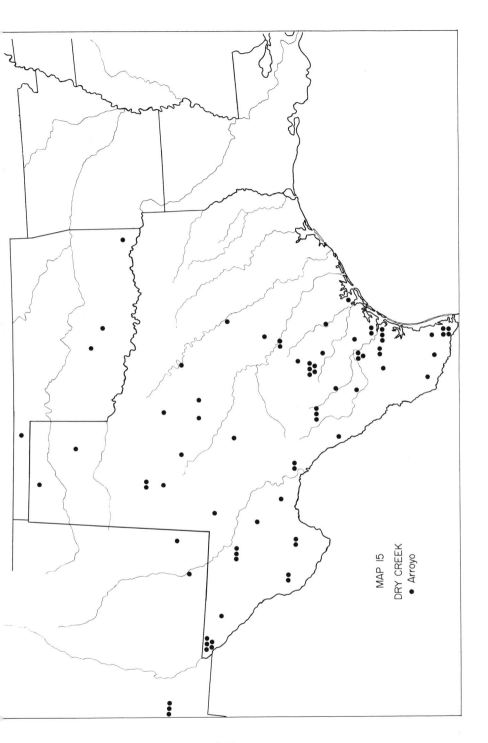

MAP 15
DRY CREEK
• Arroyo

145

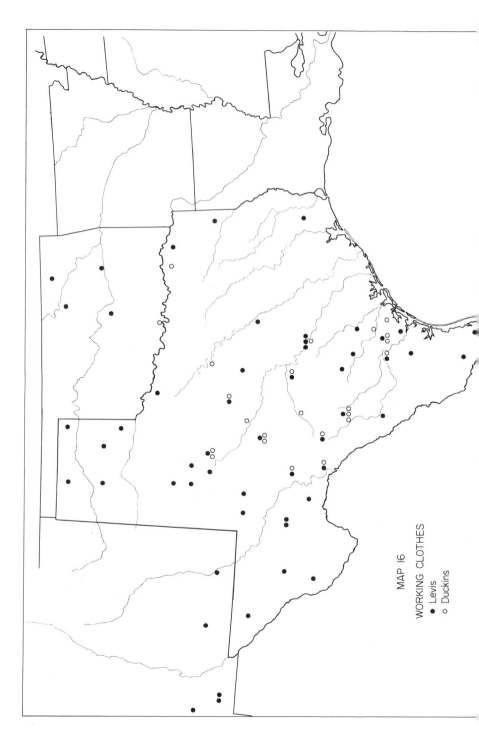

MAP 16

WORKING CLOTHES

● Levis
○ Duckins

146

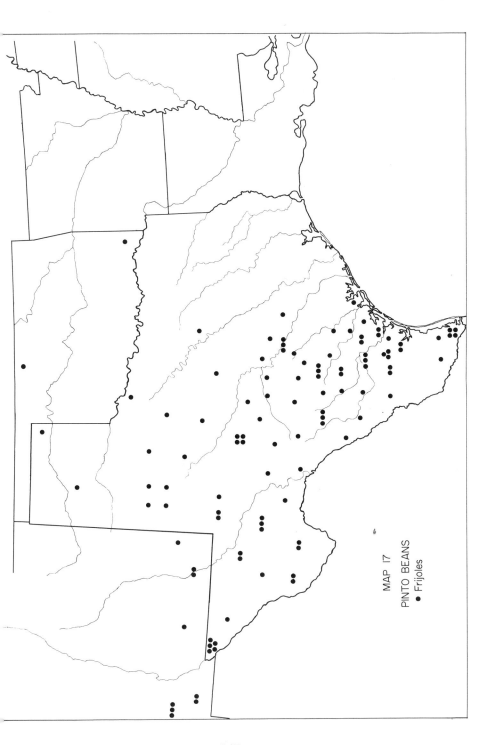

MAP 17

PINTO BEANS

● Frijoles

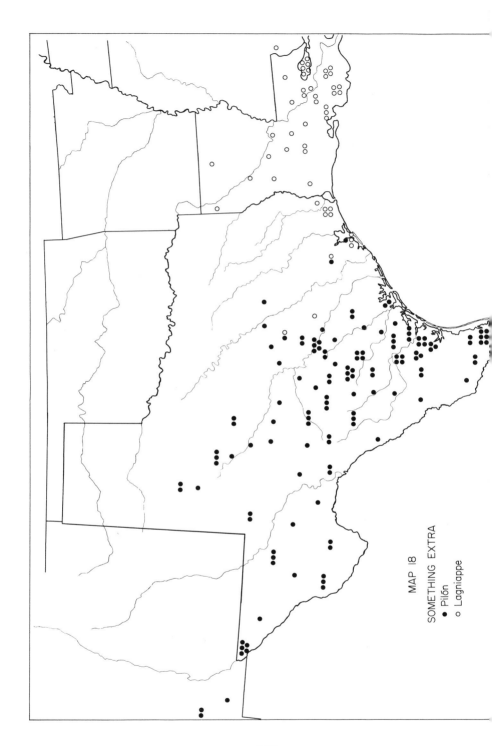

MAP 18

SOMETHING EXTRA

● Pilón
○ Lagniappe

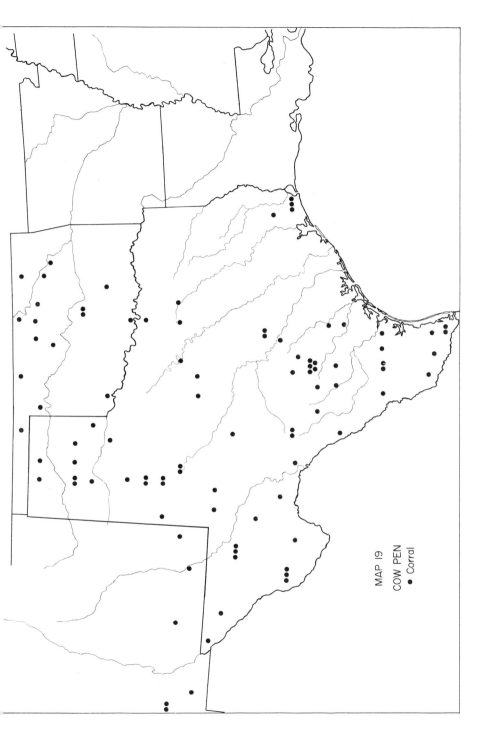

MAP 19

COW PEN

● Corral

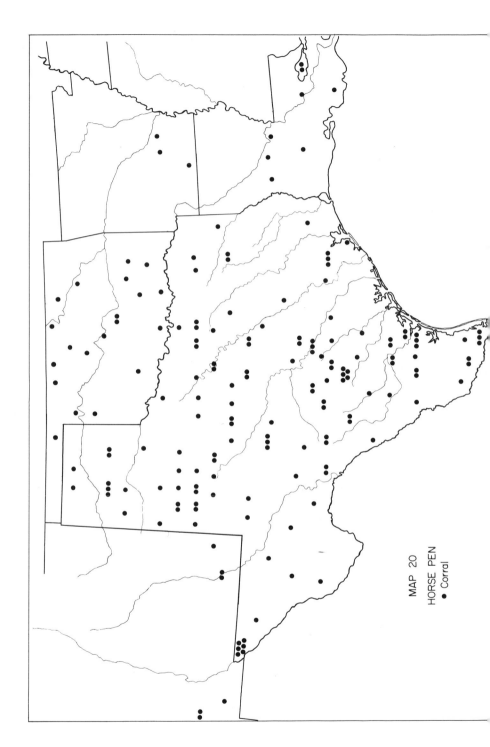

MAP 20

HORSE PEN

• Corral

150

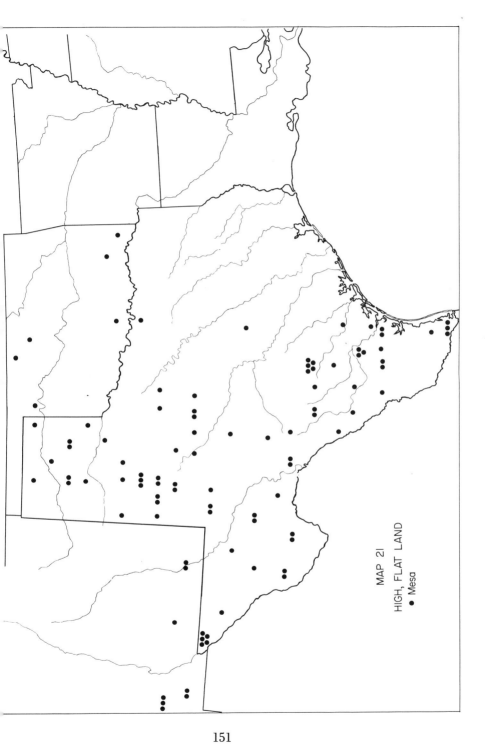

MAP 21
HIGH, FLAT LAND
● Mesa

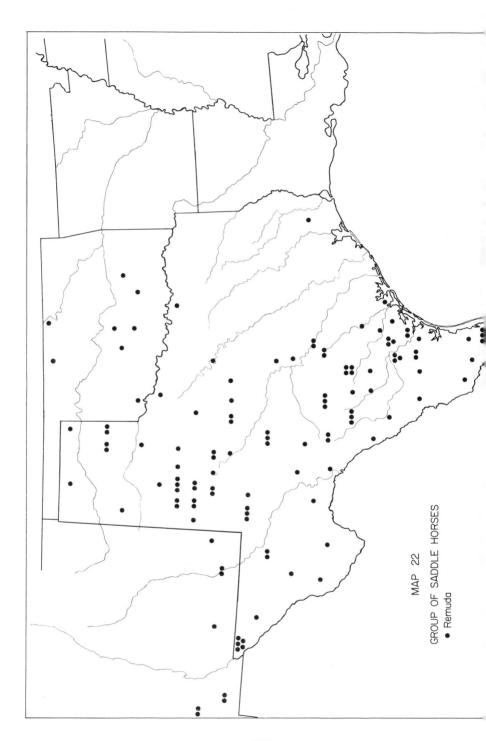

MAP 22

GROUP OF SADDLE HORSES

• Remuda

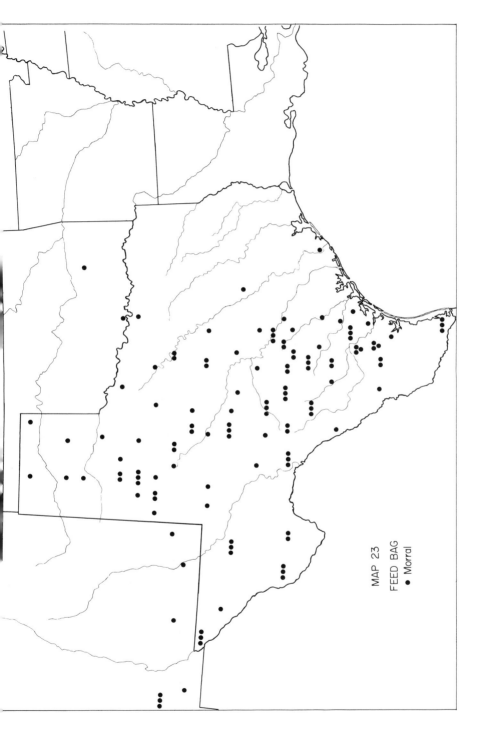

MAP 23

FEED BAG

● Morral

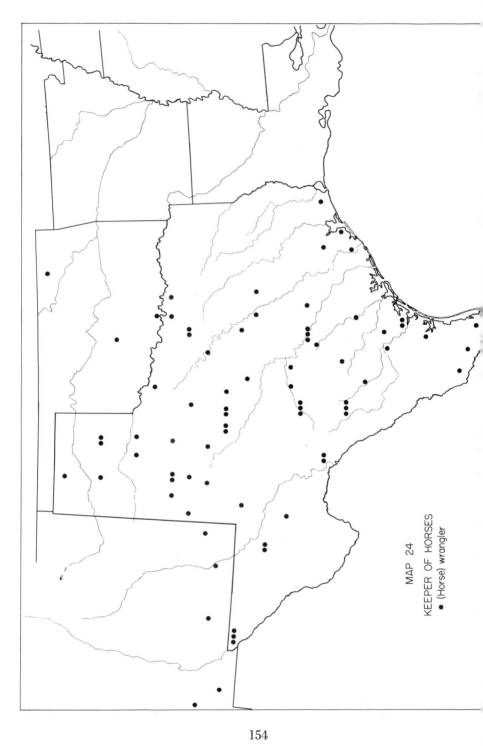

MAP 24
KEEPER OF HORSES
• (Horse) wrangler

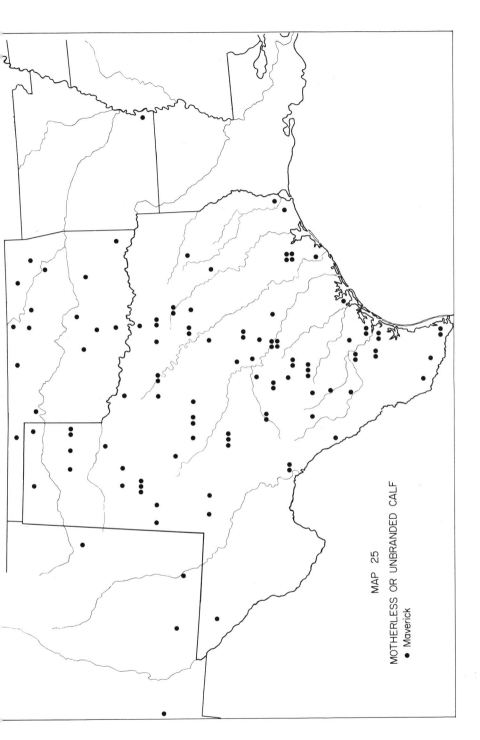

MAP 25

MOTHERLESS OR UNBRANDED CALF

● Maverick

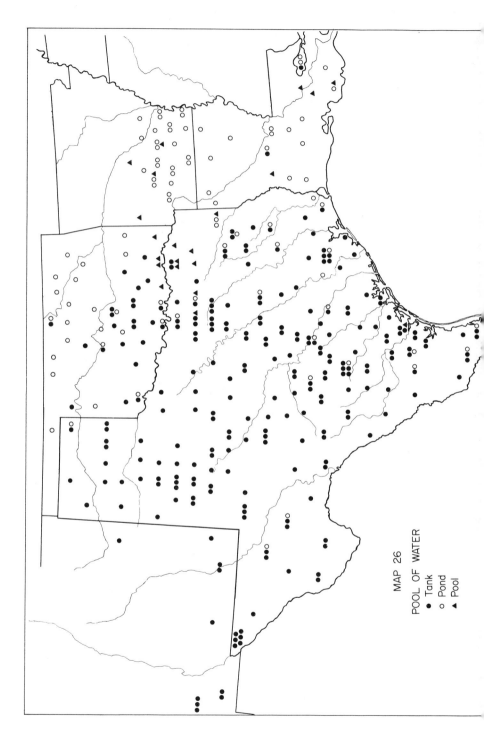

MAP 26

POOL OF WATER

● Tank
○ Pond
▲ Pool

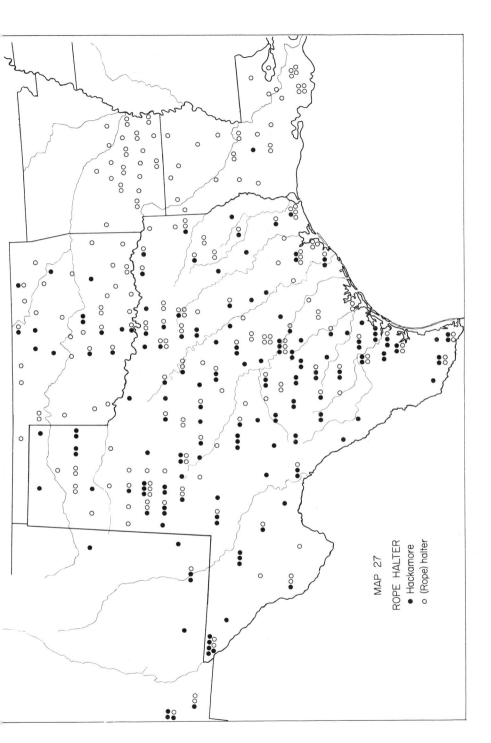

MAP 27

ROPE HALTER

● Hackamore

○ (Rope) halter

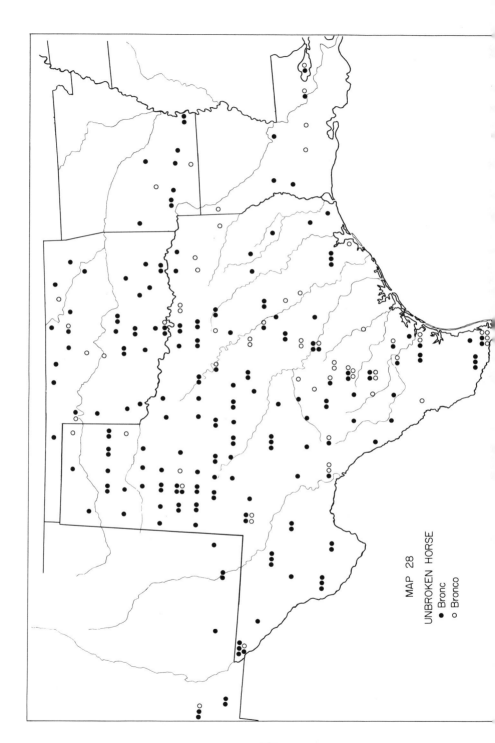

MAP 28

UNBROKEN HORSE

● Bronc

○ Bronco

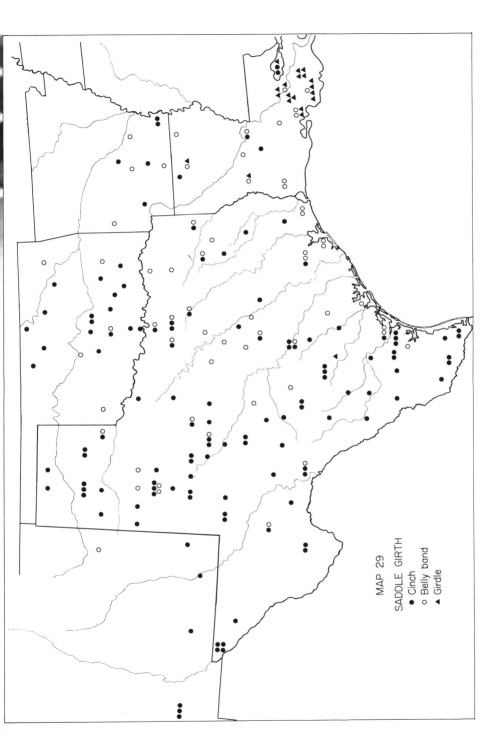

MAP 29

SADDLE GIRTH
● Cinch
○ Belly band
▲ Girdle

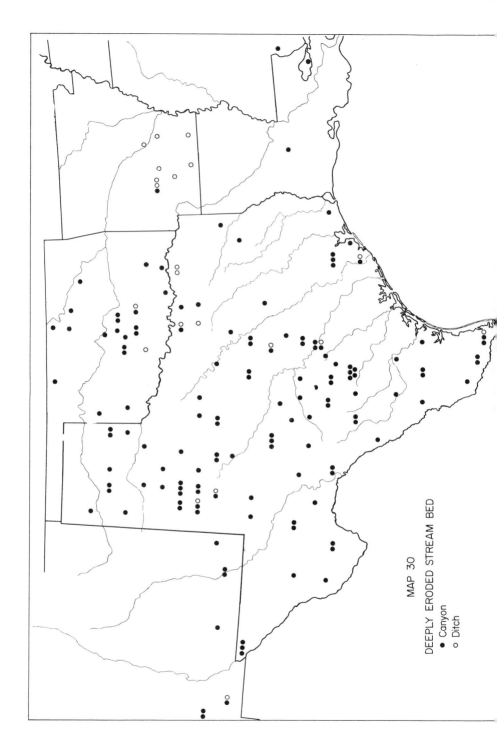

MAP 30

DEEPLY ERODED STREAM BED

- Canyon
- ○ Ditch

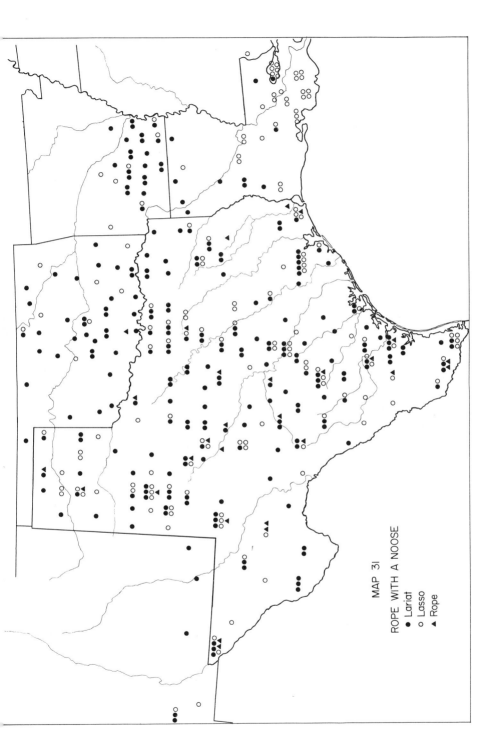

MAP 31

ROPE WITH A NOOSE

- Lariat
- ○ Lasso
- ▲ Rope

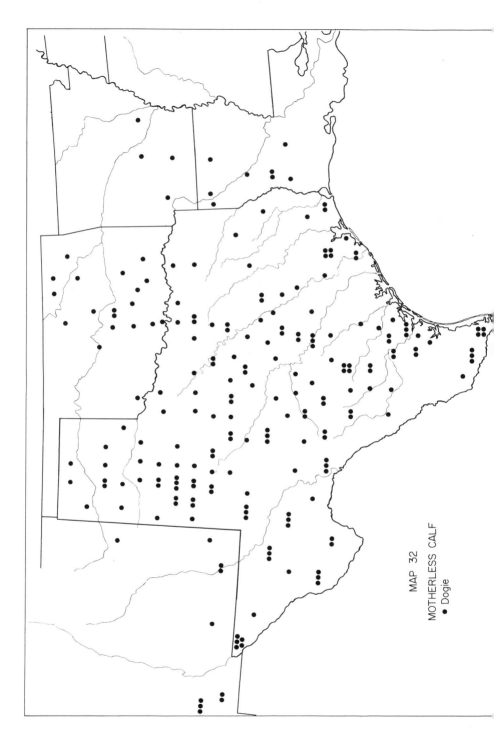

MAP 32
MOTHERLESS CALF
● Dogie

162

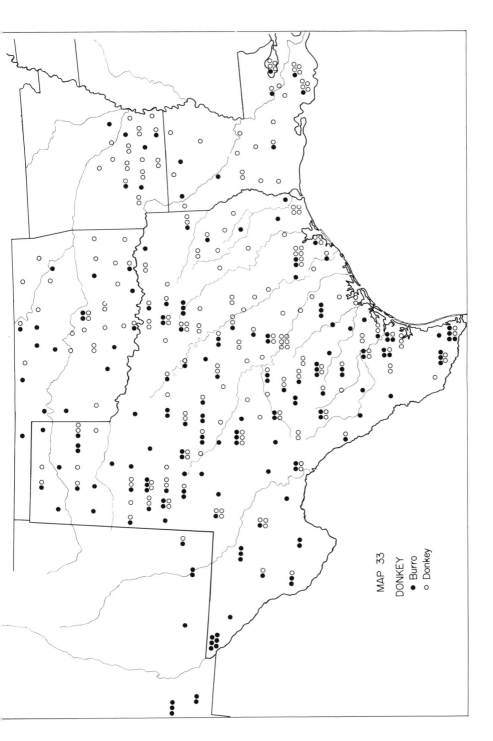

MAP 33

DONKEY

- Burro
○ Donkey

163

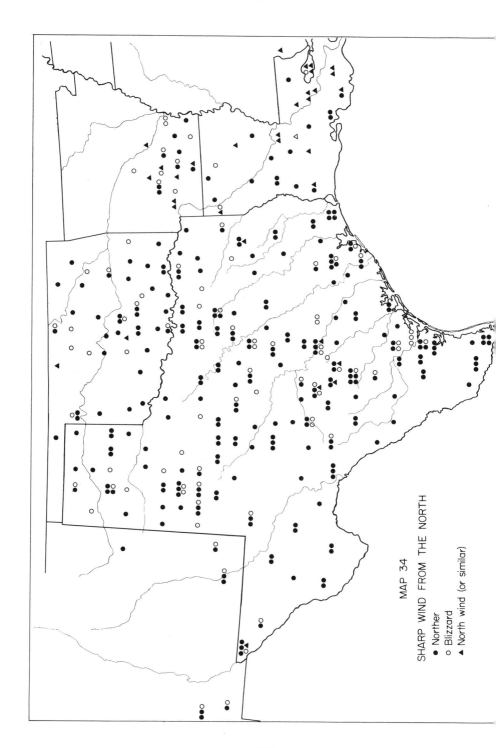

MAP 34

SHARP WIND FROM THE NORTH

● Norther
○ Blizzard
▲ North wind (or similar)

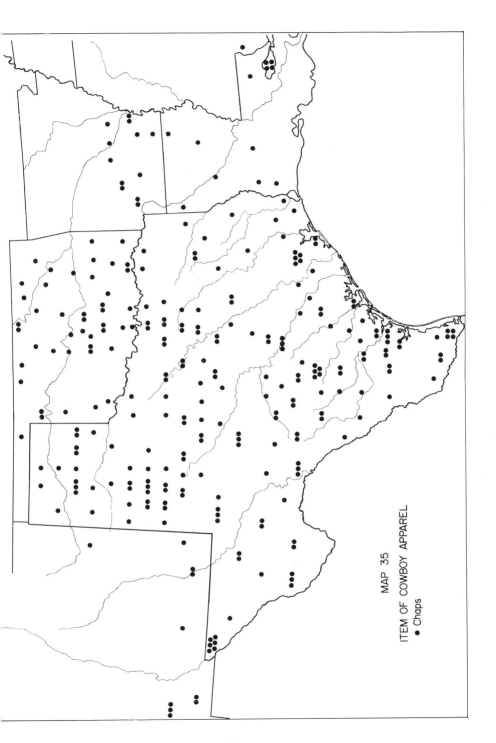

MAP 35
ITEM OF COWBOY APPAREL
• Chaps

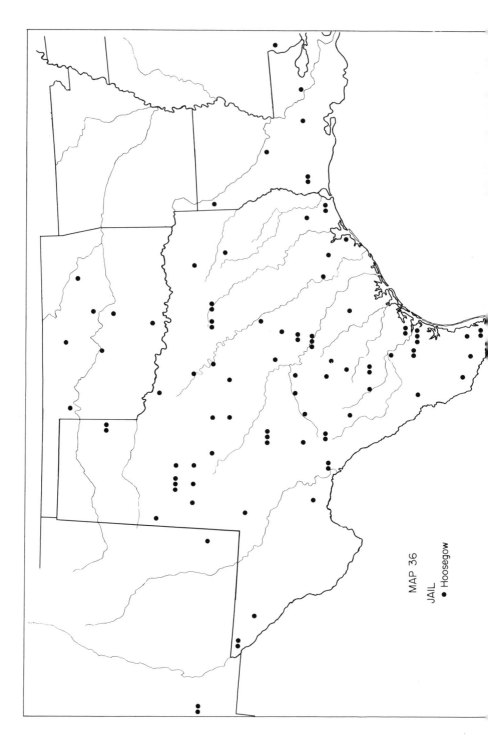

MAP 36

JAIL
● Hoosegow

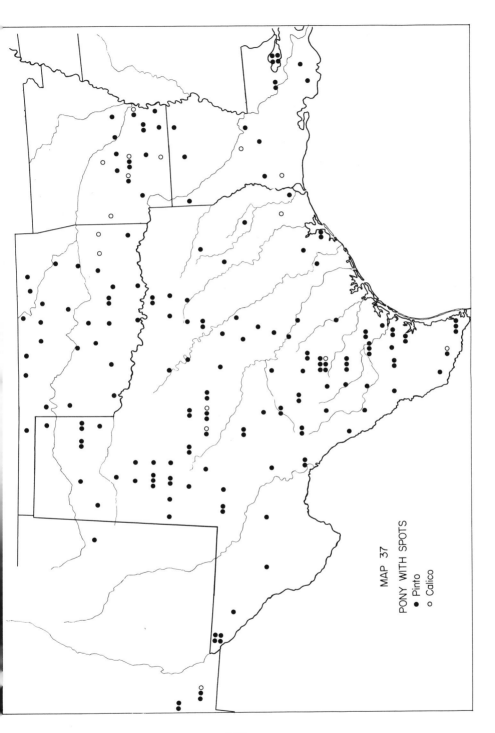

MAP 37

PONY WITH SPOTS
• Pinto
○ Calico

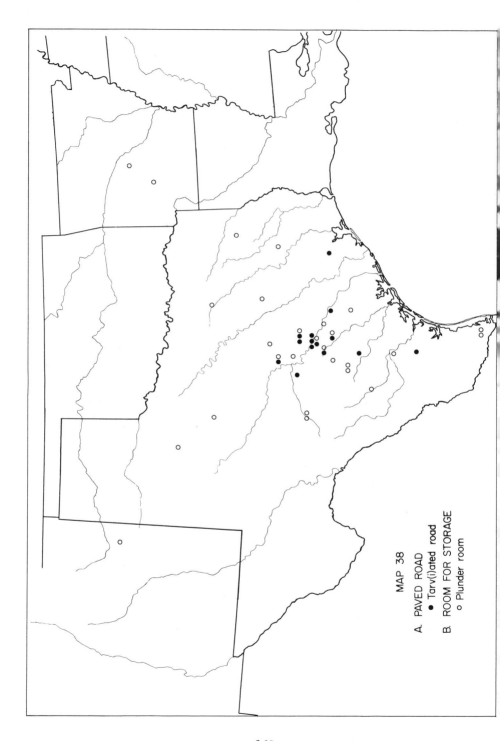

MAP 38

A. PAVED ROAD
   ● Tarv(i)ated road

B. ROOM FOR STORAGE
   ○ Plunder room

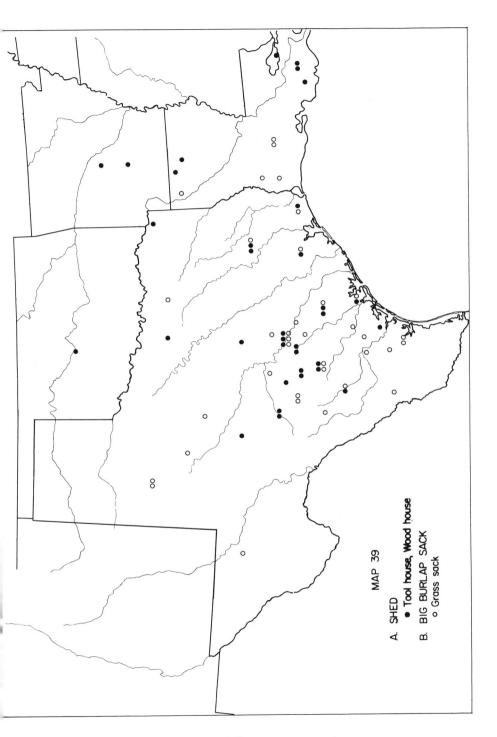

MAP 39

A. SHED
  ● Tool house, Wood house
B. BIG BURLAP SACK
  ○ Grass sack

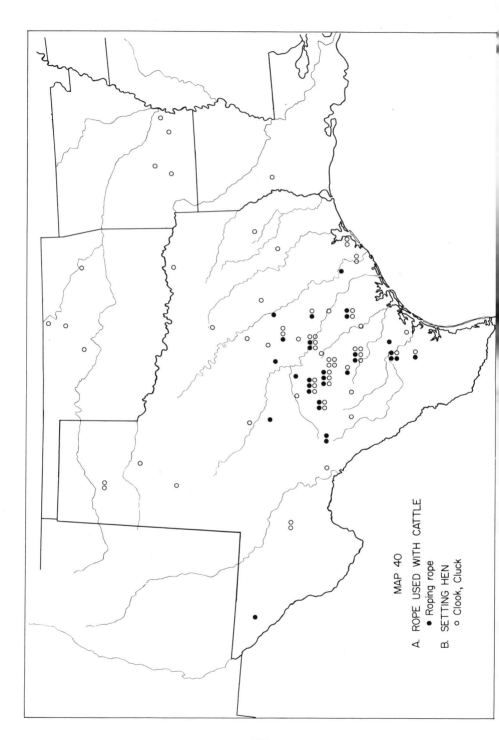

MAP 40

A. ROPE USED WITH CATTLE
   ● Roping rope

B. SETTING HEN
   o Clook, Cluck

170

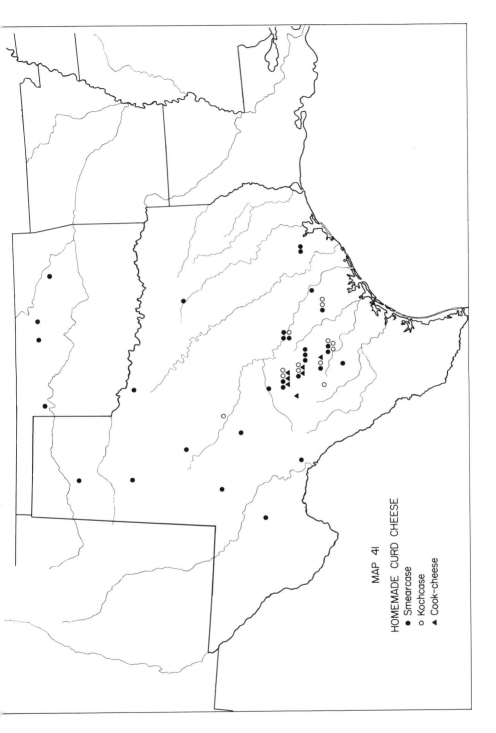

MAP 41

HOMEMADE CURD CHEESE

● Smearcase
○ Kochcase
▲ Cook-cheese

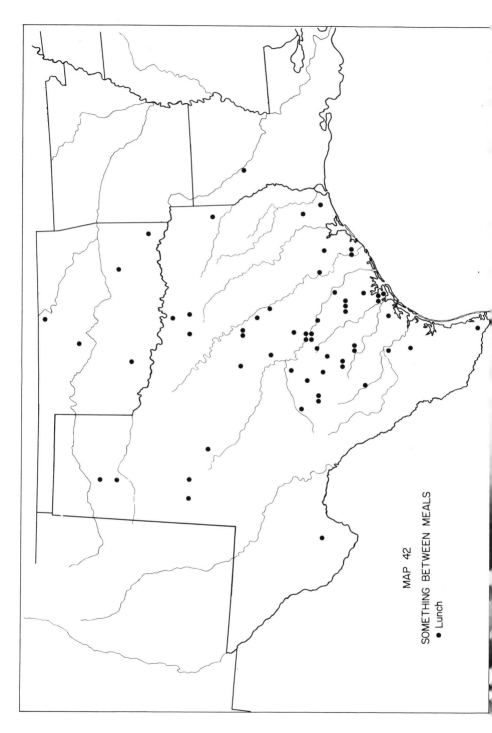

MAP 42

SOMETHING BETWEEN MEALS
● Lunch

172

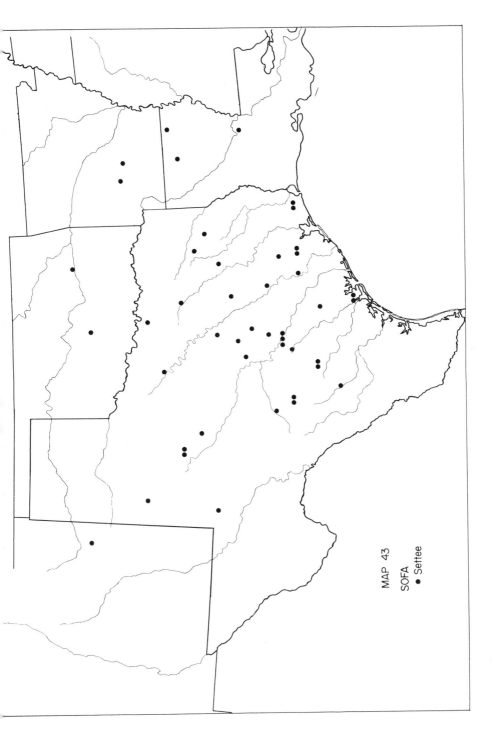

MAP 43
SOFA
• Settee

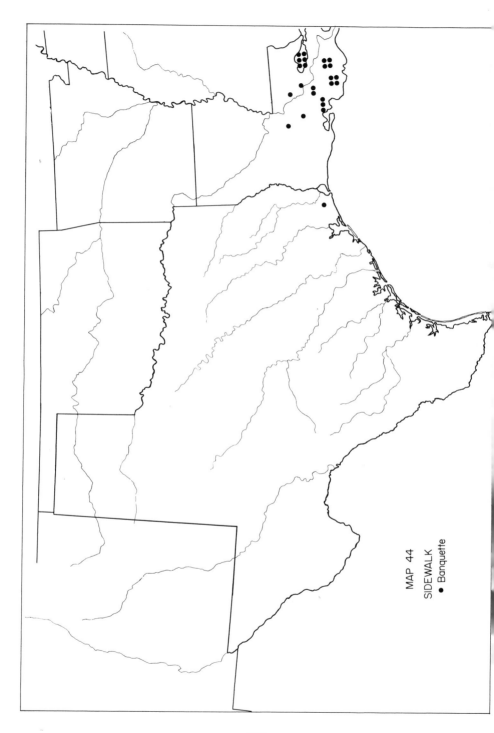

MAP 44

SIDEWALK
● Banquette

174

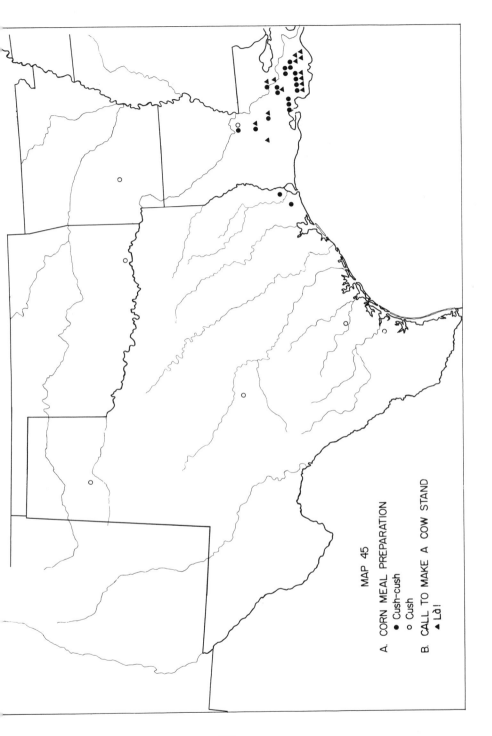

MAP 45

A. CORN MEAL PREPARATION
   ● Cush-cush
   ○ Cush

B. CALL TO MAKE A COW STAND
   ▲ Là!

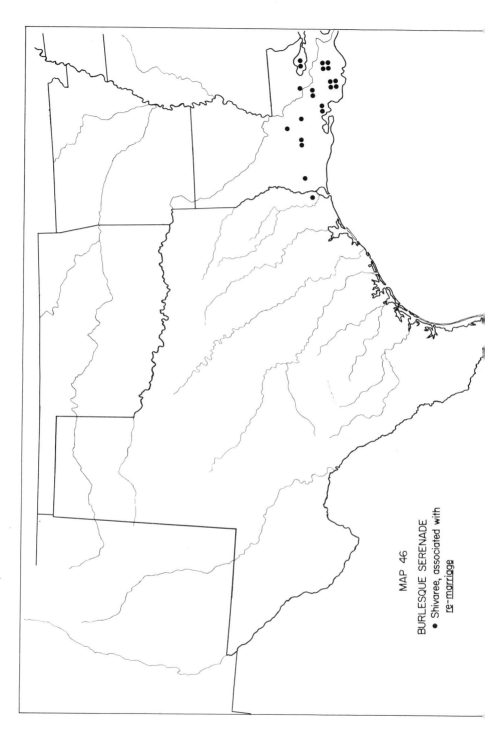

MAP 46

BURLESQUE SERENADE

• Shivaree, associated with re-marriage

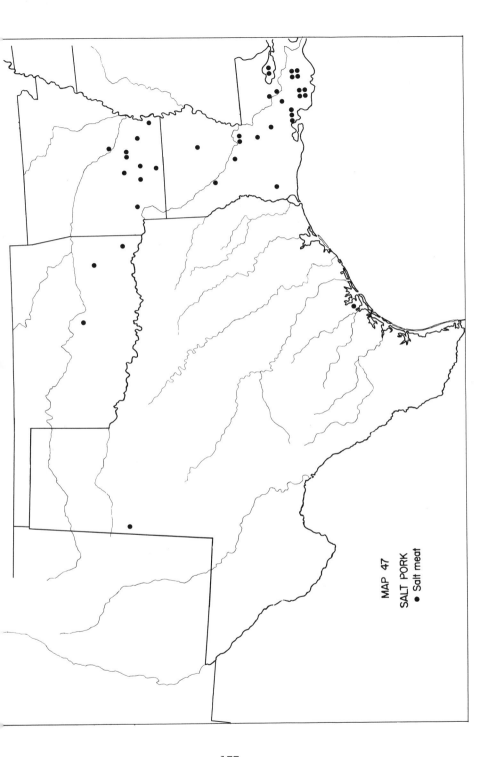

MAP 47
SALT PORK
● Salt meat

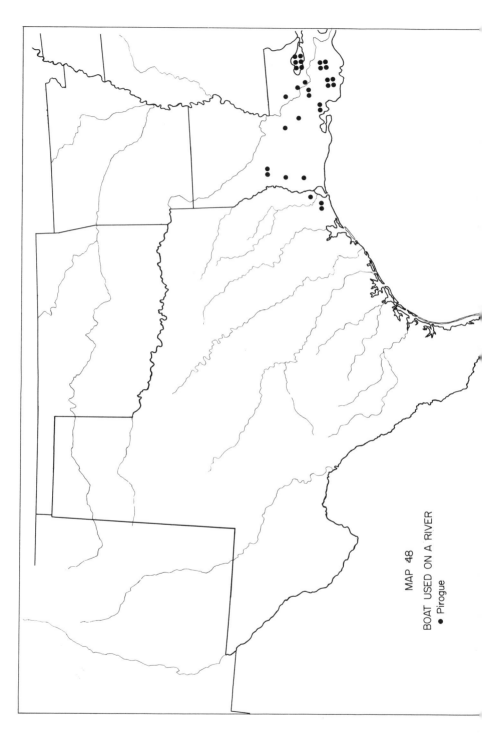

MAP 48

BOAT USED ON A RIVER

● Pirogue

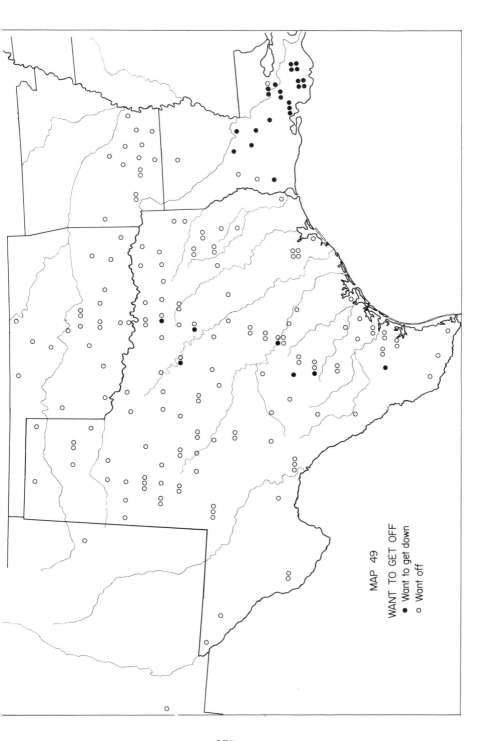

MAP 49

WANT TO GET OFF
● Want to get down
○ Want off

179

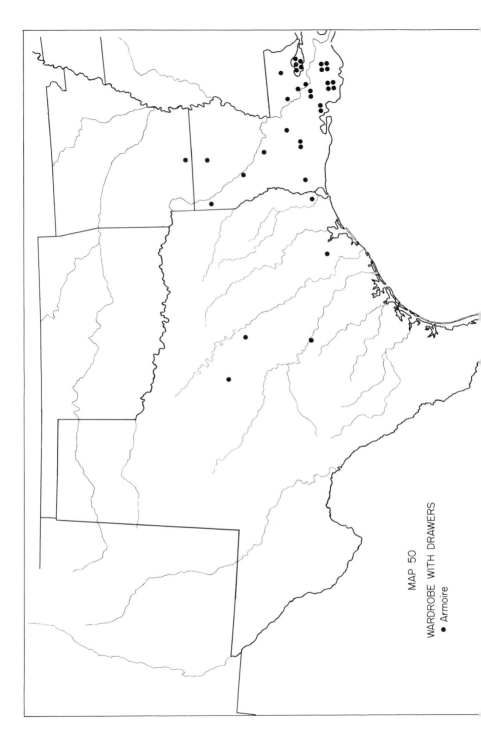

MAP 50

WARDROBE WITH DRAWERS

• Armoire

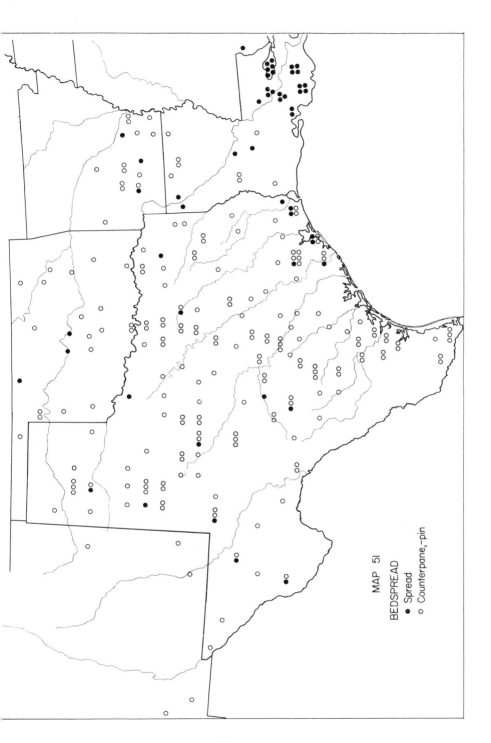

MAP 51

BEDSPREAD
• Spread
○ Counterpane,-pin

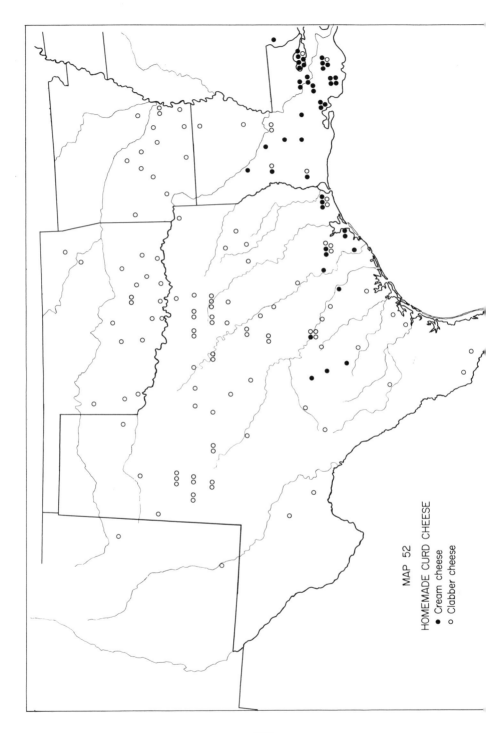

MAP 52

HOMEMADE CURD CHEESE
● Cream cheese
○ Clabber cheese

182

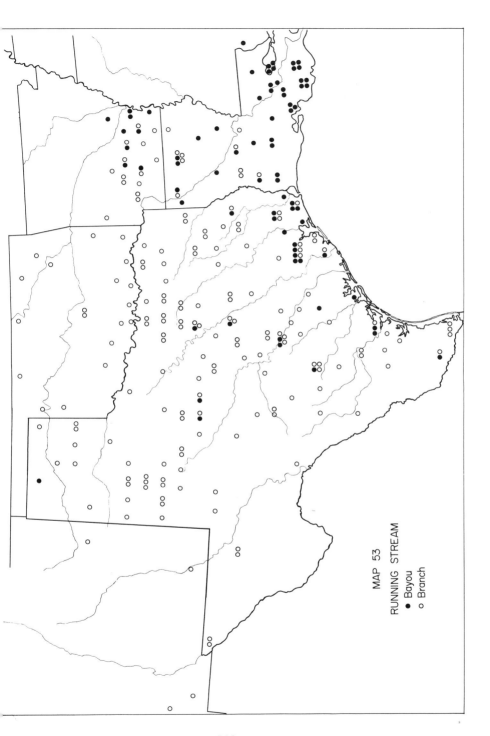

MAP 53
RUNNING STREAM
● Bayou
○ Branch

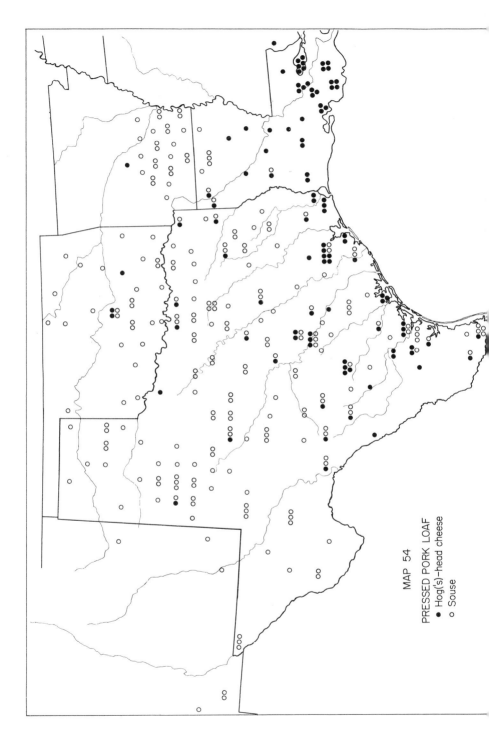

MAP 54

PRESSED PORK LOAF
● Hog(s)-head cheese
○ Souse

184

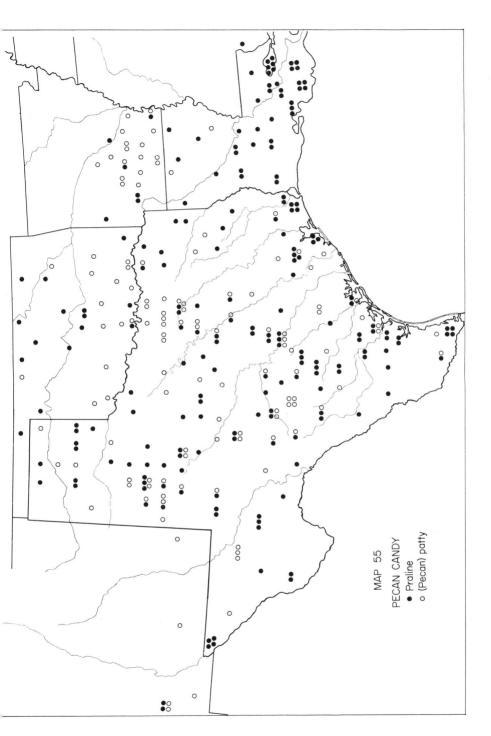

MAP 55

PECAN CANDY

● Praline
○ (Pecan) patty

185

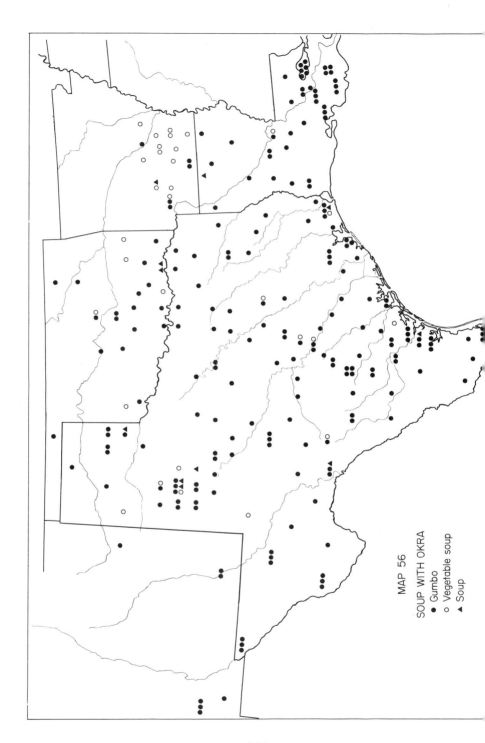

MAP 56

SOUP WITH OKRA

● Gumbo
○ Vegetable soup
▲ Soup

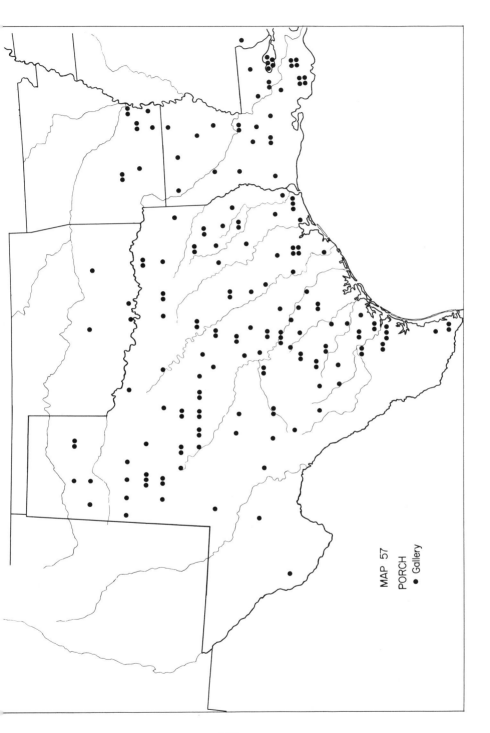

MAP 57

PORCH

• Gallery

187

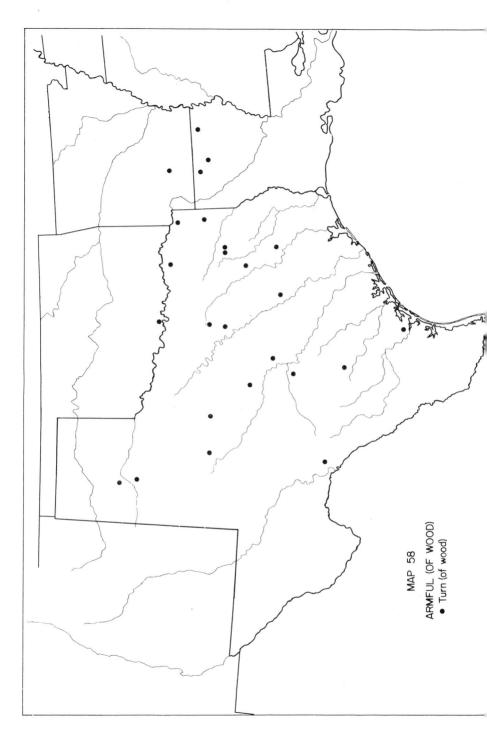

MAP 58
ARMFUL (OF WOOD)
● Turn (of wood)

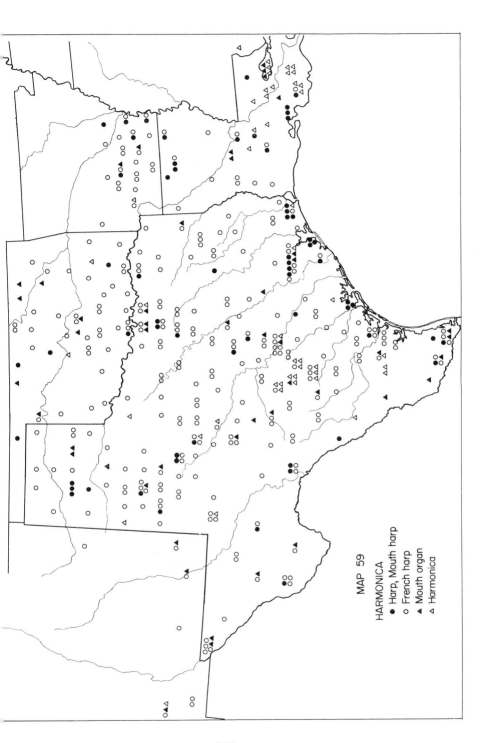

MAP 59

HARMONICA

● Harp, Mouth harp
○ French harp
▲ Mouth organ
△ Harmonica

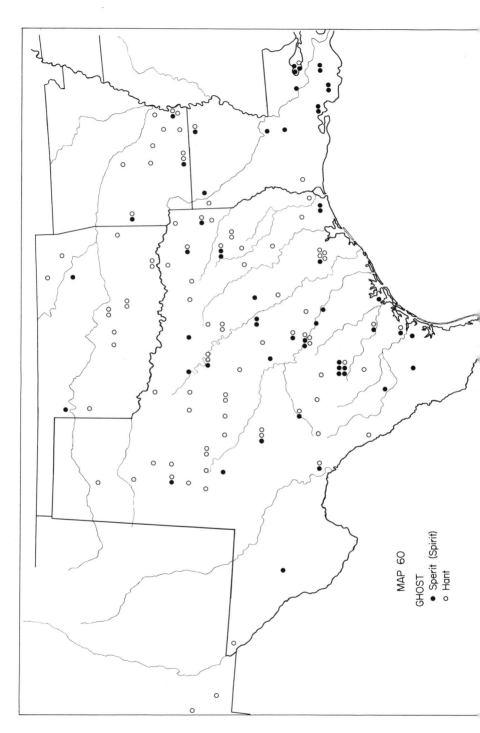

MAP 60

GHOST

● Sperit (Spirit)

○ Hant

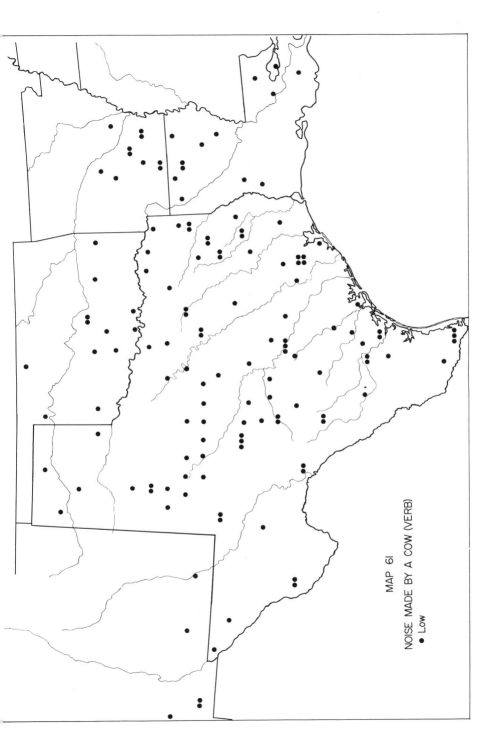

MAP 61

NOISE MADE BY A COW (VERB)

● Low

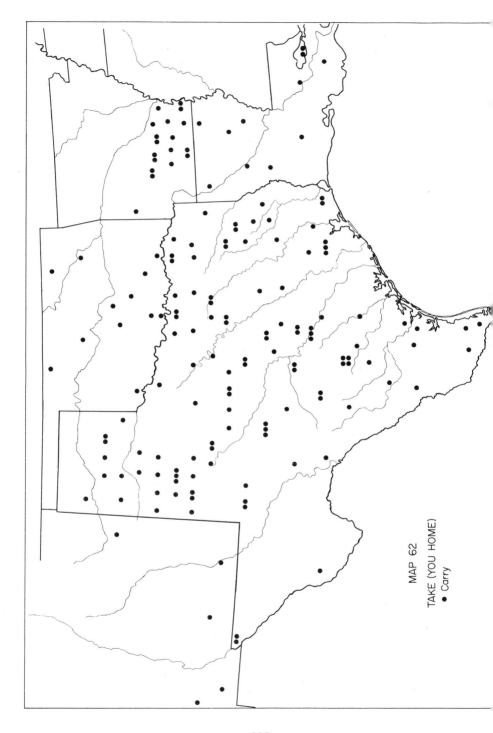

MAP 62
TAKE (YOU HOME)
• Carry

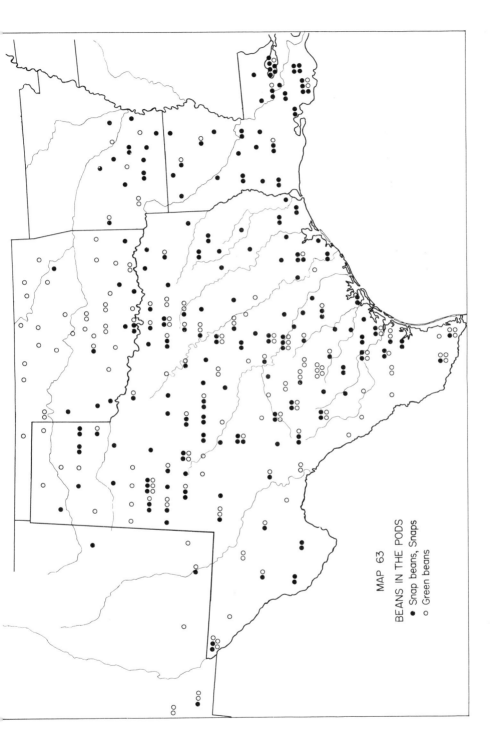

MAP 63

BEANS IN THE PODS

• Snap beans, Snaps
○ Green beans

193

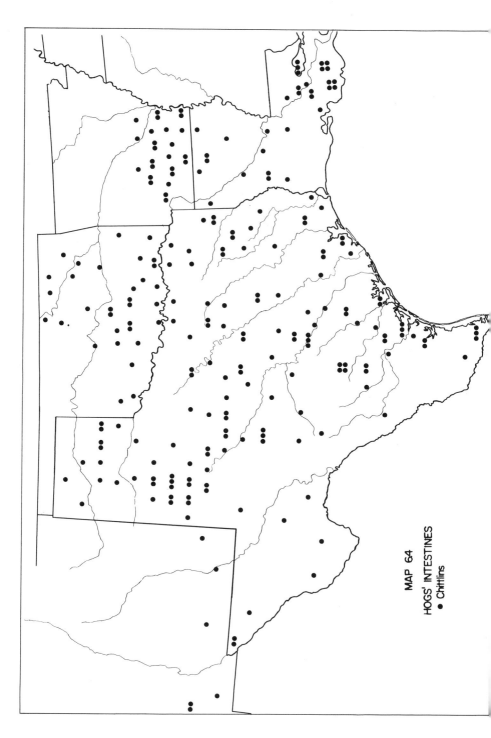

MAP 64
HOGS' INTESTINES
• Chitlins

194

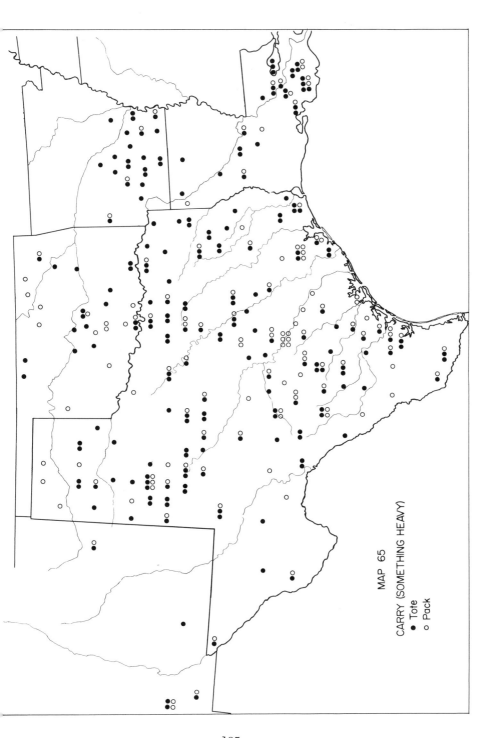

MAP 65

CARRY (SOMETHING HEAVY)

• Tote
○ Pack

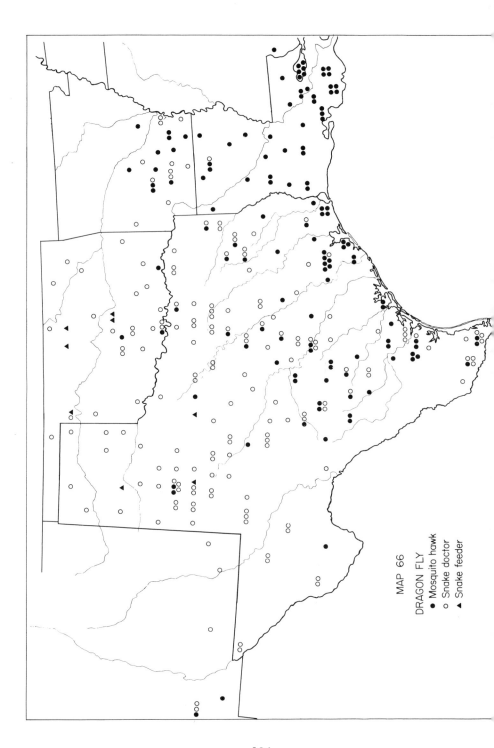

MAP 66

DRAGON FLY

● Mosquito hawk
○ Snake doctor
▲ Snake feeder

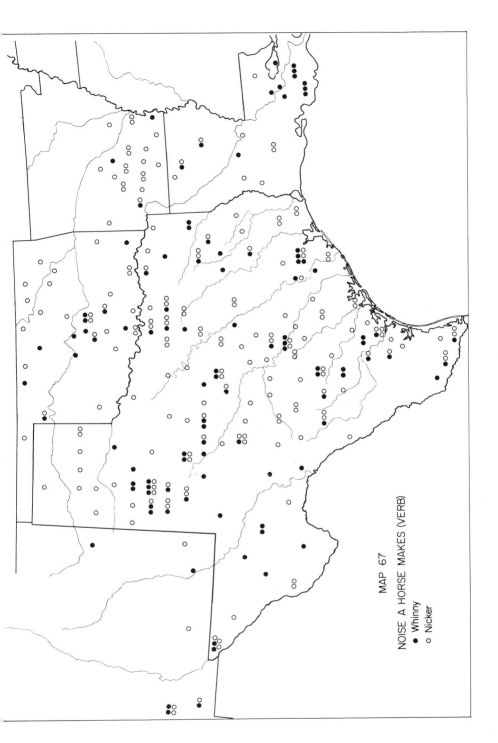

MAP 67

NOISE A HORSE MAKES (VERB)

● Whinny
○ Nicker

197

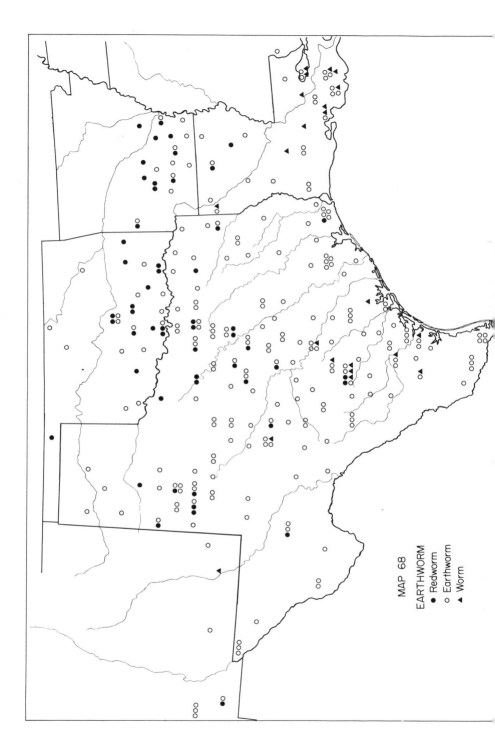

MAP 68

EARTHWORM
● Redworm
○ Earthworm
▲ Worm

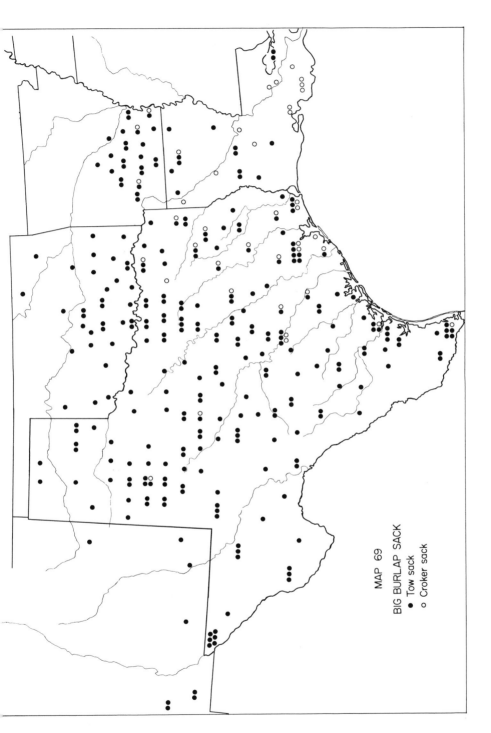

MAP 69

BIG BURLAP SACK

● Tow sack
○ Croker sack

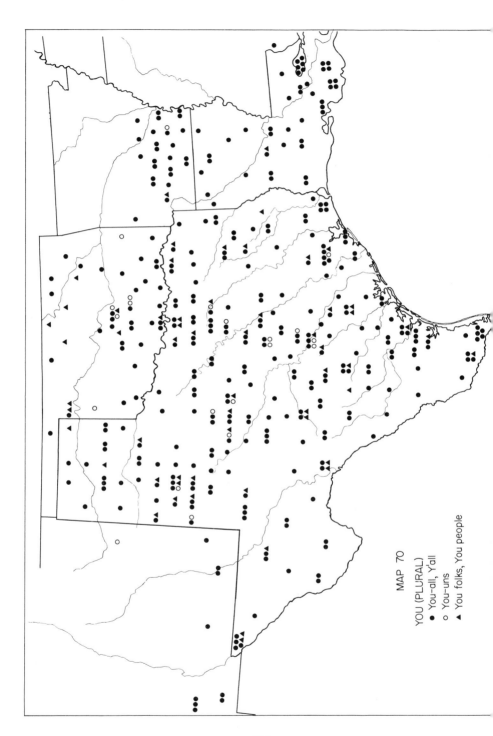

MAP 70

YOU (PLURAL)
● You-all, Y'all
○ You-uns
▲ You folks, You people

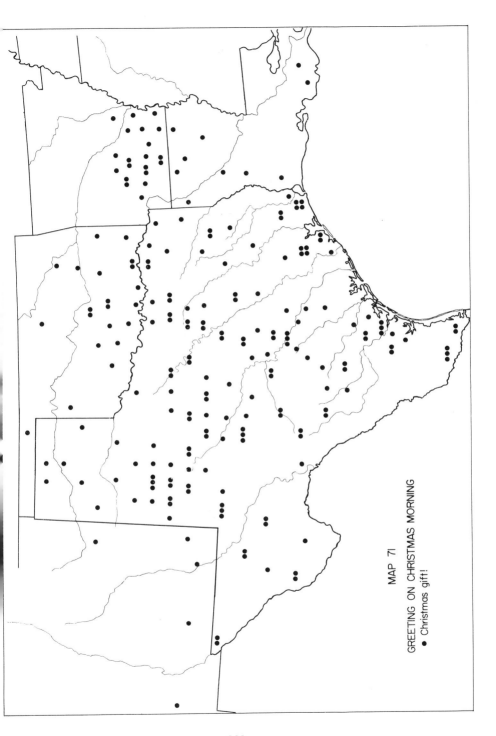

MAP 71

GREETING ON CHRISTMAS MORNING

● Christmas gift!

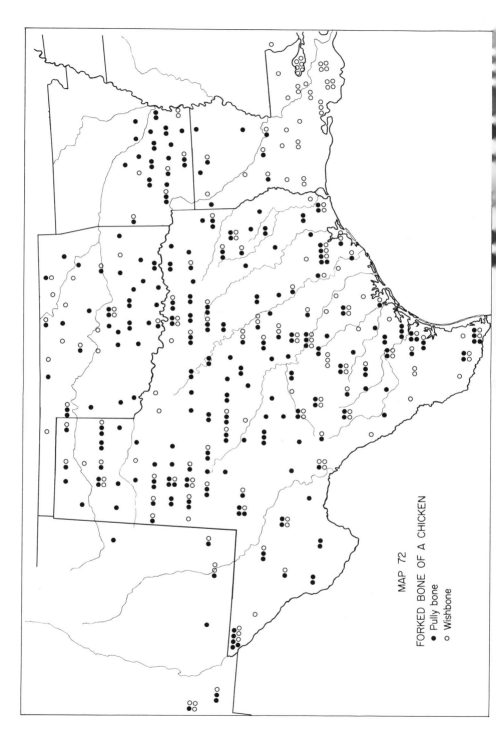

MAP 72

FORKED BONE OF A CHICKEN

● Pully bone
○ Wishbone

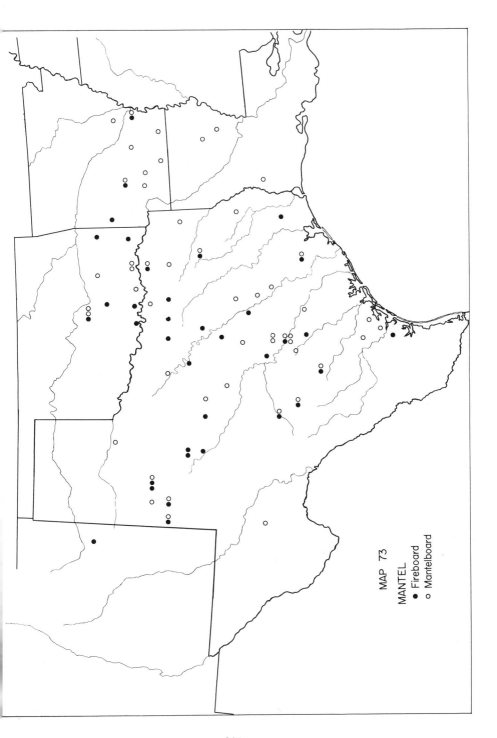

MAP 73

MANTEL
● Fireboard
○ Mantelboard

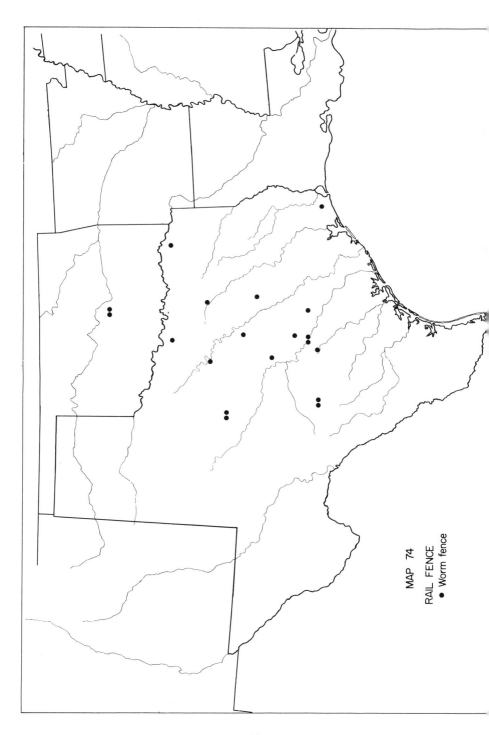

MAP 74

RAIL FENCE
● Worm fence

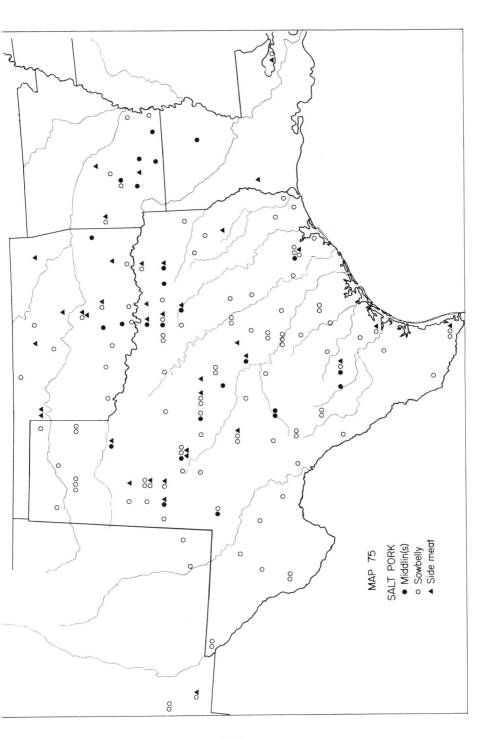

MAP 75

SALT PORK
● Middlin(s)
○ Sowbelly
▲ Side meat

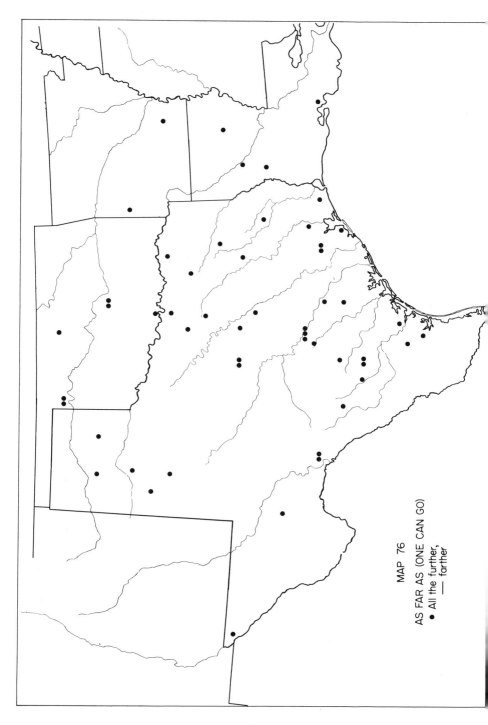

MAP 76

AS FAR AS (ONE CAN GO)
● All the further,
— farther

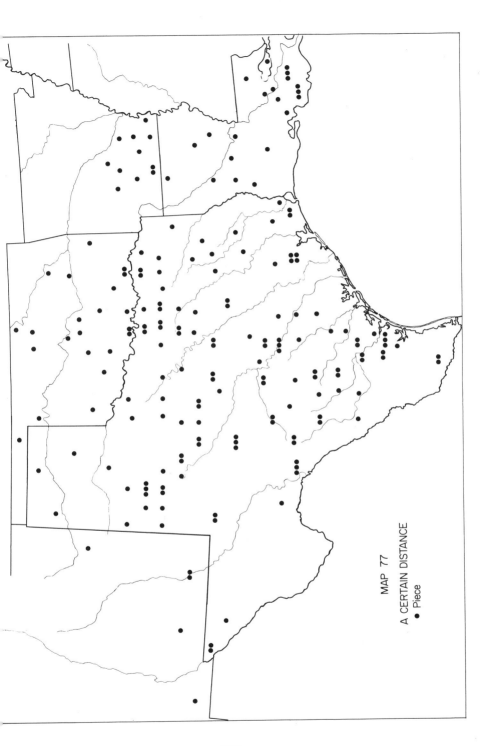

MAP 77

A CERTAIN DISTANCE

• Piece

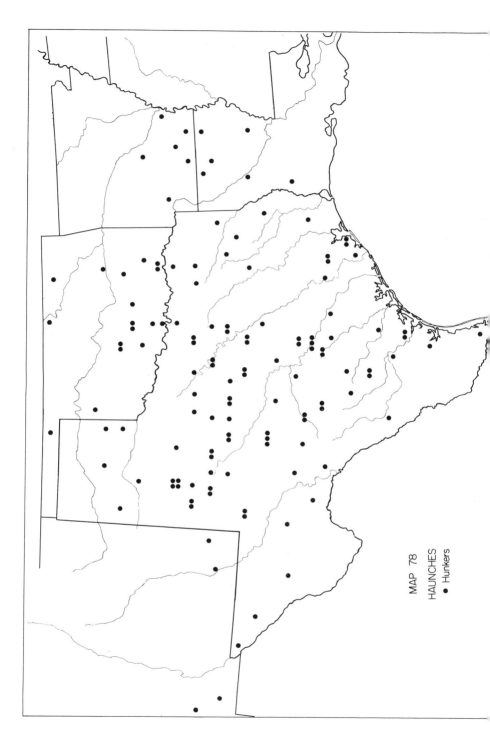

MAP 78
HAUNCHES
• Hunkers

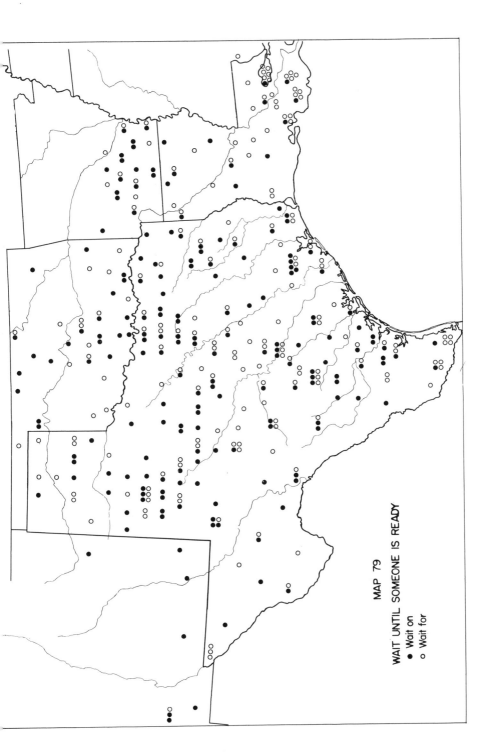

MAP 79

WAIT UNTIL SOMEONE IS READY

● Wait on
○ Wait for

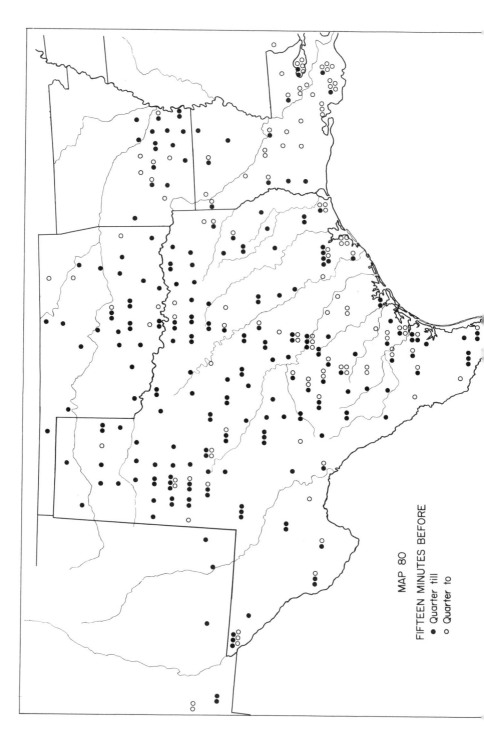

MAP 80

FIFTEEN MINUTES BEFORE

● Quarter till
○ Quarter to

210

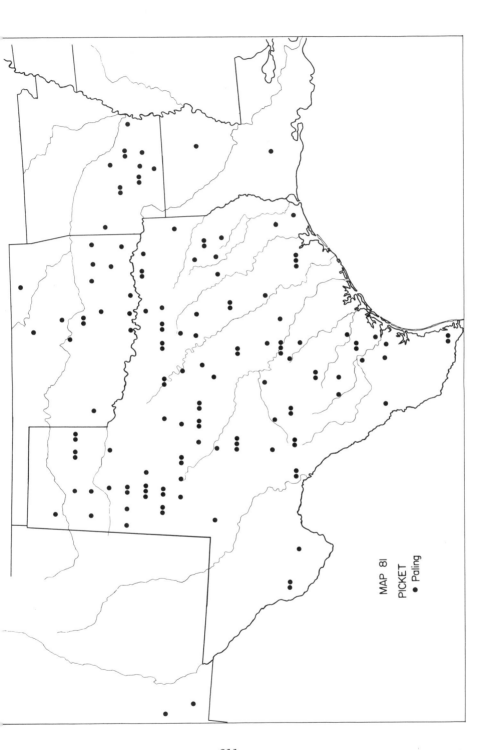

MAP 81
PICKET
● Paling

211

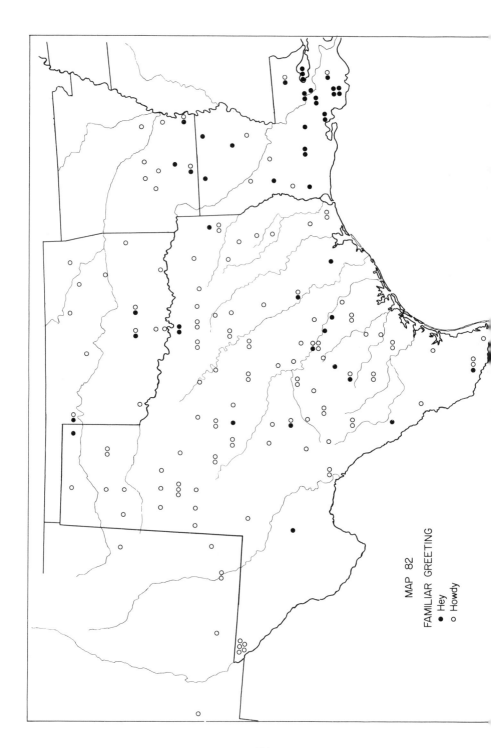

MAP 82

FAMILIAR GREETING

● Hey
○ Howdy

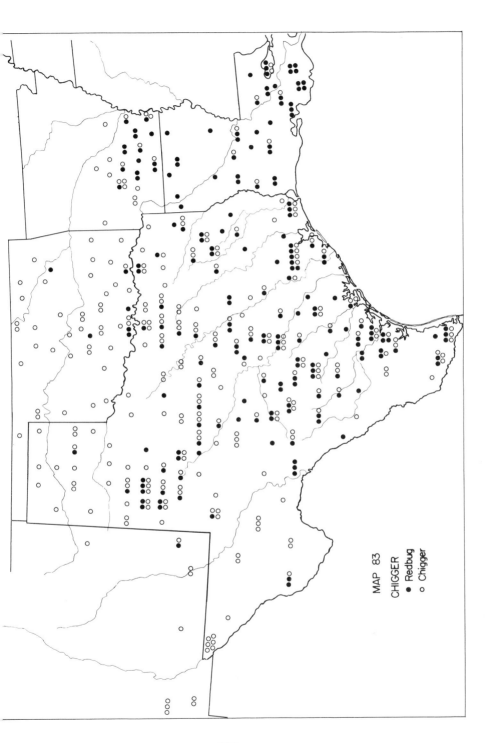

MAP 83

CHIGGER

● Redbug

○ Chigger

213

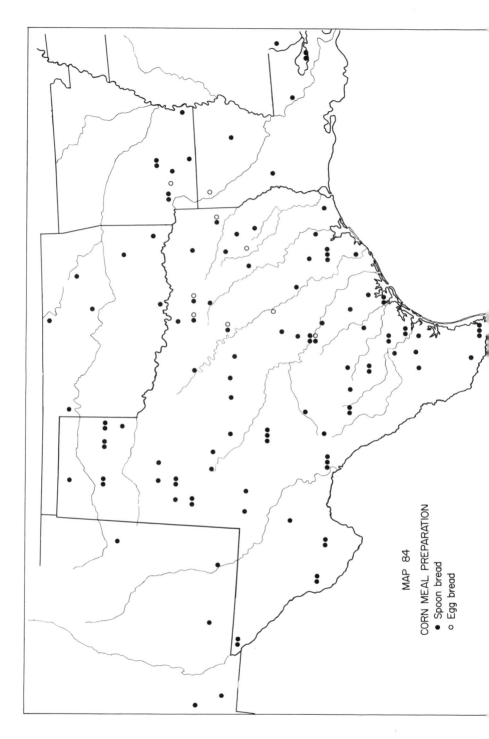

MAP 84

CORN MEAL PREPARATION

• Spoon bread
○ Egg bread

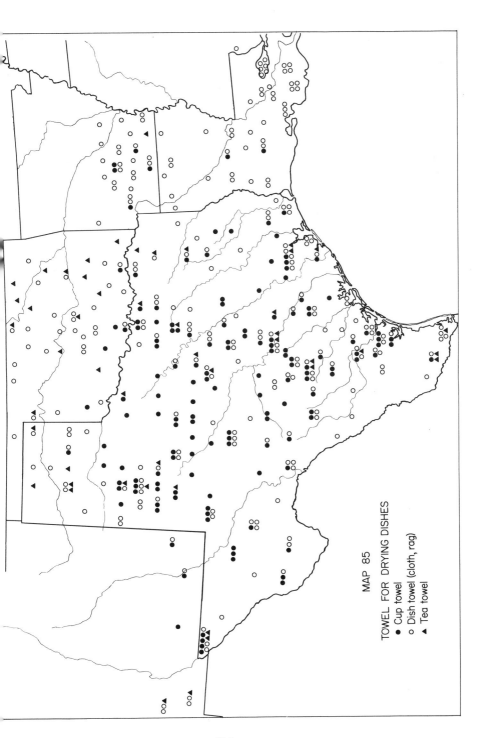

MAP 85

TOWEL FOR DRYING DISHES

● Cup towel
○ Dish towel (cloth, rag)
▲ Tea towel

215

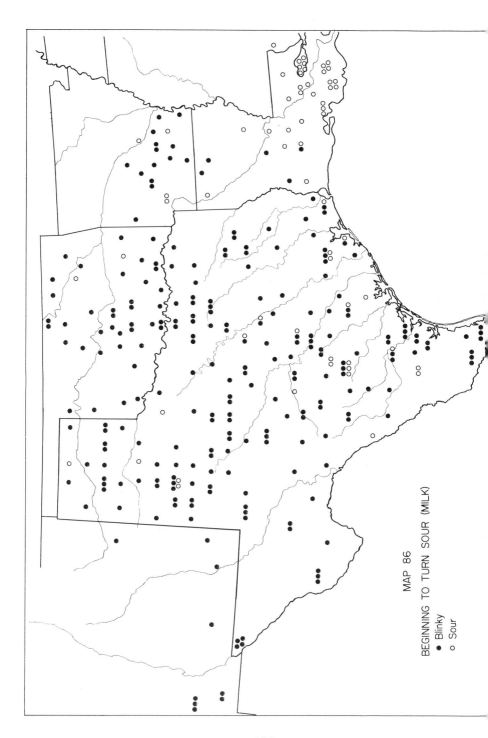

MAP 86

BEGINNING TO TURN SOUR (MILK)

● Blinky
○ Sour

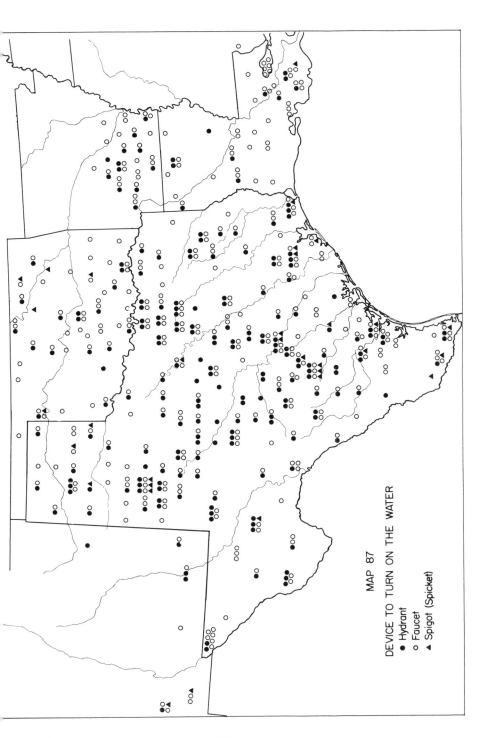

MAP 87

DEVICE TO TURN ON THE WATER

● Hydrant
○ Faucet
▲ Spigot (Spicket)

217

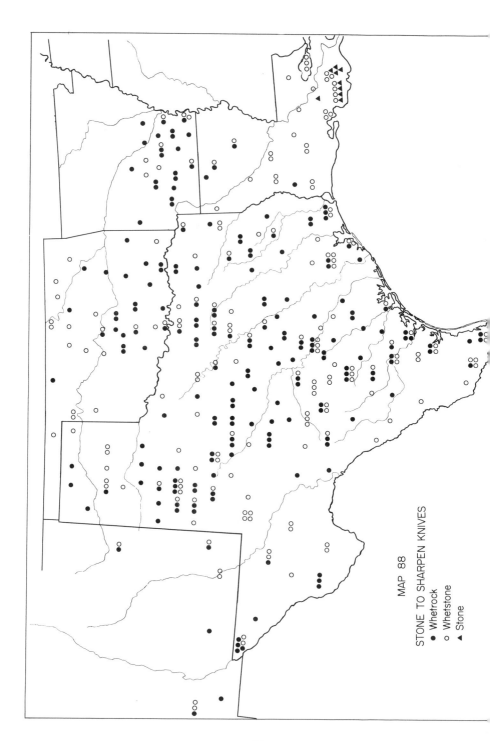

MAP 88

STONE TO SHARPEN KNIVES

● Whetrock
○ Whetstone
▲ Stone

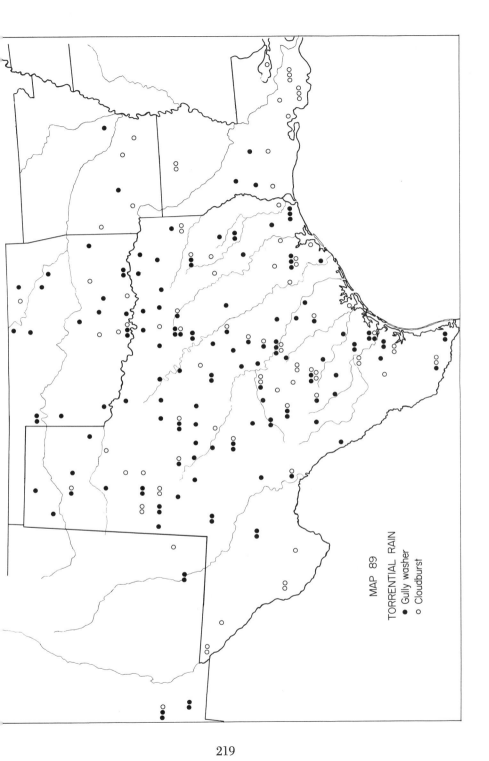

MAP 89

TORRENTIAL RAIN
● Gully washer
○ Cloudburst

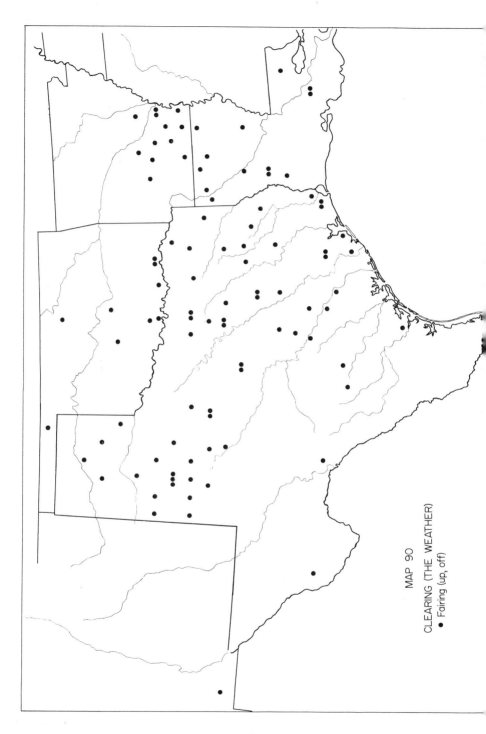

MAP 90

CLEARING (THE WEATHER)
● Fairing (up, off)

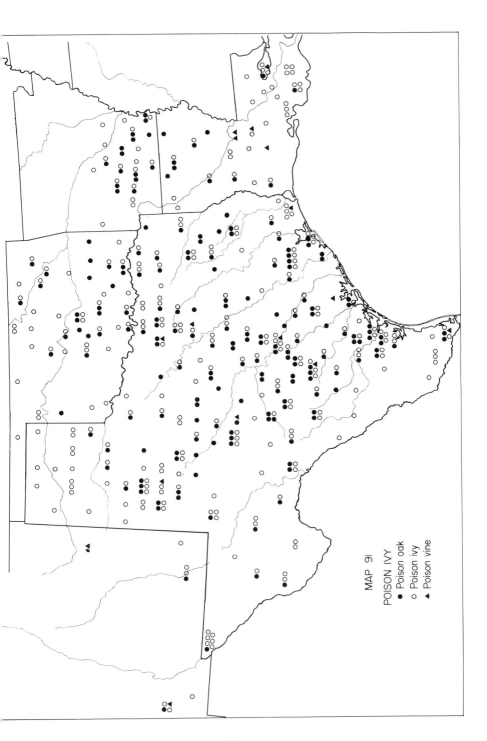

MAP 91

POISON IVY
● Poison oak
○ Poison ivy
▲ Poison vine

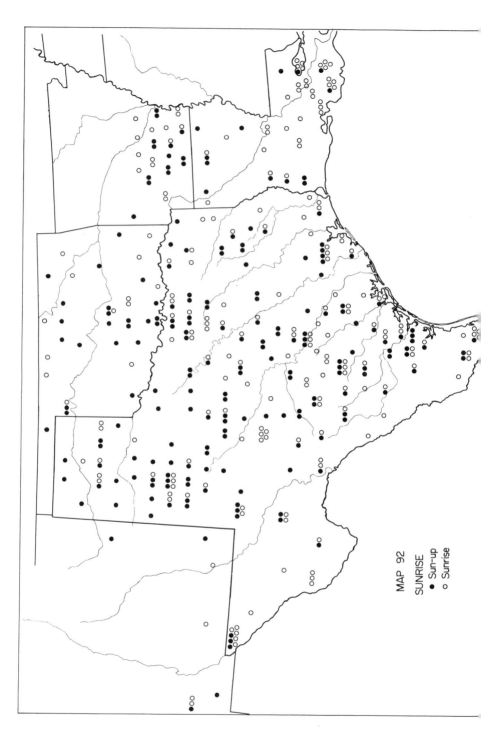

MAP 92

SUNRISE

● Sun-up
○ Sunrise

222

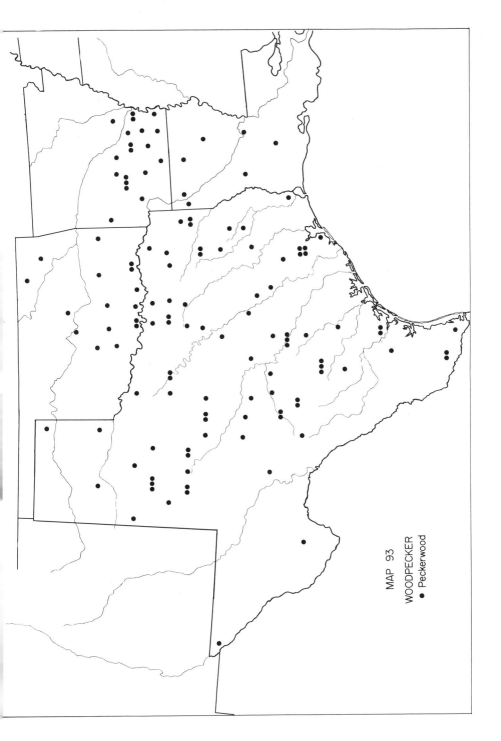

MAP 93

WOODPECKER
● Peckerwood

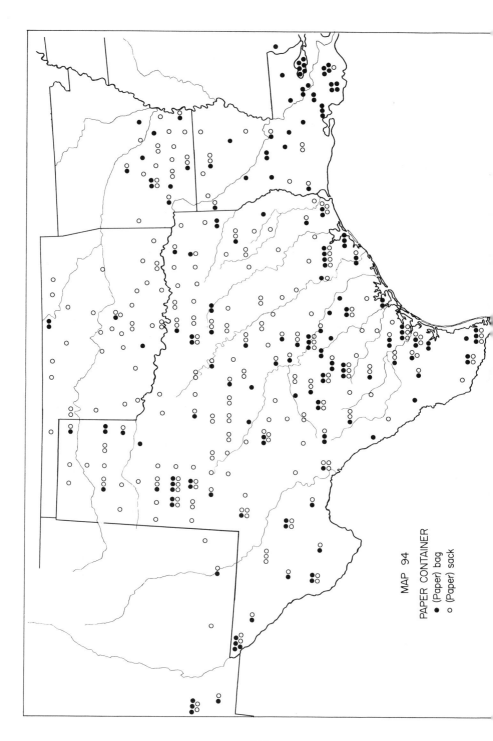

MAP 94
PAPER CONTAINER
● (Paper) bag
○ (Paper) sack

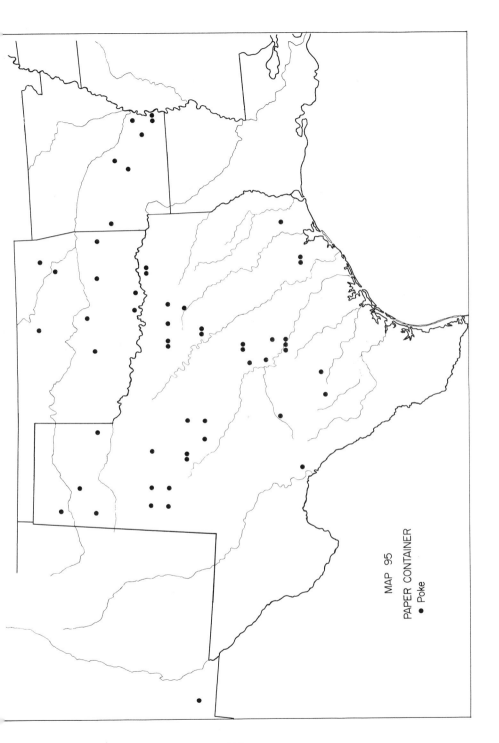

MAP 95
PAPER CONTAINER
● Poke

225

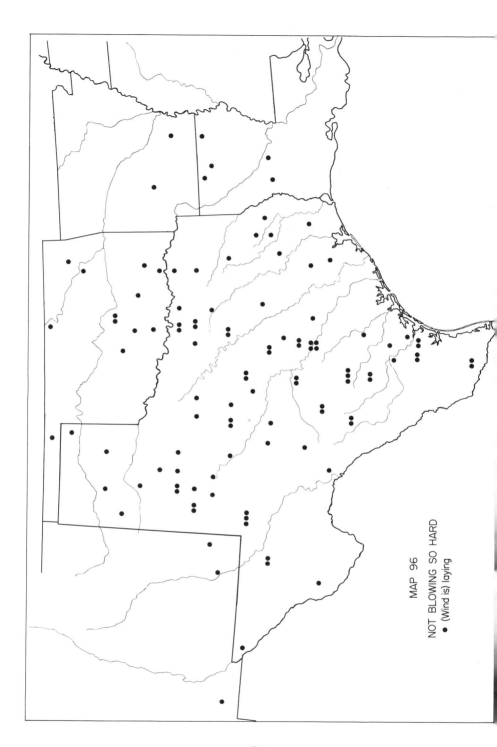

MAP 96

NOT BLOWING SO HARD

• (Wind is) laying

226

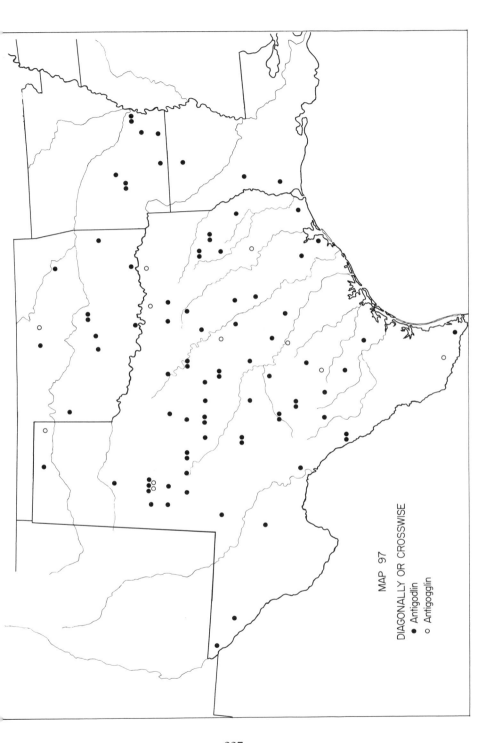

MAP 97

DIAGONALLY OR CROSSWISE
● Antigodlin
○ Antigogglin

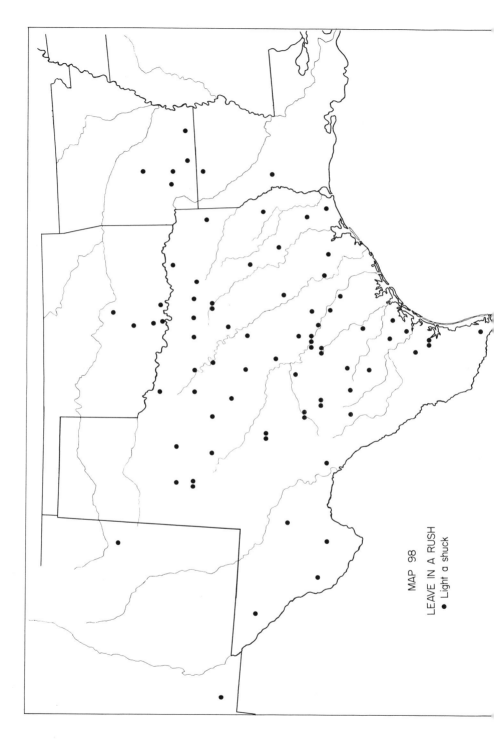

MAP 98
LEAVE IN A RUSH
• Light a shuck

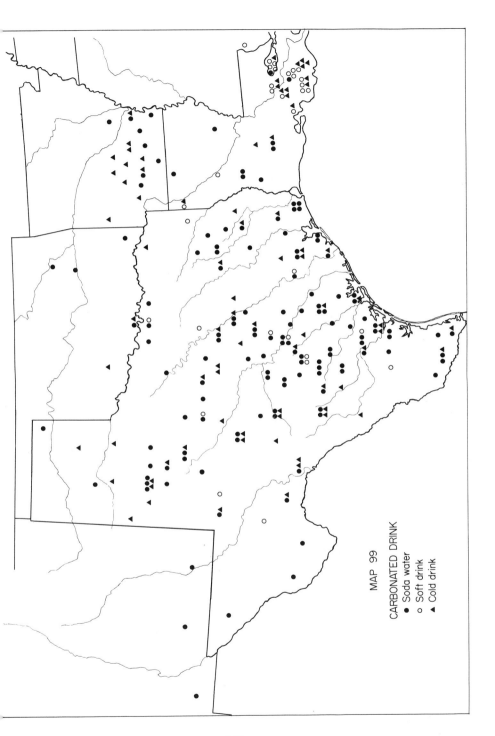

MAP 99

CARBONATED DRINK
● Soda water
○ Soft drink
▲ Cold drink

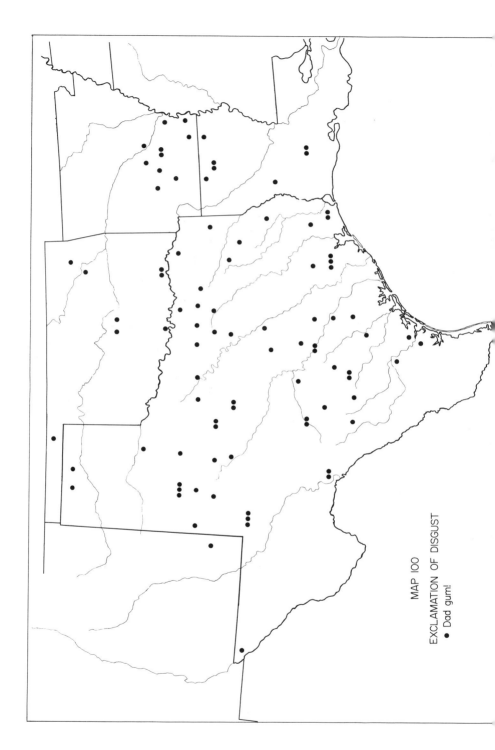

MAP 100

EXCLAMATION OF DISGUST

● Dad gum!

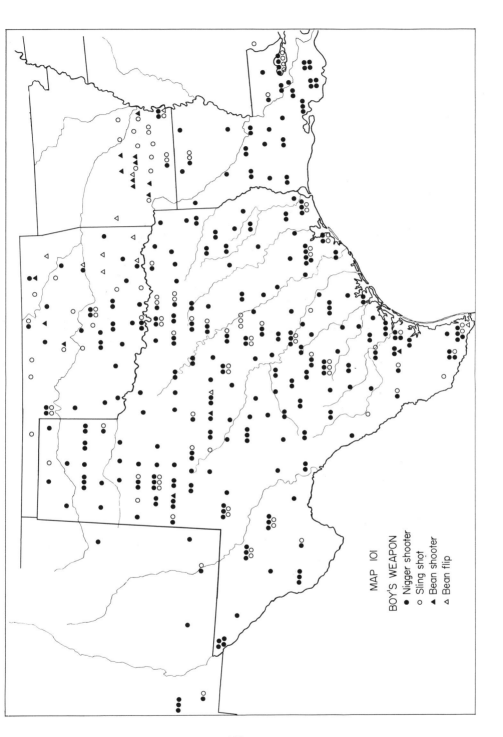

MAP 101

BOY'S WEAPON
● Nigger shooter
○ Sling shot
▲ Bean shooter
△ Bean flip

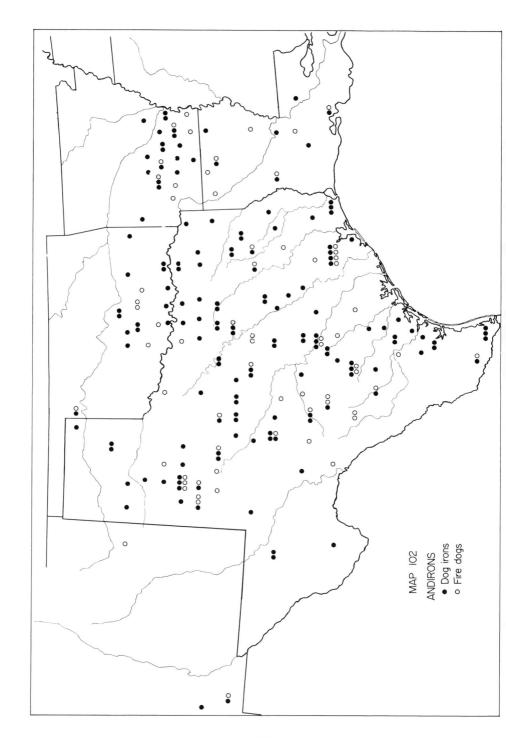

MAP 102
ANDIRONS
● Dog irons
○ Fire dogs

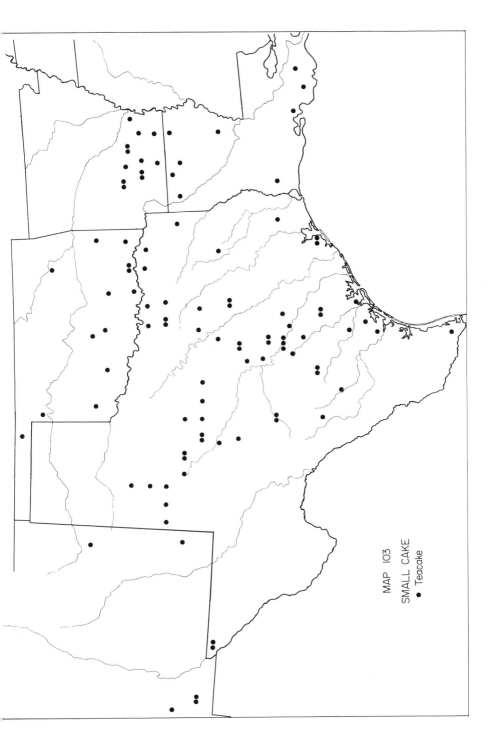

MAP 103
SMALL CAKE
• Teacake

233

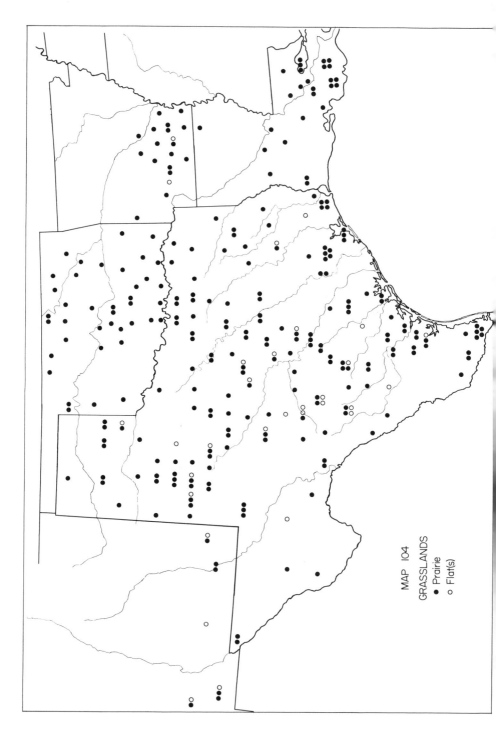

MAP 104
GRASSLANDS
● Prairie
○ Flat(s)

234

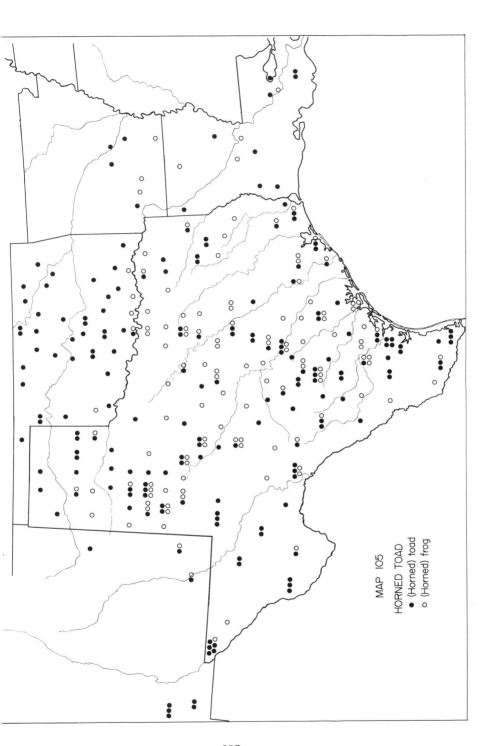

MAP 105

HORNED TOAD
● (Horned) toad
○ (Horned) frog

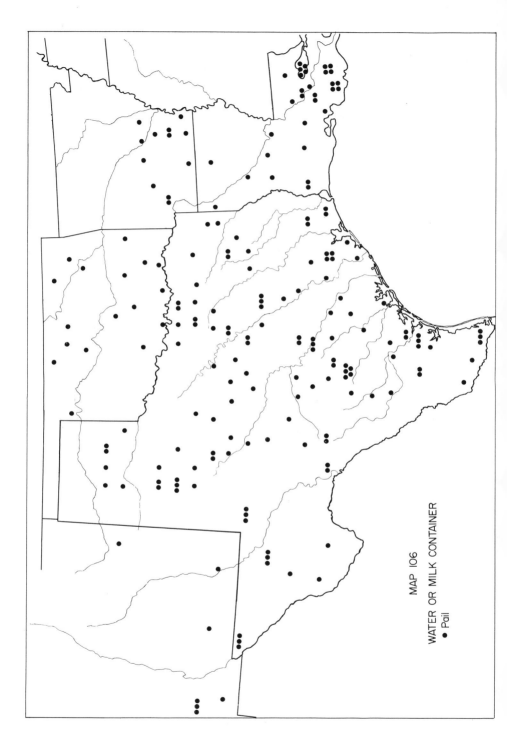

MAP 106

WATER OR MILK CONTAINER
● Pail

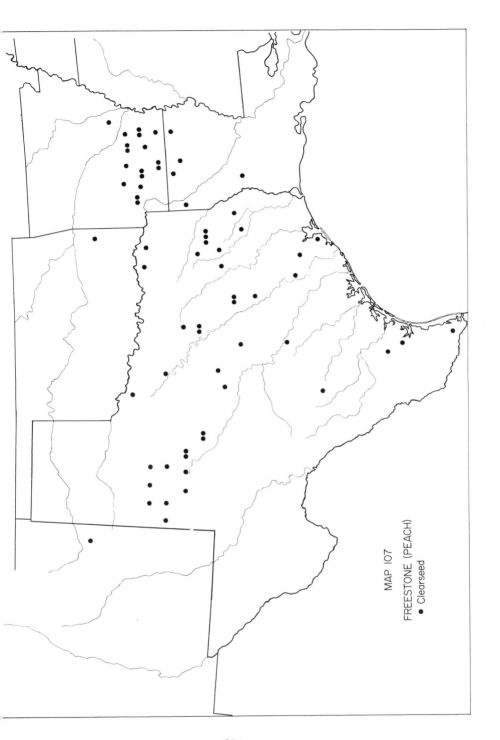

MAP 107
FREESTONE (PEACH)
● Clearseed

237

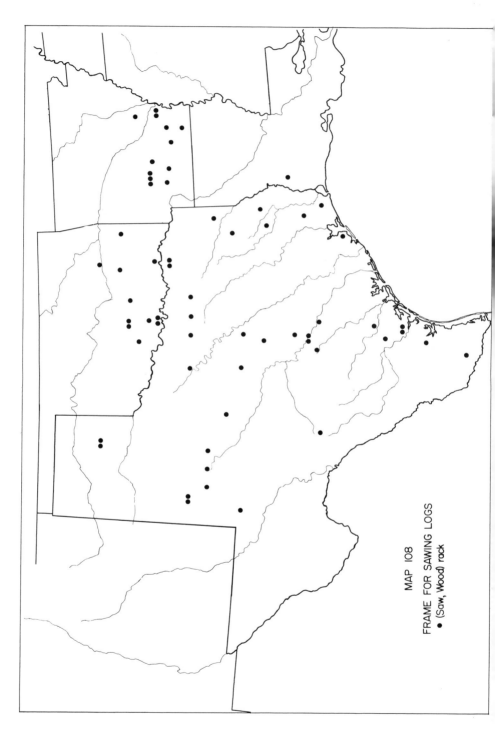

MAP 108

FRAME FOR SAWING LOGS

● (Saw, Wood) rack

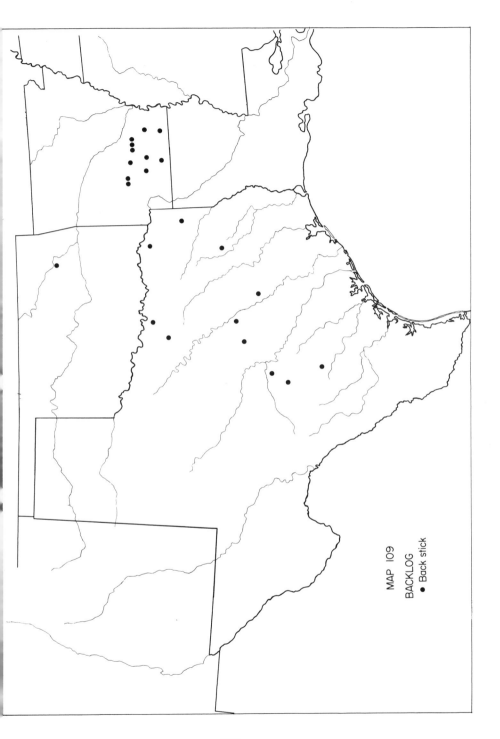

MAP 109

BACKLOG

● Back stick

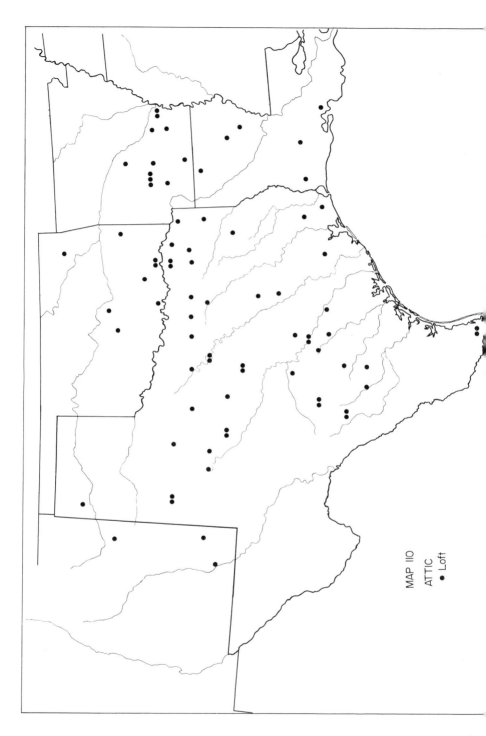

MAP IIO

ATTIC

• Loft

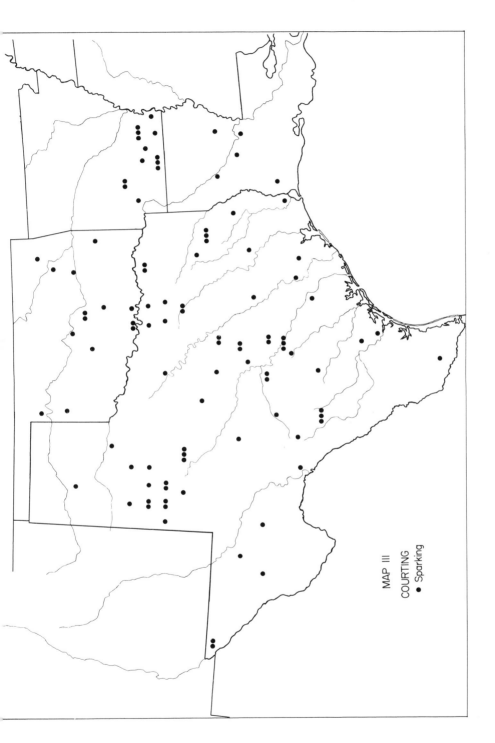

MAP III

COURTING

• Sparking

241

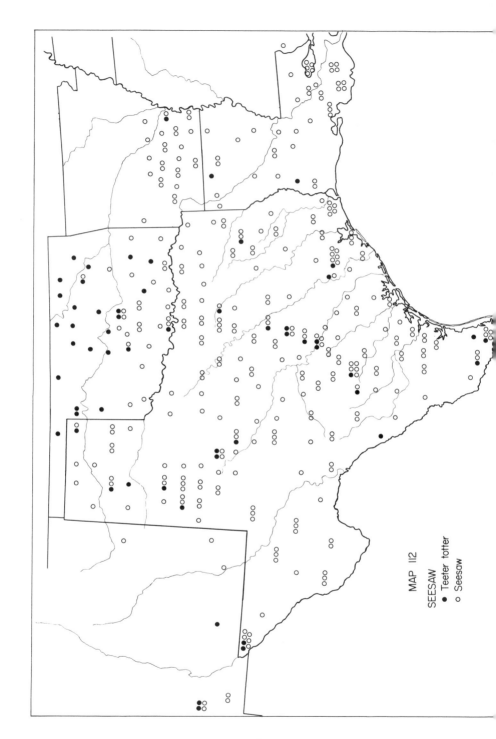

MAP 112

SEESAW
● Teeter totter
○ Seesaw

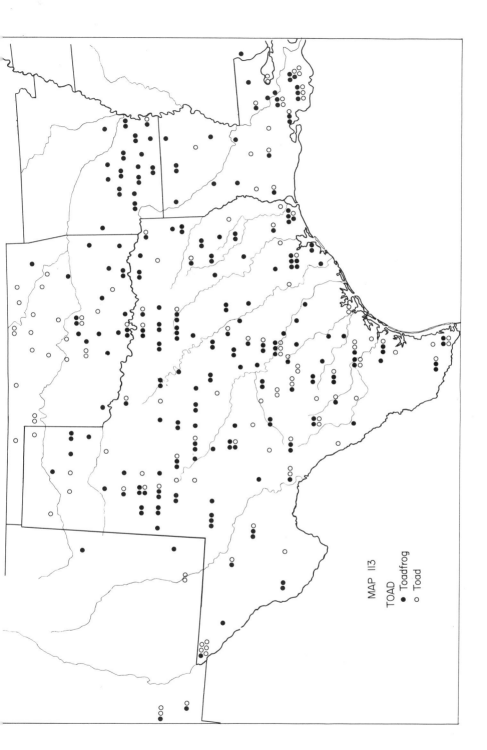

MAP 113

TOAD
● Toadfrog
○ Toad

243

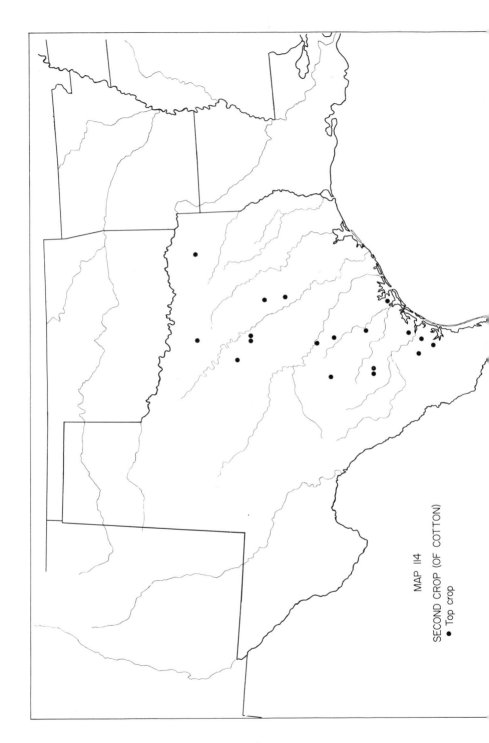

MAP 114

SECOND CROP (OF COTTON)
● Top crop

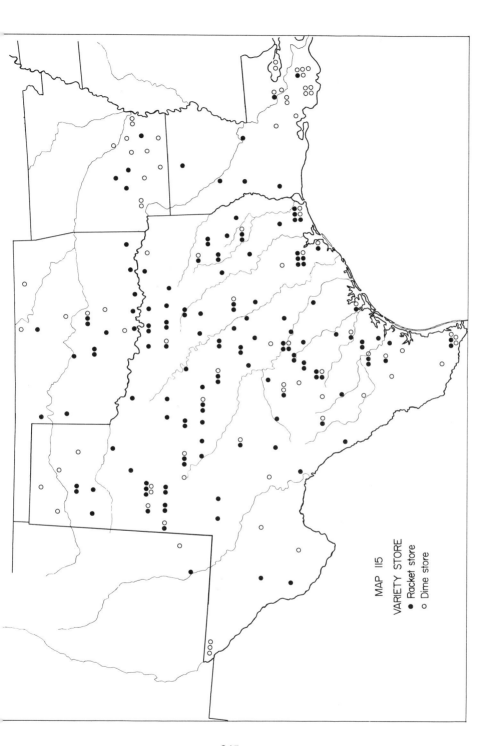

MAP II5

VARIETY STORE

● Racket store
○ Dime store

245

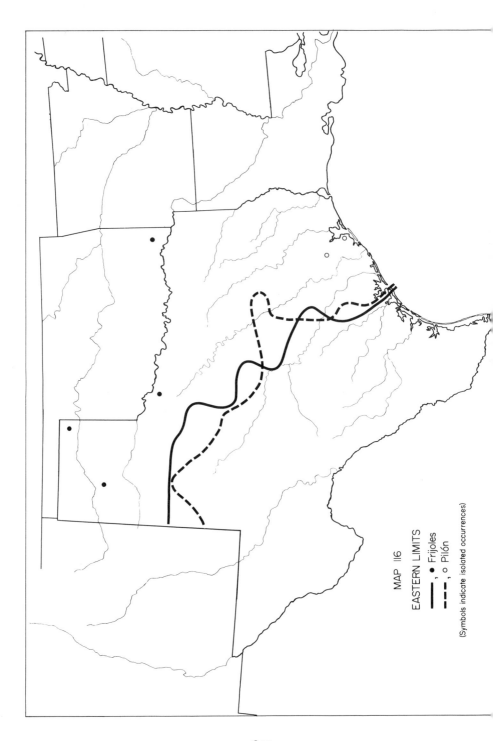

MAP 116

EASTERN LIMITS

● Frijoles
○ Pilón

(Symbols indicate isolated occurrences)

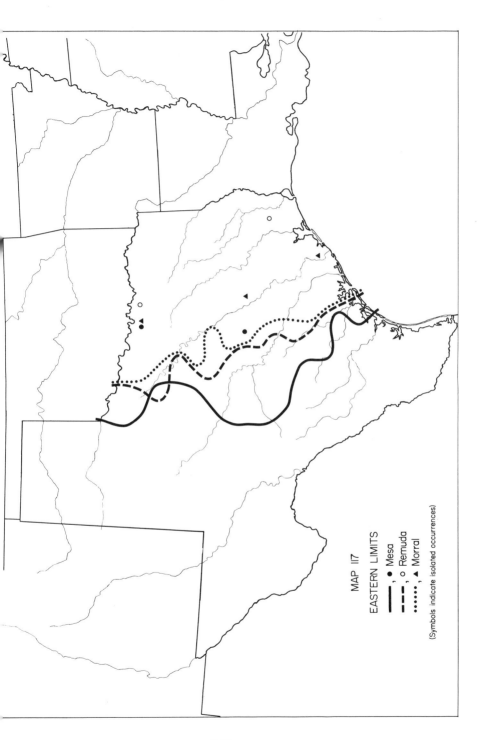

MAP 117

EASTERN LIMITS

- ● Mesa
- ○ Remuda
- ▲ Morral

(Symbols indicate isolated occurrences)

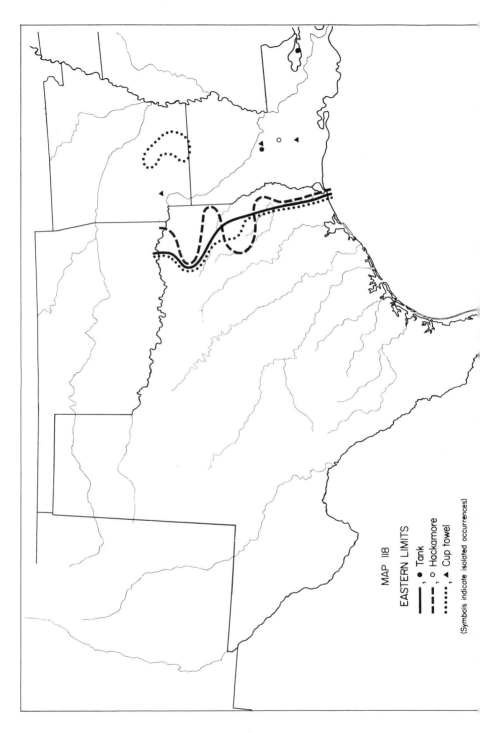

MAP 118

EASTERN LIMITS

——— , ● Tank
▬ ▬ , ○ Hackamore
··········· , ▲ Cup towel

(Symbols indicate isolated occurrences)

248

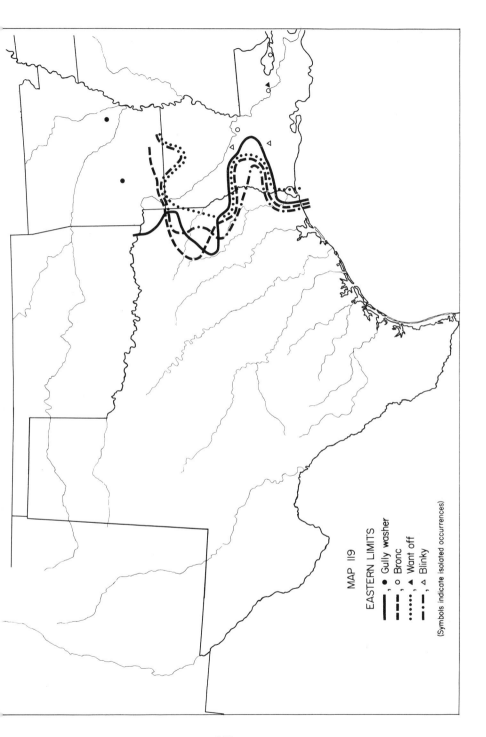

MAP 119

EASTERN LIMITS

- Gully washer
- ○ Bronc
- ▲ Want off
- △ Blinky

(Symbols indicate isolated occurrences)

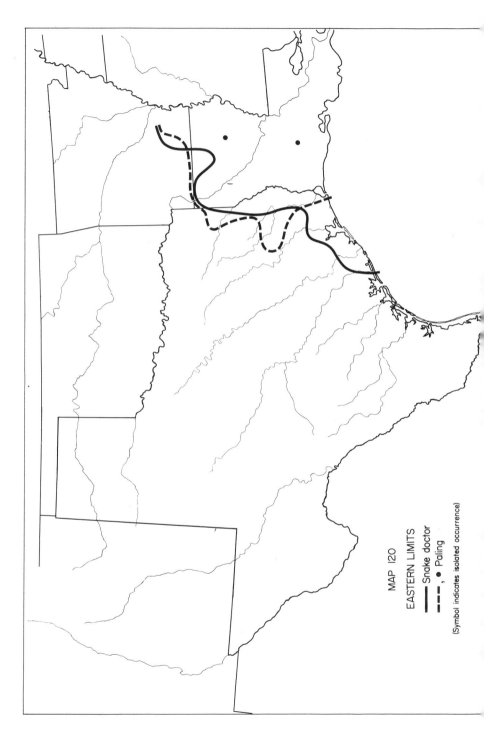

MAP 120

EASTERN LIMITS

━━━ Snake doctor

▬ ▬ ▬ ●, Paling

(Symbol indicates isolated occurrence)

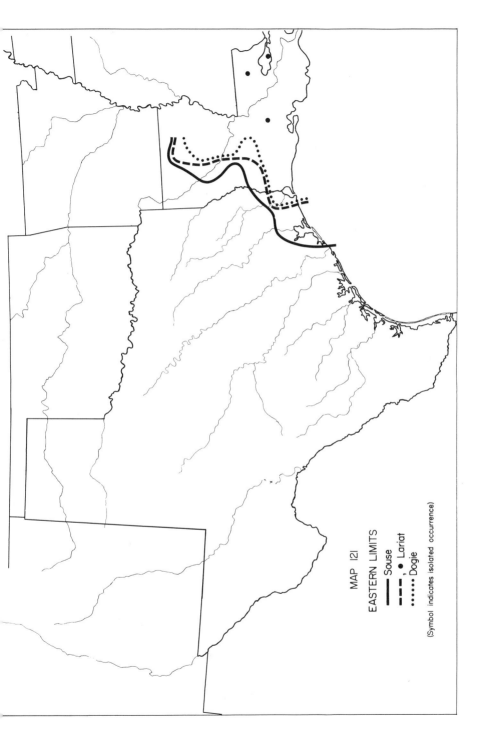

MAP 121

EASTERN LIMITS

—— Souse

– – , ● Lariat

· · · · · · Dogie

(Symbol indicates isolated occurrence)

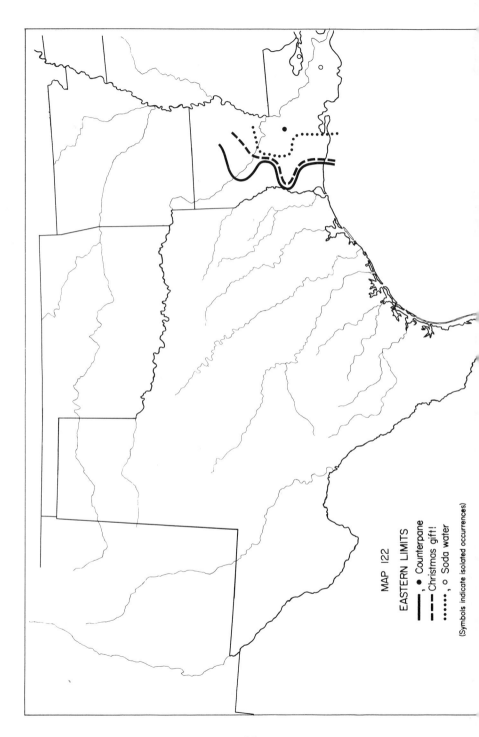

MAP 122

EASTERN LIMITS

———, • Counterpane
——— Christmas gift!
·········, ○ Soda water

(Symbols indicate isolated occurrences)

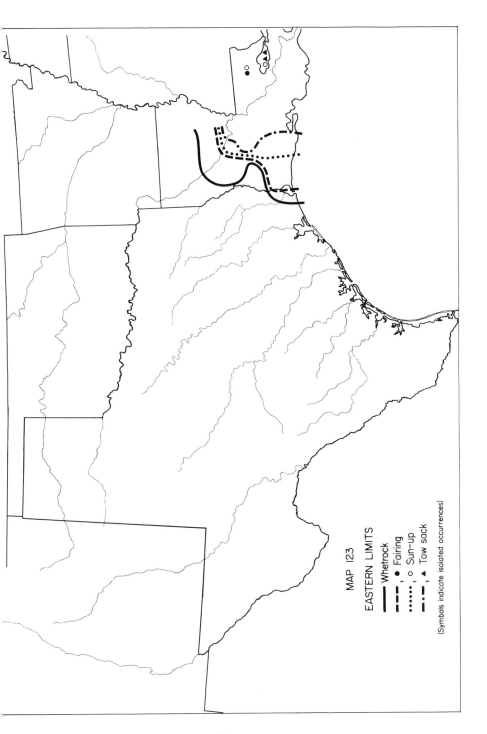

MAP 123

EASTERN LIMITS

Whetrock
Fairing
Sun-up
Tow sack

(Symbols indicate isolated occurrences)

253

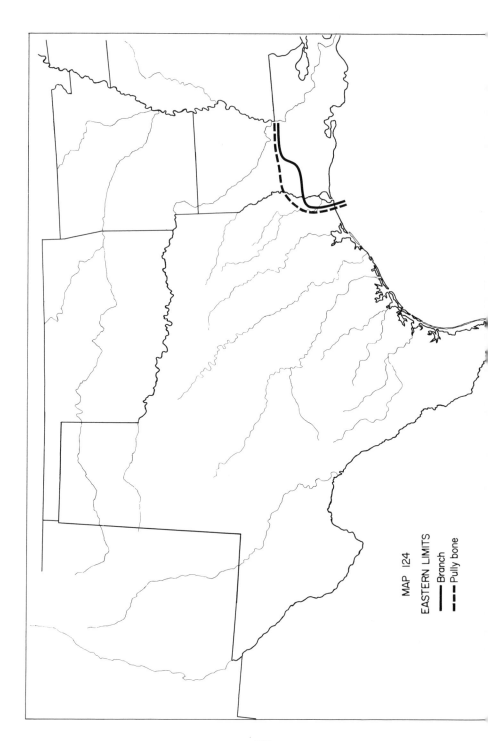

MAP 124

EASTERN LIMITS

——— Branch
━ ━ ━ Pully bone

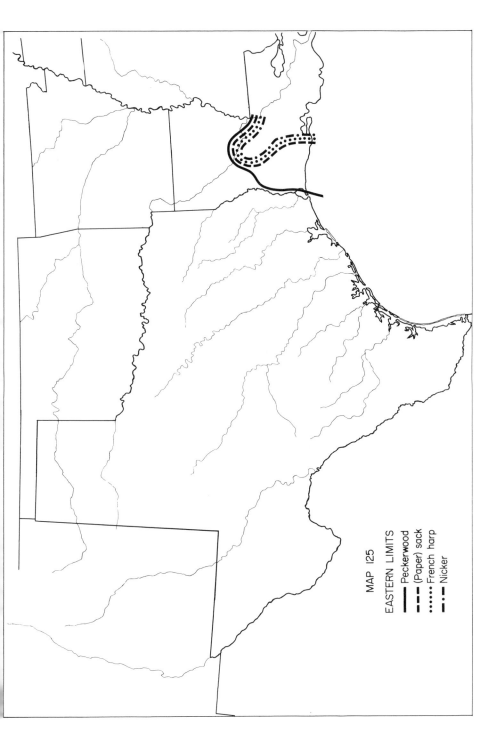

MAP 125

EASTERN LIMITS

—— Peckerwood
– – – (Paper) sack
······ French harp
–·– Nicker

255

APPENDIX

MACHINE HANDLING OF THE DATA

As mentioned in Chapter II, most of the arranging of materials for this study was accomplished by IBM machines. Since the venture was, in a sense, a pioneering one, some of the processes were imperfectly carried out, so that the best possible use of the machines was not always achieved. The steps in this type of handling are as follows:

Editing. The first stage in editing is to identify the actual responses to an item, as distinguished from various comments that were occasionally recorded by the fieldworkers. Thus, "hants" is to be marked as the response, "don't believe in sech" as the comment. Many of the comments had to be shortened in order to have room on the cards for them.

The other necessary steps in editing were often not sufficiently thorough, principally because of the influence of a traditional view that altering a field record is almost equivalent to forgery.

Words which are sometimes written as one, sometimes as two, sometimes with a hyphen, should always be treated alike. It is rare that such separations, or the lack of them, signifies anything of importance linguistically. Failure to apply this procedure rigorously left me, for example, with a list of 61 occurrences of *bed spread* and another list of 77 occurrences of *bedspread*, which then had to be added together manually.

Words which are spelled differently should be standardized, unless a phonemic difference can be deduced. Thus, I should always have changed *gulley* to *gully*, in order to avoid the producing of two lists for what is really the same word. On the other hand, I think I was right in preserving such differences as *counterpin* and *counterpane*, since the two are apparently pronounced differently, and since they show distinct differences in social distribution.

Words which are recorded now as singular, now as plural, should be regularized. Otherwise, one will find himself with, for example, one set of occurrences of *redbug*, another set of the plural *redbugs*.

Failure to observe some of these practices did not ultimately affect the accuracy of the results, but it left a great deal of work to be done manually that could otherwise have been done by machine. It is strongly recommended that others who wish to apply this method should standardize the materials as rigorously as possible.

Coding and Punching. The information that was coded and punched into the cards has been described in Chapter II. The arrangement of the numbered and lettered material is shown on the accompanying diagram, which represents one of the actual cards.

Informant no.	County	Section of state	Age (decade)	Sex	"Race"	Education	Page of workbook	Item	
									Response CORN PONE
									Definition or comment MADE WITH JUST WATER
0 1	1	3 5	4	6	1	1	2	1 1	0 4

A complete interpretation of this card would run as follows: the first informant in Lamar County, located in North Texas; between 60 and 69 years of age, male, "Anglo" or native-born white, of high-school education (two years or more); in answer to page 11, item 4, gave the response *corn pone*, followed by the comment, "made with just water."

The cards were prepared on a Model 026 IBM Printing Key Punch, equipped with certain controls to permit the instantaneous repetition of portions of preceding cards. The operator was able to punch these cards, from the edited workbooks, at the rate of approximately 340 an hour, or about one every ten and a half seconds. This is clearly the most time consuming of the various processes.

Sorting. The arranging of the cards was done on a Model 082 IBM Sorter, which has a rate of about 600 cards a minute (newer models are somewhat faster). Of course, a good many "runs" are required in order to achieve any useful classification of materials. The arrangement of cards as used in this study was as follows: all the responses to a single item were grouped together, then alphabetized through the first five letters. Thus, the responses to the item which sought terms for the earthworm would first list the occurrences of *angleworm,* then *earthworm,* then *fish worm,* then *fishing worm,* and so on. The decision to alphabetize only through five letters (as a matter of economy) was unfortunate, since such variants as *thunderstorm* and *thundershower* could not be differentiated without further alphabetizing, which had to be done by hand.

Listing and Tabulation.   The final printing of the lists of responses was done on a Model 402 IBM Accounting Machine. This entered on large sheets all of the data punched on the cards, but in a different order, with the actual response coming first, the code numbers last. The Accounting Machine was also wired to keep running counts of certain items, and to print those counts at the end of each set of occurrences. For example, after all the occurrences of *battercake* are listed, there is a figure indicating the total number of times this word occurs, and other figures indicating the number of occurrences in each area of the state and in each age group. An ordinary slide rule may be used to convert these numbers to percentages. For the purposes of this study it was found that the Perrygraf circular slide rule was quite convenient and sufficiently accurate.

WORD INDEX

Not all of the words entered here are part of the Texas regional vocabulary, but they are commented on in the text for one reason or another. Meanings are meant to be only approximate.

blinds. Window shades; also shutters: 45, 82
blinky. Beginning to turn sour (milk): 62, 95, 96, 100, 114, 115, Maps 86 (p. 216), 119 (p. 249)
blinky john. Milk beginning to turn sour: 100
blizzard. A severe north wind: 39, 121, Map 34 (p. 164)
blue jeans. Outer working garment(s): 51
bluejohn. Milk beginning to turn sour: 62, 100, 114, 115, 120
blue norther. A severe north wind: 39
bohunkus. What you squat down on: 70
bolster. A long pillow: 77
bonny-clabber. Clabber: 62, 81
booger. A ghost: 71, 121
Boogerman. A bad man that "gets" little children: 71
Boogieman. Same as **Boogerman**: 71
bosal. A kind of headstall: 52, Map 8 (p. 138)
bosque. A thicket: 41. Map 8 (p. 138)
bracero. A Latin American: 73
branch. A stream: 39, 84, 86, 90, 96, 101, 103, 109, 117, 121, Maps 53 (p. 183), 124 (p. 254)
brat. An illegitimate child: 66
Braunschweiger. A kind of sausage: 114 n.
bread. White bread: 64
breaking up. Clearing; said of the weather: 38
brig. A jail: 71
bronc. An unbroken horse: 56, 92, 96, 109, Maps 28 (p. 158), 119 (p. 249)
bronc buster. One who breaks horses: 53
bronco. Same as **bronc**: 56, 109, 125, Map 28 (p. 158)
brook: 40, 81
brown beans. Pinto beans: 60
brush (land, country). Terrain covered with mesquite or similar vegetation: 41
buck. To try to throw off the rider: 36, 56, 101
buckaroo. A cowboy: 53
bucket: 45, 46, 100, 102, 122
bull: 57, 122
bunch (of horses): 55

bunk. A kind of bed: 47
bureau. A chest of drawers: 44, 102, 110, 112, 119
burlap sack: 53
burrhead. A Negro: 73
burro. A donkey: 30, 36, 57, 92, 109, Map 33 (p. 163)
bush child. An illegitimate child: 66
bussing. Kissing: 67, 116, 120
butt. What you squat down on: 70
butter beans. Lima beans: 60, 103, 113, 115
butter macaroon. A kind of cookie: 114 n.
buttonwood. A sycamore: 81

caballada. A group of horses: 55
caballerango. A keeper of horses: 125
caballero. A horseman: 125
cabinet. A piece of kitchen furniture: 45, 111, 113
Cajun. An Acadian: 73
calaboose. A jail: 71
calico. A horse with spots: 55, Map 37 (p. 167)
calming down. Abating; said of the wind: 39
calves. What you squat down on: 70
came up. Rose; said of the sun: 76
can. A jail: 71
canal. An irrigation ditch: 41
canyon: 40, 92, 109, Map 30 (p. 160)
car house. A garage: 77
carry. To transport; also to take or escort: 68, 69, 83, 86, 87, 90, 120, Map 62 (p. 192)
catawba worm. A worm used for fish bait: 58 n.
catch rope. A lasso: 50
catty-cornered. Diagonally: 71
catty-wampus. Diagonally: 71
caviard. A group of horses: 55
cavvy. A group of horses: 55, 121
ceasing. Abating; said of the wind: 39
ceasting. Same as **ceasing**: 39
cedar bucket: 45
cedar chopper. A type of rustic: 74
chamber. A chamber pot: 77
chaparral. Terrain covered with brush, often mesquite: 41, 91, 109, 125, Map 5 (p. 135)
chaparro. An oak: 125

chaparro amargoso. A thorny bush: 125

chaps. Leather devices worn by cowboys: 51, 92, Map 35 (p. 165)

charcoal burner. A type of rustic: 74

charivari. A mock serenade after a wedding: 67

charro. A fancy cowboy: 129

cherry pit. The seed of a cherry: 79, 81

cherry seed: 60

cherry stone: 61

chest of drawers: 44, 110, 122

chick! A call to chickens: 54

chickee! A call to chickens: 54

Chic Sale. An outdoor toilet: 53 n.

chiffonier. A chest of drawers: 44, 102, 110, 112

chifforobe. A wardrobe with drawers: 44, 110, 112

chigger: 59, 96, Map 83 (p. 213)

chihuahua! An exclamation of disgust: 70

chili beans. Pinto beans, Mexican style: 60

chinchy. Stingy: 72, 119

chipmunk: 54

chips. Kindling: 48

chitlets. Same as chittlins. Possibly confused with giblets: 100

chitterlings. Hogs' intestines: 64 n.

chittlins. Hogs' intestines: 64, 83, 86, 100, 113, 114, 120, Map 64 (p. 194)

chocolate drop. A Negro: 73–74

Christmas gift! A greeting on Christmas morning: 68, 83, 86, 90, 96, Maps 71 (p. 201), 122 (p. 252)

chunked. Threw: 75

chunk floater. A torrential rain: 38, 103

chunk mover. A torrential rain: 38

cinch. A saddle girth: 50, 92, 109, 118, 123, Map 29 (p. 159)

civet cat. A skunk or similar animal: 54

civvy cat. Same as civet cat: 54

clabber: 62, 113, 115

clabber cheese. Homemade cottage cheese: 36, 61, 84, 86, 106, 113, 115, 119, Map 52 (p. 182)

clabber(ed) milk. Clabber: 62

clapboards. Split boards; siding: 44, 79 n., 81, 110, 111, 119

clean your plow. To give a good whipping: 77

clearing off. Said of the weather: 38

clearing up. Said of the weather: 38

clearseed peach. A freestone peach: 60, 94, 100, 113, 115, 120, Map 107 (p. 237)

clim. Climbed: 75

climbed: 75

cling (peach) : 60

clingstone (peach) : 60

clink. A jail: 71, 100

clinker. A jail: 100

clod roller. A torrential rain: 38, 103

clook. A setting hen: 57, 83, 93, Map 40 (p. 170)

close. Stingy: 72

close-fisted. Stingy: 72

closet. An outdoor toilet: 53; a place for clothing: 43

(clothes) closet: 43

clothes press. A closet or wardrobe: 43, 82

cloudburst. A torrential rain: 38, 103, Map 89 (p. 219)

cluck. A setting hen: 57, 93, Map 40 (p. 170)

clucker. A setting hen: 57, 93

clum. Climbed: 75, 118

clump (of trees) : 42

co, boss! A call to cows: 54, 81

(coal) bucket: 46

coal oil. Kerosene: 47

(coal) scuttle: 46

cob floater. A torrential rain: 38

coconut bar. A kind of cookie: 114 n.

cold drink. A carbonated drink: 33, 63, Map 99 (p. 229)

colored (man, person). A Negro: 73

come up. Came up; said of the sun: 76

comfort. A bedcover: 47

comforter. A bedcover: 47, 79, 81

Congress. An outdoor toilet: 53 n.

consarn (it). An exclamation of disgust: 70

cook. A ranch employee: 53

cook-cheese. A kind of homemade cheese: 61, Map 41 (p. 171)

cookie: 61

cooler. A jail: 71, 100

coon. A Negro: 73, 118, 121

coonass. An Acadian: 73

cooter. A turtle: 84

div. Dived: 75, 118
divan. A sofa: 45, 118, 119
dived: 75
doggone (it); An exclamation of disgust: 70
dogie. A calf: 36, 56, 92, 96, 103, 109, Maps 32 (p. 162), 121 (p. 251)
dog irons. Andirons: 45, 105 n. 110, 111, 119, Map 102 (p. 232)
dominie. A preacher: 81
donkey: 57, Map 33 (p. 163)
doubletree. A bar to which singletrees are attached: 52, 109, 120
doughnut: 63
dove. Dived: 75
downpour. A torrential rain: 38, 103
dragged: 74
dragon fly: 58, 109, 118
drat (it). An exclamation of disgust: 70
draw. A stream bed, usually dry: 40, 93, Map 11 (p. 141)
dreamed: 75, 116, 117, 122
dremp. Drempt: 75, 118
drempt: 75, 116, 119
dresser. A piece of bedroom furniture: 44
drought: 39
drouth: 39
drug. Dragged: 74
dry branch. A dry creek: 40
dry creek (bed) : 33, 40
drying cloth. A dish towel: 46
drying rag. A dish towel: 46
dry norther. A severe north wind without rain: 39
dry salt. Salt pork: 62
dry spell: 39
duck drencher. A torrential rain: 38, 103
duckins. Outer working garment(s): 51, Map 16 (p. 146)
dumplin mover. A torrential rain: 38
duofold. A kind of sofa: 45
durn (it). An exclamation of disgust: 70
duster. A sandstorm: 77
Dutch cheese. Cottage cheese: 81
dying down. Abating; said of the wind: 39

earthworm: 58, 84, 258, Map 68 (p. 198)

easing up. Abating; said of the wind: 39
eaves trough. A gutter for a house: 43, 81
egg bread. Soft corn bread: 63, 113, 114, 121, Map 84 (p. 214)
electrical storm: 38
enriched bread: 114
escort. To take someone (home) : 69
escusada. An outdoor toilet: 53 n.
evener. A doubletree: 52
evening. Afternoon: 48, 116, 119

fair (to middling). Reasonably good or well: 72
fairing (up, off). Clearing; said of the weather: 38, 96, 121, Maps 90 (p. 220), 123 (p. 253)
fartherest. Farthest: 49
farthest: 48
fatback. Salt pork: 62
fat-cake. a doughnut: 83
Father: 66, 116 n.
fatherless child. An illegitimate child: 66
fatwood. Kindling: 84
faucet: 36, 46, 103, Map 87 (p. 217)
favor. To resemble in appearance: 65
Federal Building. An outdoor toilet: 53 n.
feed bag. A bag to feed a horse: 50, 118
feed sack. A burlap sack: 53
fetch. To bring: 77
fiddlesticks. An exclamation of disgust: 70
fifteen till. Fifteen minutes before a given hour: 48
fig bar. A kind of cookie: 114 n.
fig newton. A kind of cookie: 114 n.
fills. Shafts (of a buggy) : 52, 81
fireboard. A mantel: 43, 82, 100, 101, 110, 111, 121, Map 73 (p. 203)
firebug. A firefly: 100
fire dogs. Andirons: 45, 110, 111, 121, Map 102 (p. 232)
firefly: 58, 100, 109, 122
firemantel. A mantel: 100
fishing worm. An earthworm: 58, 258
fish worm. An earthworm: 58, 258
five-and-ten (store) : 69, 122
flapcake. A pancake: 100

oughtn't. Ought not: 76
outhouse. An outdoor toilet: 53, 110
outside child. An illegitimate child:
   66
overalls. Outer working garment(s):
   51
overhalls. Same as overalls: 51
over there: 49
over yonder: 49

Pa. Father: 66, 107, 115, 116, 117, 119
pack. To carry: 69, 79 n., 82, Map 65
   (p. 195)
Paddy. An Irishman: 73, 116, 121
pail: 45, 46, 79, 81, 100, 102, Map 106
   (p. 236)
paint (pony). A horse with spots: 55
pair. A string (of beads): 67
paling (fence): 49, 87 n., 96, 109,
   121, Maps 81 (p. 211), 120 (p. 250)
pallet: 47, 83, 86, 87 n.
panas. A kind of pork mixture: 83
pancake: 62, 100, 113, 114, 122
Papa. Father: 66, 107, 115, 116, 121
Papaw. Grandfather: 66
paper bag: 47, 101, Map 94 (p. 224)
paper sack: 47, 90, 96, 101, Maps 94
   (p. 224), 125 (p. 255)
Pappy. Father: 66, 107, 115, 116, 121
pardner. A term of address: 70
parents: 65, 118
parlor. A living room: 42, 100, 105 n.,
   110, 111, 119
parlor room. A living room: 100
parson. A preacher: 69, 116, 121
partera. A midwife: 66, 109, Map 8
   (p. 138)
pastor: 69, 116
patio: 106
patty. A kind of pecan candy: 61, 90,
   106, Map 55 (p. 185)
Patty. An Irishman: 73
pavement. A highway: 41, 93, Map 10
   (p. 140)
peach seed: 60
peaked. Unwell: 77
peart. Spry: 72, 120
pecan patty. A kind of pecan candy:
   61, 90, 106, 113, 115, 120, Map 55
   (p. 185)
pecan sandy. A kind of cookie: 114 n.

peckerwood. A woodpecker: 58, 87 n.,
   90, 95, 96, 117, 120, Maps 93 (p.
   223), 125 (p. 255)
pee. A call to turkeys: 55
peep. A call to turkeys: 55
pee turk. A call to turkeys: 55 n.
pelado. A Latin American: 73, 91, 128,
   Map 3 (p. 133)
penny pincher. A miserly person: 72
peon. A Latin American: 73
pepper-belly. A Latin American: 73
Pepperoni. A kind of sausage: 114 n.
perspired: 75, 119
petered out. Very tired: 70
pfannhase. A pork mixture: 83 n.
phooey. An exclamation of disgust: 70
picket (fence): 49, 109, 123
piece. A snack: 61, 82; a certain distance: 48, 82, Map 77 (p. 207)
pig pen: 50
pig sty: 50, 81
pike. A highway: 41
pillow bier. A pillow case: 47
pillow case: 47, 105 n., 111, 113, 117,
   122
pillow sham. A kind of pillow covering: 121
pillow slip. A pillow case: 47, 105 n.,
   111, 113, 120
pilón. Something extra: 30, 34 n., 68,
   92, 95, 109, 126, 128, Maps 18 (p.
   148), 116 (p. 246)
piloncillo. A kind of candy: 128
pinders. Peanuts: 84
pine. Kindling: 48
pinto beans: 60
pinto (horse). A horse with spots: 55,
   92, 109, Map 37 (p. 167)
pintos. Pinto beans: 60
pirogue. A kind of boat: 53, 89. Map
   48 (p. 178)
pit. The seed of a peach: 60; the seed
   of a cherry: 60, 61, 79, 81
pitch. To try to throw off the rider: 36,
   56, 101
plague take it. An exclamation of disgust: 70
plain: 14 n.
plains: 40, 93, Map 12 (p. 142)
plateau: 40, 109, 122
played out. Very tired: 70, 121
play-party. A party with games: 77

sweet corn. Fresh corn on the cob: 59
swill. Food for pigs: 46, 52, 81, 120
swingletree. A bar to attach a horse's traces: 101

table land. A plateau: 40, 109, 121
tacky. Untidy; in bad taste: 72
take after. To be like (a parent): 65
take off. To leave in a rush: 71
take (you home): 69, 122
tank. A pool of water: 41, 92, 96, Maps 26 (p. 156), 118 (p. 248)
tarv(i)ated road. A kind of paved road: 41, 93, Map 38 (p. 168)
tarvey. A kind of paved road: 41
teacake. A kind of cookie: 61, 113, 114, 120, Map 103 (p. 233)
tear out. To leave in a rush: 71
tea towel. A dish towel: 46, Map 85 (p. 215)
teeter saw. A seesaw: 100
teeter totter. A seesaw: 70, 81, 100, Map 112 (p. 242)
ten-cent-store. A variety store: 69
terrace: 106
thick milk. Clabber: 62, 81, 83
thigh(s). What you squat down on: 70
thills. Shafts (of a buggy): 52, 81
threw. Past of throw: 75
thribbletree. A bar to which three horses are attached: 52
throwed. Past of throw: 75, 118
thundershower: 38, 258
thunderstorm: 38, 258
Thuringer. A kind of sausage: 114 n.
tight. Stingy: 72
tightwad. A stingy person: 72
tin bucket: 46
toad: 54, 118, Map 113 (p. 243)
toadfrog: 54, 88, 118, Map 113 (p. 243)
toad strangler. A torrential rain: 38
tobacco worm. A kind of worm used for fish bait: 58 n.
toilet. An outdoor toilet: 53
tol(er)able. Reasonably good or well: 72, 119
tomato worm. A kind of worm used for fish bait: 58 n.
tool house. A toolshed: 50, 93, Map 39 (p. 169)
toot. A paper bag: 83

top crop. A second crop (of cotton): 42, Map 114 (p. 244)
toro. A bull: 57, 91, Map 4 (p. 134)
tote. To carry: 69, 83, 86, 120, Map 65 (p. 195)
touchous. Sensitive: 72, 122
touchy. Sensitive: 72
tow sack. A burlap sack: 53, 83, 96, Maps 69 (p. 199), 123 (p. 253)
trap. A kind of enclosure for horses (or cows): 49, 93, Map 12 (p. 142)
trash. People of low repute: 74
trash floater. A torrential rain: 38
trebletree. A bar to which three horses are attached: 52
trestle. A device for sawing boards: 51
trifling. Lazy, worthless: 72, 120
tripletree. A bar to which three horses are attached: 52
trundle bed. A bed that slides under a larger bed: 77
tuckered (out). Very tired: 70, 121
turk. A call to turkeys: 55
turkee. A call to turkeys: 55
turn (of wood). An armful: 52, 83, 86, 87, 110, 111, 117, 120, Map 58 (p. 188)
turpentined cat (leave like a). To leave in a rush: 71

unwanted child. An illegitimate child: 66

vamoose. To leave in a rush: 71
vanilla sandwich. A kind of cookie: 114 n.
vanilla wafer. A kind of cookie: 114 n.
vaquero. A cowboy: 53, 91, 109, 129, Map 2 (p. 132)
variety store: 69, 116, 122
varmint. A small, undesirable animal: 77
vegetable soup: 64, Map 56 (p. 186)
veranda: 43, 117, 119
vinegarone. A kind of scorpion: 77
vittles. Any kind of food: 77
volunteer crop. A second crop: 42

waffle cream. A kind of cookie: 114 n.
wait for: 76, 102, Map 79 (p. 209)
waiting on. Courting: 67